WESTMINSTER ABBEY
RE-EXAMINED

WESTMINSTER ABBEY
RE-EXAMINED
BY W. R. LETHABY

BENJAMIN BLOM, INC.
Publishers New York 1972

First published London, 1925
Reissued 1972 by
Benjamin Blom, Inc.
New York, N.Y. 10025

Library of Congress
Catalog Card Number 69-13244

Printed in the
United States of America

PREFACE

WESTMINSTER ABBEY and the Kings' Craftsmen, *published in* 1906, *has been out of print for several years. In the meantime the author has had opportunities, in upwards of a thousand visits, for closer study of the famous church, and now embodies his observations in the present volume. It is a supplement to, rather than a reprint of, the former book, which is only referred to as other existing works are used. The special subject of this, as of the earlier study, is the form and details of the Abbey Church and other buildings as first wrought and the Craftsmen who worked at them. The older volume remains a fuller study of the Royal Masons and other artists, while this is a completer account of the Buildings. The illustrations are not repeated ; the larger part of those in the present volume are from sketches by the author. Most of these chapters appeared in* The Builder *during the year* 1924.

Recent works on the Abbey are the following :

Westminster Abbey, the Church, etc., of St. Peter, 2 *vols.*, 1923, *by Minor Canon H. F. Westlake. This important work is cited here as* " Church of St. Peter."

Royal Commission on Historical Monuments : An Inventory, etc., Westminster Abbey, 1924.

Westminster Abbey, *by Francis Bond*, 1909.

PREFACE

Westminster Abbey and the Kings' Craftsmen, 1906. *This is referred to here as " Craftsmen."*

Notes and Documents relating to Westminster Abbey, *by Dr. Armitage Robinson. This series includes Flete's History.*

Monks of Westminster, *in the same series by Dr. E. H. Pearce.*

The Nave of Westminster Abbey, *by the Rev. R. B. Rackham, Proceedings of the British Academy,* 1909.

Building at Westminster Abbey, 1298–1348, *by the same, Archæological Journal,* 1910.

111 INVERNESS TERRACE, W.
October 1925.

CONTENTS

CHAPTER   PAGE

I. THE CONFESSOR'S CHURCH   1

Foundation Legend and the Site—Existing Remains—
Description—The Nave and Tower—St. Margaret's.

II. EARLY ABBEY BUILDINGS   21

The Dormitory—The Chapter House—The Infirmary—
The Cloister—The Refectory.

III. FIRST AND SECOND WORKS OF HENRY III   .   38

The Lady Chapel and Belfry—The Two Works—Origins
—Original Forms—The Exterior: Second Work—The
Interior—Planning.

IV. THE TRANSEPT FRONT AND GREAT PORTALS .   64

North Transept Front—Great Portals—Colouring, etc.

V. THE ARCHITECTS OF WESTMINSTER ABBEY   .   81

Master Henry the Mason—Master John of Gloucester—
Master Robert of Beverley—Master Richard Crundale and
other Master Masons.

VI. THE CHAPTER HOUSE   98

Vault and Tie-bars—Windows, Arcade, and Floor—
The Annunciation Door—Jesse-tree Doorway—Glass and
Painting—Crypt—Exterior—The Mason.

VII. LATER BUILDING MASTERS   133

Repairs—The Nave—The Abbot's House—Later
Building Masters.

CONTENTS

CHAPTER   PAGE

VIII. HENRY THE SEVENTH'S CHAPEL . . . 155

         Original Forms—The King's Masons.

IX. HENRY THE SEVENTH'S CHAPEL (*continued*) . 167

         Decorations and Fittings: Sculpture—Stalls and Pavement—Glazing.

X. SCULPTURE AND SCULPTORS . . . 184

         Master John of St. Albans, Sculptor—Portrait Heads—Arcade Sculpture—Royal Portrait Statues—Master Alexander of Abingdon, the Imager—Later Sculptures.

XI. ILLUMINATION 204

         Whitening, Gold, and Colour.

XII. THE ITALIAN MOSAICS 217

         The Pavement of the Presbytery—The Confessor's Chapel—The Confessor's Shrine—Tombs.

XIII. THE STAINED GLASS 234

         Grisaille — Shields — Quarries — Kings — Medallions — Later Glazing.

XIV. ALTAR, SHRINE, AND CHOIR . . . 254

         The Altar—The Shrine—The Crossing—The Choir.

XV. RELICS AND TOMBS: WOOD, METAL, TILES . 275

         Relics and Royal Tombs—Funeral Effigies—Tomb Slabs—Brasses—Inscriptions — Woodwork — Metalwork—Bells—Tiles—Heraldry—Seals—Regalia.

NOTES 296

CHAPTER I

THE CONFESSOR'S CHURCH

Seint Pere, du ceil claver,
Va sa iglese dedier,
Des angeles mut grant partie
Li junt servise e grant aie
Li angele chantent au servise
La nuit quant dedient liglise.
Life of the Confessor, Cambridge.

Foundation legend and the site.—The church of St. Peter was built on the river-side between the branches of a small stream, and at high-water the site was probably entirely insulated by the tide. We get an interesting and probably a true reference to the topographical facts in the legendary account of the consecration of the church by St. Peter himself. The monk Sulcard, writing about 1075, says: " The Thames with its tides surrounded Thorney Island. Here a wealthy citizen of London erected the church and asked Bishop Mellitus to consecrate it. A day was fixed and the folk were summoned. Tents were fixed half a mile from the church, for the inundation of the river prevented nearer access. While all were asleep St. Peter appeared on the bank of the Thames and called to a fisherman to take him across, for doubtless he desired, as an eye witness, a man of his own craft. The apostle landed and proceeded to the church, attended by celestial choirs, while heaven opened to behold the apostle's work. To the fisherman he revealed his name and bade him tell Mellitus, who would find signs of consecration. Then the apostle was withdrawn from his sight. Mellitus found the walls signed with sacred unction and marks of candles fixed upon them, and gathering the people he celebrated mass. The church obtained the

B

name of Westmonastery and was no longer the Isle of Thorns." * The church to-day occupies the highest ground of the immediate neighbourhood, and the sand is found only a few feet below the modern surface. Round about, however, at the entry to Tothill and Victoria Streets, excavations show that the levels have been much made up, and there is every reason to suppose that a marshy belt intervened between Thorney and firmer land.

On the actual site of the church sufficient remains have been found to show that it must once have been occupied by important Roman buildings, and there is much evidence to show that the great Roman road, later called the Watling Street, passed close by to a river ford. The road is represented by Tothill Street, the line of which produced passes close and *parallel* to the north front of the church between it and St. Margaret's. Close to this line the fine Roman tomb, now in the entry to the Chapter House, was found. It is not unlikely that, in the legend given above, St. Peter was supposed to have appeared at the end of the Roman road on the south bank, which was later called Stoney Gate. The King's Palace of Westminster was built between the monastery and the river, and the ancient road gave access to it as well as to the Monastery. Later, when the great Hall of the New Palace was built, the road appears to have been diverted along Horseferry Road.

A charter, purporting to be a grant by King Offa (illustrated in *Church of St. Peter*) exists, but it is of doubtful authenticity, and it may be one of a series of attempts to fill up the void between the legendary foundation and firm record. A document of 1122, printed by Dr. Armitage Robinson (*Notes and Documents*, Gilbert Crispin), which gives the names of persons to be prayed for, began with that of Edward the Confessor; but the names of King Offa and King Edgar were written in above as a contemporary correction. This might be the more significant of a change

* Condensed from Dr. Armitage Robinson's edition of Flete's *History*. The name Sebert had not yet, it seems, been attached to the supposed founder.

of tradition, but King Edgar was certainly a real benefactor of the Monastery.

Dean Robinson writes in *The Times of St. Dunstan* (1913): "After Edway's death in 957, the kingdoms were reunited under Edgar, and Dunstan became Archbishop of Canterbury. The monastic movement now went forward rapidly." At Westminster were many precious relics, which were said to be the gift of King Athelstan. "Now it was not until Athelstan had been in his grave for twenty years that Dunstan took Westminster in hand, and brought monks, probably from Glastonbury, to dwell there. Till then there was but a small church there of no significance. Dunstan himself is not among the donors of relics . . . but it is possible that he had part of King Athelstan's treasury of relics at his disposal, and may have given some of the items mentioned in his old master's name."

In the first half of the thirteenth century, Abbot Barking gave some hangings for the Choir on which the life of Christ was figured, and also the story of St. Edward. The last subject of the latter represented the founders of the Abbey. In a copy of the inscriptions (seventeenth century), the writer says: "The ffounders names of Westminster were theis: King Edgare, King Edward, and ye Archbishope Dunstane." This information he doubtless found on the tapestry itself, and it gives the early thirteenth-century tradition.

Edward the Confessor rebuilt the church in emulation of the great monastic buildings of Normandy. In *Gleanings*, Sir G. Scott discussed a description of the church—given in a *Life of the Confessor*, written not later than 1070— and its relation with the existing "Norman" buildings. He came to the conclusion that the scale of the plan was much the same as that of the existing church, but that the Confessor only built the eastern part, including the crossing and transepts.

Existing remains.—In 1866, Scott found the bases of

3

some piers of early Norman form, under the mosaic floor of the Presbytery, which, as he saw, could only be actual remnants of the Confessor's Church. In 1894, Micklethwaite planned these piers in their relation to the existing " Norman " buildings, and set out a tentative reconstruction of the whole church.

In 1906, I suggested that, if we seek for a direct prototype, it is probable that we should look to Jumièges, a famous church, founded by Robert, who became Archbishop of Canterbury. Like Jumièges, its prototype, Westminster probably had an effective triforium story. In a letter written to the Pope to obtain Edward's canonisation, in 1165, it is described as a noble building, which the King had *beatissima consummavit*. A spurious charter of later days mentions one Godwin Gretsyd as having been the master-mason (*cementarius*).* I accepted the view that the Confessor had not completed the church.

In November 1909, I published a short study of the Confessor's Church (*Journal*, R.I.B.A.), following an account of excavations at Jumièges in *Bulletin Monumental*, July 1909. This is now given in a condensed form. " The stumps of the piers of the Confessor's Church have convinced me that they were probably parts of wall-piers once attached to a closed-in presbytery. They consisted of pilaster-strips with bold half-rounds in front; although in themselves they might have belonged to isolated piers, it is almost impossible to imagine the chance which should have led to just these members surviving, while the rest of such isolated piers were entirely grubbed up. Of the two piers on the north side, being the first and second from the crossing, the second is different in having to the *west* an additional member, so that it projects forward or south about a foot in front of the other pier. These facts can best be explained by supposing that the second pier represents the respond of an apse terminating a closed presbytery (Fig. 1). The force of the evidence will be appreciated by

* On building organisation from Roman days see *The Legacy of Rome.*

4

comparing it with the plan of Cerisy, and the prototype of Cerisy was Jumièges. According to this reading the bays of the Confessor's Church would have been about 17½ ft. wide. The old presbytery would have been of the normal two-bayed type found in early Norman churches. The plan so obtained coincides perfectly with that of Jumièges. The word *ambitus* in the description of the church referred to the aisles [and not, as had been supposed, to an ambulatory round the apse : see below]. In the Jumièges type they

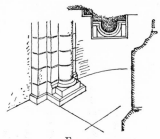

Fig. 1.

were continued even across the ends of the transepts. The ambulatory plan did not reach England till about 1070 or 1080. The form of the piers and the profile of the bases bear out the evidence of the plan ; the base made only of two hollows, is found at Caen, and it is the typical base at Jumièges. All the facts gathered up show that Westminster was a copy of Jumièges."

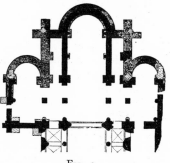

Fig. 2.

In February 1910, Dr. Armitage Robinson, then Dean of Westminster, read a paper before the Antiquaries, in which he gave the results of a visit to Jumièges. From measurements taken there he prepared a restored plan of the Confessor's Church. " It appeared certain that at Jumièges the original presbytery consisted of two bays and an apse." A little before this time M. Roger Martin du Gard had written a monograph on the

5

Norman Abbey, giving the result of recent excavations. From this my Fig. 2 is taken. Dr. Robinson, in his paper, analysed all known written sources regarding the Confessor's Church and came to the conclusion that it had been entirely completed before King Edward's death, although in the eleventh-century description the older Saxon church is said to have been left standing to the west.

After Dean Robinson had read his paper, I suggested that a search might be made for the foundations of the Confessor's apse under a disturbed piece of pavement just behind the present altar screen. I had observed that " of the two stumps of piers on the north side, the more eastward one had an additional break on its western face and projected further, so that the space between the eastern piers on opposite sides must have been 2 ft. 6 in. less than the space between the piers farther west. It seems obvious that the pier to the east must have been one of the responds to the arch opening to the apse, and a comparison with a series of early Norman plans fully confirmed this view " (Figs. 1 and 3).

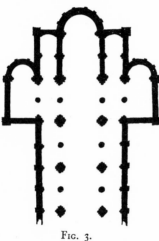

Fig. 3.

In searching for the apse, we found that under the mosaic floor the ground had been made up for several feet by a filling of stone chips from a mason's yard ; at a depth of 5½ ft. " we reached the flat surface of a hard mass following a concave curve. We now dug deeper along the curved front of this hard mass and found that it was a foundation-wall of concreted rubble largely of flints. The upper surface of what remained was in part covered with broken

6

Roman tiles. A total depth of 7 ft. 8 in. was reached, and here we seemed to come to undisturbed sandy loam. The foundation must have projected about 1 ft. 6 in. from the surface of the apse wall. In digging the hole, several large pieces of Roman tiles (bricks) were found, also one fragment of a Roman roof-tile with flanged sides, and some lumps of a floor of *opus signinum*—that is, of mortar and broken tiles about 3 in. thick. There must once have been an important Roman building on the site" (*Archæologia*, lxii.).

Since the plan of Westminster (Fig. 3) was established, other churches of similar form have been explored. Mr. Bilson described the plan of the early "Norman" church built at Lincoln in *Archæologia*, lxii. The presbytery with its aisles was of the same form, but a bay longer, and the apse was narrower than the presbytery, as at Westminster; the aisles ran on past the transepts, as at Jumièges and Bayeux (see an original plan by Bouet in the Print Room at South Kensington Museum), and probably at Westminster. Quite recently the foundations of an eleventh-century (?) "Norman" church of the type have been excavated at Wenlock (Fig. 4, based on *Archæologia*). The least certain parts of the plan, Fig. 3, are the eastern terminations of the aisles. At Jumièges the form here is not quite certain, and foundations in a similar position were sought for at Westminster in vain (October 1909). Possibly there were rounded apses not so far to the east.

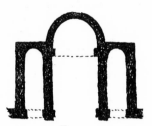

Fig. 4.

. . . . .

Description.—The eleventh-century description of Westminster contained in the *Life of the Confessor* was first printed by Camden "from an ancient manuscript." Wren put it into English thus :

"The principal area or nave of the church, being raised

7

high, and vaulted with square and uniform ribs, is turned circular to the east; this on each side is strongly fortified with a double vaulting of the aisles in two stories, with their pillars and arches; the cross building contrived to contain the choir in the middle, and the better to support the lofty tower, rose with a plainer and lower vaulting, which tower, then spreading with artificial winding stairs, was continued with plain walls to its timber roof, which was well covered with lead."

In Howel's *Londinopolis* 1657, I have found a version earlier than Wren's, given from " an old manuscript book," doubtless through Camden: " The principal plot or groundwork of the building was supported with most lofty arches, cast round with four-square work, and semblable joints. But the compass of the whole, with a double arch of stone on both sides, is enclosed with jointed work, firmly knit and united together, every way. Moreover, the cross of the church, which was to compass the mid quire of those that chaunted unto the Lord, and with a two-fold support-ance, that it had on either side to uphold and bear the lofty top of the tower in the midst, simply riseth at first with a low and strong arch; then mounts with it higher, with many winding stairs, artificially ascending with a number of steps. But afterwards with a single wall, it reacheth up to the roof of timber, well and surely covered with lead."

When the *Life of the Confessor* was edited in the Rolls' series, it was found that the description of the church in the MS. used differed a little from that given by Camden. Camden's began: " *Principalis domus area* "; the other had " *aræ.*" The new text also had an additional passage.

The description in the *Life* has often been printed and analysed—most fully in Dean Robinson's paper in *Archæologia*. I am quite incompetent to deal with it as a whole, so I only print here the first part as a necessary key to what follows: (1) Principalis aræ domus altissimus erecta fornicibus quadrato opere parique commissura circumvolvitur; (2) ambitus autem ipsius ædis duplici

8

DESCRIPTION

lapidum arcu exutroque latere hinc et inde fortiter solidata operis compage clauditur; (3) porro crux templi. . . . This has been interpreted in several quite different ways, but there is general agreement as to the latter part not given here.

The new text was printed in *Gleanings* (1863), and the editor (J. H. Parker) observed of it: " *Domus aræ*, literally the house of the Altar, obviously means the choir, whereas Wren had taken it for the area or nave. From other passages it is clear that the Choir was the only part finished at the time of the dedication." (The text mentions the cross and the central tower over the *Choir*, and hence Parker must have used this word to include the crossing.)

In 1894, Mr. Micklethwaite adopted this interpretation in a version which otherwise closely followed Wren's. I give his opening sentences corresponding to the part of the text printed above : " The main building is rounded and built with very high and uniform arches of ashlar work, and the aisle enclosing that part is strongly vaulted with a double arch of stone springing from either side, right and left. Then the cross of the church. . . ."

In 1909, the late Mr. Francis Bond objected that it was a mistake to imagine that *arcus* meant " a vault," and *fornix* " an arch." " The meaning of the words *principalis aræ domus altissimus erecta fornicibus circumvolvitur* is that the sanctuary (home of the high altar) is built with vaults very high and is surrounded by them." These vaults, he goes on to say, can only have been those of the ambulatory, for there were no high vaults in 1050.

Micklethwaite supposed that the arches or " vaults " in question must be those of the main building (Parker's *Choir*), and that, therefore, they could be no other than the four great arches under the Lantern-tower, which, as all agree, surmounted the crossing of the church.

Dean Robinson, in 1910, followed Mr. Bond in making the description begin with the presbytery, but he claimed that " the very high vaults " must be those of the presbytery

and the apse. It had now been discovered that, at Westminster, there had been no ambulatory around the apse,
such as Mr. Bond assumed. I copy here this latest translation in full :

" The sanctuary of the high altar rises up with very high
vaults ; it is made with squared stones and even jointing,
and is brought round in a curve.

" But the main church is compassed about with a double
stone arching on both sides, and is closed in, this way and
that, by solid work of strong construction.

" Then the crossing, which is to contain, in the middle,
the choir of those who sing God's praises, and with its
two-fold abutment on either side to steady the lofty
summit of the tower in the middle, rises simply at first with
a low and sturdy vault, swells with many a winding stair
of elaborate artifice, but then, with a simple wall, reaches
the wooden roof, which is carefully covered with lead.
Above and below projecting chapels are arranged, to be
consecrated by their altars to the commemoration of
apostles, martyrs, confessors, and virgins.

" Now the whole of this vast and elaborate work was
started so far east of the ancient church that the brethren
of the place might not have to cease, in the meantime, from
the service of Christ, and also that some part of the porch,
which was to be set in between, might have room to follow
on."

What does the opening phrase of the description, *principalis domus aræ*, refer to ; the highest and most characteristic
part of the whole structure, as Parker and Micklethwaite
supposed, or to the eastern limb of the building ?

I am not competent to deal with the question and should
not pretend to do so were it not for fresh evidence. This I
find in what Enlart tells us of early churches in France :
" At times a lantern-tower, giving light to the church, surmounted the crossing ; it may have been a Gaulish version
of a central dome. It was called *turris, domus altaris*, or
domus aræ, the altar being placed below ; the tower had a

DESCRIPTION

pointed roof, *turritus apex*" (*Manuel*, vol. i, p. 118. See also " Cabrol under *Domus* ").

The lantern-tower of a Romanesque cruciform church, like a Byzantine Dome, rose over the centre of the structure, having windows through which much of the light was derived. Wilfrid's Church at Hexham is described as a round *tower* with four projections surrounding it. The late Saxon church at Durham had two towers, one of which contained the choir. The Saxon church at Ramsay also had two towers—one being central. The characteristic feature of the Saxon cathedral at Winchester was " a lofty *temple* full of light—a sparkling tower reflecting the rising sun." The picture in the " Benedictional of St. Ethelwold " shows clearly that the church had a tall central tower as well as a second one, which was doubtless at the west end.

The lantern, with its windows, is here identified with the temple or main structure, just as in the Westminster description it represents the *domus*. The same general idea seems to be followed in a description of the Saxon cathedral at York, about 970, also given by Willis :

" A wondrous basilica was completed. This house of appropriate altitude is supported by solid columns set under curved arches . . . within its beauty shines environed with many aisles (or apsidal chapels). It has a great number of apartments, which contain thirty altars."

This leads off naturally as, I suppose, the Westminster account does, with the height of the " house," and, in fact, it might be the model for the Westminster description. Of Lanfranc's Church at Canterbury, we are told, although it had a long nave, " the tower, raised upon great pillars, is placed in the midst of the church like the centre of a circle. . . . A gilded corona hangs in the midst of the church."

The relation of Domus, Dome, and Lantern-tower is well brought out in Walcott's *Sacred Archæology*. " *Dome* : A cupola, probably so called as being the distinguishing ornament of the cathedral ; the Italian *Duomo*, the German *Dom*, and Latin *Domus dei*, God's house, the *Dominicum* of St. Jerome. . . . It became the lantern of English Gothic art, but is closely approached in the superb lantern at Ely." "*Lantern*: An open central tower, as at Ely, Coutances, Lisieux, Evreux, Lincoln, and York, for showering down light on the choir and rood. On festivals, an immense lamp was suspended from the vault of the tower of Beauvais, and was visible at great distances at night— a beacon that could not be hid."

It is curious that Howel, who was quoted above, uses the word "dome" for Old St. Paul's and also for Westminster Abbey.

John Carter, a century ago, noted of lantern-towers: "There is a part of our antiquities which seems to have escaped general observation—the interiors of central towers. Hiding them by ceilings seems to have been first resorted to, *temp.* Henry VI. and Henry VII., and many fine groined ceilings were then set up, as at Canterbury, Gloucester, and Wells. The central tower at Durham, still open, is the diadem of masonic power." The name Lantern-tower occurs in the Rites of Durham, and in the Will of Henry VII. it is used for Westminster.

We are now better prepared to understand what the writer of the *Life* must have meant by the opening words of his description. We should note first of all that there were no other introductory phrases dealing with the main building. The account begins by saying that the King rebuilt the monastery not far from the walls of London, and then at once proceeded as above quoted. I venture now, by comparing the several versions, and with the help of a dictionary, to put down what I suppose the writer must have meant.

The House of the High Altar (sacred structure, or, as below, "temple") is raised extremely high with vaults (or broad arches) of squared work evenly jointed (round about the four sides of the central space). The edifice is also enclosed on both sides by double arches of wrought stone, solid and strong. Moreover, the cross (or transept) of the temple, which contains in its midst the choir of those who sing to God, with twin supports from each side, upholds the lofty middle tower : first (on either side) it has a low and strong vault, then rises with many winding stairs, artfully ascending, and continues with a simple wall up to the wooden roof, which is well covered with lead. Below and above chapels are thrown out, to be consecrated by their altars to the memories of apostles, martyrs, confessors, and virgins. All this vast and complex work was planned so far to the east of the old temple that the brethren need not cease from the service of Christ, and so that a sufficiently spacious vestibule might be placed between them.

The great arches of the crossing under the lantern would have been five to seven feet broad on the soffit, and an untechnical writer even now might be confused in describing them as to the precise use of the words " arches " and " vaults." As the word *fornicibus* is plural, Dean Robinson explained it as applying to high vaults over the whole of the presbytery and its apse. If I could believe the presbytery had high vaults, then I could also think that the little transepts were also vaulted, and thus again we should be free to suppose that the description started with the main building. Apart from other considerations, the existence of high vaults at this time seems to me more unlikely than the use of the word *fornicibus* for the arches—great and high and altogether remarkable—which were about the square crossing.

Further, it is these arches or " vaults " which appear to be described as constructed of carefully wrought stone. Now arches would have been so built while main vaults would not. Dean Robinson alone makes this wrought masonry apply to the walls.

Again, Dr. Robinson understood the second sentence, *Ambitus autem ipsius ædis* . . ., which he rendered, " But the main church is compassed about . . . ." to apply to the nave, while the third sentence came back to the choir. Yet in a monk's church the nave hardly counted, while the choir was essential. The great altar was the altar of the Blessed Peter, Prince of the Apostles; Sulcard, *c.* 1075, says that the Confessor was buried before the altar *principis apostolorum.* The phrase discussed above—*principalis domus aræ*—is another way of saying the House of St. Peter. It is not improbable that, at so early a date, the chief altar would have been well forward under the light of the Lantern, and that an altar of relics stood in front of the apse.

Besides describing the Confessor's work at Westminster, I want to bring out the thoughts which conditioned the design of our ancient churches. The dominating position in every way of the central tower and its parallelism with the eastern dome has hardly been realised. It was much more than a handsome feature in " a design." In some of our smaller Saxon churches the body of the work is a tower with a projection for the altar at one end and a porch at the other, and these have been well named " Tower churches." It is part of the same tradition that, in churches like Westminster, the choir of singers is in the western limb of the building.*

The Nave and Tower.—The *Life* description of the Church is usually said to have been written about 1070, but Dean Robinson pointed out that there is no reference to the Conquest, and that it is quite possible it was written before the end of 1066. In any case, " the writer's description does not come at the end of Edward's life, but while the work is still in progress. . . . But we may not assume from this that, when he wrote, the things described were only in contemplation. He is describing the process of building." Dean Robinson also pointed out that Sulcard, who wrote about 1080, said " the work that had been

---

* While speaking of Saxon cruciform churches, I may add that the foundations at Peterborough may be explained by supposing that the transepts were not wider than the nave, but had sacristies or chapels which made up the greater width found. Were not the foundations at York, which Micklethwaite supposed to be Saxon, part of Bishop Roger's work ?

14

begun was pushed forward by the King's command, and after a few years, supported on divers columns and vaulted with manifold arches (*multiplicibus volutum hinc et inde arcubus*), being finished to the very porch (*vestibulum*), it was shown forth to the bishops for consecration." I wonder whether *vestibulum* here and in the earlier description necessarily means a western porch ? I find it hard to think that the older Saxon church was still farther to the west than the *completed* nave of the Confessor's church. Dean Robinson speaks of " room for the Saxon church between the Norman west front and the Long Ditch, a distance which may be reckoned as from 300 to 350 ft." If we could suppose that *vestibulum* might here stand for nave, which otherwise does not seem to be mentioned, then we might understand that a part of it was first interposed between the old church and the new, and that the former was pulled down for its completion. Sulcard, indeed, says that the old monastery " which we have all seen, was purposely destroyed that the nobler one might rise, which now we see." In Parker's *Concise Glossary*, it is said that vestibule sometimes meant nave, but this meaning is not given by Ducange. (See also *Inventory* of the Monuments Commission.)

A slight confirmation of this view may be found in the fact that, in the Confessor's *completed* church, there was an altar dedicated to the Trinity. Now a legend told that it was at the altar of the Trinity that the Confessor saw one of his visions. This would mean in the old Saxon church, for the Confessor never entered his new church after its consecration. It seems probable, therefore, that the site of the older Trinity altar (possibly in a lateral eastern apse) was considered to be represented by a nave altar in the church built by the Confessor. The event is represented by one of the sculptures on the back of the existing altar-screen, and it there looks like a nave-altar. The Trinity altar is mentioned, in 1246, as being the place where the Confessor saw, as in a vision, the King of the Danes drowned. (B.M. Cal. " Charter Rolls.")

THE CONFESSOR'S CHURCH

Again, remains of Roman building have been found half-way down the nave, and the Saxon church is likely to have been on a Roman site, which seems to have been the highest point of very low ground.

This reading of the evidence, however, requires that the Vestibule spoken of, between the Confessor's work and the old Saxon church, should be understood to mean a part of the incompleted nave to the west of the Choir gates. Possibly only the actual altar, and not the chapel of the Trinity, was preserved.

That the Confessor built at least a considerable part of the western limb of the church is confirmed by the Bayeux embroidery, on which the church is carefully represented. In a study of this in the *Archæological Journal*, about ten years ago, I convinced myself that it was an English work wrought to the instructions of Odo, Bishop of Bayeux, soon after the Conquest, for his cathedral. (Its subject was Harold's oath on the relics, and what followed, rather than the Conquest of England seen politically.)*

Of several buildings indicated on the embroidery, the only one which is represented, with any appearance of accuracy, is the Confessor's church. It is properly shown close to the palace, which lay just to the east, and it is familiarly named " the Church of St. Peter." It is possible that the embroidery was wrought in London.

Five bays of the western limb of the church are shown. These, it is true, might stand for a greater number, but no

* Mr. R. S. Loomis, in the latest examination of the evidence, concludes that the embroidery was English work prepared in time for the dedication of Bayeux Cathedral in 1077. " When it reached its destination, it was found to be too long. The end shows no border corresponding to the beginning. The designer presents Edward enthroned in the first scene, Harold in the middle, and evidently intended to present William enthroned at the end. An embroidery which belonged to the Conqueror's daughter, Adele, must have been planned by the designer of the Bayeux hanging. Every scene is found also at Bayeux, except the last two. It follows that these two were in the Bayeux hanging before it was cut down." (American *Art Bulletin*, vol. vi., No. 1.)

16

completion by western towers is indicated. The view correctly represents the facts that the church was cruciform and had a tall central tower standing over high arches. The upper stories of the tower were reached by turret stairs projecting at the angles, and above it was finished by a steep leaded roof. The western limb had arcades and upper windows, but the eastern limb, which was short, had no arcades.

All this agrees with the evidence otherwise gathered. The tower had two stages of lights, and it cannot be doubted that it was a "lantern." It may be compared with the noble early lantern-tower of St. Albans, and also with that of Jumièges, the parent of both.

The importance of the lantern-tower at Westminster, as brought out both in this view and the old description, is confirmed by the fact that Matthew Paris, telling in the *Major Chronicle* of the beginning of the new work of 1245, says that the eastern part of the old church was pulled down, and adds, in the margin, " *cum turris.*"

FIG. 5.

Another little detail, which may be gathered from the embroidery, is that the church had a weathercock (Fig 5). To the east of the transept no aisle extension appears, but rather apses are indicated (see what is said above as to the eastern terminations of the aisles). It is doubtful whether the square external terminations to the aisles had been developed so early; at Bernay they were round.

It has been held hitherto that the scale of the Confessor's plan was nearly the same as that of the present church, but this may, I think, be proved to be a mistake. One piece of evidence is the fact that the south wall of Henry's III.'s Church against the Cloister must have been built outside the older church. About ten years ago, we found, by an excavation in the north walk of the Cloister, that the outer wall of the west walk of the Norman cloister ran for some feet under the present north walk of the cloister, and it was not traced to the angle. Again, the tombs of early Abbots may have been shifted under Henry III. to the south walk of the cloister. Possibly they originally lay by the wall of the church, but were displaced when it was widened.

The dimensions of the Confessor's work at Westminster, which may be stated with fair accuracy, are these : Internal width of the presbytery, 31 ft. 2 in. ; its external width about 40 ft. Internal length of presbytery, comprising two bays and the apse, about 56 ft. Width of bays in presbytery 17½ feet. The external width of the existing Dormitory range, which ran away from the south transept (and was probably of the same dimension) is 39 ft. ; that is about the same as the presbytery, as might be expected. Now these agree closely with the dimensions of the similar parts at Jumièges, and we may not doubt that the two churches were closely alike in size. So we may transfer other dimensions from the Norman church to Westminster, with high probability of their being correct. At Jumièges the nave was about 66½ ft. internally, and about 74 ft. externally. Dean Robinson, however, gave a width of 72 ft. to the Confessor's nave at Westminster, nearly as much as the present width, which is 73½ ft. The width of 66½ ft. seems to be the greatest known for contemporary Norman churches (see J. Bilson's " Lincoln," in *Archæologia*, lxii.), and it may be doubted whether Westminster was so great.

Other probabilities, which may be gathered by the comparison with Jumièges, are that the aisles ran on past the transepts, and that the remaining parts of the north and south limbs were vaulted at the same height as the aisles. The nave had large piers and columns alternately following from the treatment at the transepts. There was an important triforium stage. The great lantern-tower had two stories above the roof. Compare St. Albans lantern-tower, which is so like that of Jumièges, that I think it must have copied Westminster. The existing pier bases at Westminster are like bases at Jumièges, and some very early Norman capitals from the Dormitory windows (c. 1075) are also of a Jumièges type. (See Fig. 6, p. 23.) In M. Roger Martin du Gard's book on Jumièges, the presbytery and transepts are dated 1040–52, and the Nave 1052–67. There is a late statement that the Confessor began his church in 1049, but this is doubtful. I noted above that the master mason was said to be one Godwin Gretsyd. The late Dr. Scott wrote to me, in 1913, that "the Dean of Wells has just found him and his wife Wendelburh in the list of people to be prayed for in Hyde Abbey at Winchester." Only the other day Mr. Westlake told me he had found a reference to "Teinfrith mine Churchwright."

These both look like Saxon names, but the records are not contemporary documents, and I cannot think that any other than a Norman master could have built this great church in a fashion new to England. The material of the existing bases seems to be Caen stone.

.   .   .   .

St. Margaret's.—Until recently, it has been generally accepted that this church, close by the Abbey, was founded by the Confessor. It has been urged, however, that such a dedication, in the name of the Martyr of Antioch, could hardly be earlier than the middle of the twelfth century. A charter of Abbot Herbert (1121–40) refers to the church of St. Margaret "standing in our cemetery," and it has been suggested that it was probably erected by that Abbot. But the claim for the foundation by the Confessor goes back to an early time. In Bentley's *Cartulary*, among fourteenth-century documents, I find the heading "Of the foundation of the parish church of St. Margaret, Westminster, by S. Edward Confessor."

The similar dedication of a church at Rochester may be cited as evidence that it was in use at an earlier time than is alleged. "The earliest mention of the church in the Rochester records is found in a charter of Bishop Gundulf, which may be assigned to the period 1107–1108. The

THE CONFESSOR'S CHURCH

Bishop grants to the monks the parish altar of St. Nicholas [in the nave of the Cathedral] the church of St. Margaret which is appendant thereto" (Mr. G. M. Livett, in Parish Magazine). Then, further, we have the fact that an English princess, granddaughter of Edmund Ironside, and a relation of the Confessor, was named Margaret (afterwards to become St. Margaret of Scotland). The parish of St. Margaret's, in the city of London, is mentioned in the first half of the twelfth century (Cal. St. Paul's Manuscripts).

CHAPTER II

EARLY ABBEY BUILDINGS

An excellent foundation for a full study of the Abbey buildings was laid by Mr. Micklethwaite in a paper printed in the *Archæological Journal*, 1875.

On the east side of the Cloister, extending southwards from the Chapter House entry, is a long range of buildings once occupied by the Dormitory, with vaulted cellars beneath. On the south side of the Cloister was the Refectory, now ruined. The Dorter range runs on beyond the east end of the Refectory for some distance. It was terminated by a transverse building, the Rere Dorter. The west end of this, where it overlapped the end of the passage extension from the Cloister, was destroyed about a generation since, when the usual recessed compartments of a Rere Dorter were found. These buildings are of early Norman character.

The undercroft of the Dorter, now the Abbey Museum, is divided into two spans by a row of stout, low cylindrical pillars, from which spring arches supporting vaults of concreted rubble. The original capitals had a single steep chamfer following the form of the shaft, with a square mass about twice as high above ; the bases are a flatter chamfer projecting farther. Most of the capitals were altered in the century following the first building ; some of them, one in the Pyx Chapel especially, have interesting carvings. In the east and west walls of most of the bays were single windows about 3 ft. wide on the inside. All the arches of the windows and vaults were built of two varieties of stone, a coarse tufa and chalk or Caen stone, set alternately. At the north end—the Chapel of the Pyx—the " Norman " work has been broken into by the newer building. At the south end there is a " respond " in the centre similar to those on the side walls.

In a comparison with the crypt of Winchester Cathedral, begun in 1179, Mr. Bilson pointed out that our work is a little less advanced. At Winchester, the lower member of the capitals is slightly convex, the square-planned abacus has a hollow chamfer, and there are impost mouldings to the wall piers. At Westminster, the arches of the vault are, as usual, set out from a semi-circle, in this case to the slightly narrower wall arches east and west of the Pyx Chapel ; the arches of wider span are segments of circles struck from centres a little below the springing line, so that all the arches rise to the same level at their crowns. The same system is followed at Winchester. The vaults were evidently built, as usual, on a through-running barrel-centering, with sections of centering applied on either side. The crowns of the vaults are level.

" These advances at Winchester justify our placing the Westminster undercroft a little earlier in date. . . . We may conclude that the monastic buildings would be pushed forward after the Conquest, and this eastern range would be the earliest work. If not a little earlier, it may be the work of Abbot Vitalis, whom the Conqueror brought from Bernay about 1076, and, in any case, to judge from Winchester, it cannot be later than his time." (*Archæological Journal*, 1910).

The old Dormitory is now occupied by Westminster School. On both sides within, there are traces of the original ancient windows, some or all of which were sub-divided in the repairs which followed on the fire of 1298, and one of these still serves its purpose. A doorway, which remains near the south-west angle of the Dorter, has alternate voussoirs of tufa and freestone, showing dark and light, like the arches of the cellars below, and, doubtless, the upper windows had similar arches. The external head of the window, next the south-west angle, is preserved in a class room ; this has the capitals of the nook shafts still in place, and the lower arch rim has the two different sorts of stone. This great room, eleven or twelve bays long, with a handsome window in each bay, must have been a fine and impressive thing.

On taking out a decayed and fractured capital from the outside of a hidden window on the east side of the Dormitory (October 23, 1910), we found that the back of it still retained its carved form, which was entirely similar to those near the south-west angle just mentioned. This capital is preserved in the Museum, where there is also another, which is as fair and fresh as the day when it was wrought. All were evidently of the same form. They were only set on the shafts, and not bonded into the jambs, except for the

Fig. 6.

abacus courses (Fig. 6). They are of a type used at Jumièges and at the Tower of London. We found that the window shafts were 6 in. in diameter, in separate stones 4 ft. 8 in. long, which rested on bases having flat chamfers. The arch stones were of tufa and freestone or chalk (Fig. 7). A day or two later, part of a second window arch was found on the same side, at a distance of about 14½ ft. (or one bay) from centre to centre. There were three and a half courses of masonry here above the window arch, and on the other side more remained. The windows of Westminster Hall were very similar, having recessed jambs and nook shafts. These facts give very complete knowledge of this range of buildings.

A view of the Rere Dorter (under destruction) is given by Mr. Westlake, together with an enlarged detail of the arched recesses along the walls. Even these little arches were formed with dark and light stones alternately, as evidently were all the arches of the Dorter range. The walls within were plastered, but the angles of the arches

FIG. 7.

would, I think, have shown margins of the stones, as certainly was the case in the Refectory and the later work of St. Katherine's Chapel. The scheme of having arch stones of two kinds, set alternately, must have been carried through this work systematically. Hudson Turner has pointed out that masonry of two colours is indicated on some of the buildings which appear on the Bayeux embroidery (c. 1070). For examples in France, see Enlart's *Manuel*, pp. 180 and 214.

In the south-west angle of the Little Cloister is a portion of the external wall of the east end of the Rere Dorter. Above a small eleventh-century window is a band formed of stones and tiles about 8½ in. square laid diagonally. The tiles are in the upper row, next a fourteenth-century cornice, and it may be that they were set in at that time. In the Deanery, what seems to have been the external face of the west wall of the Refectory is preserved, and this has a similar diagonally chequered facing of tiles and stone. Here, all the dark squares are of tile. This wall is surmounted by a band of fourteenth-century work, and I find it difficult to convince myself whether the chequers here

24

are of this date or of the eleventh century. A photograph of this masonry is given in Dr. Armitage Robinson's *The Abbot's House*. The wall may be of the earlier date, but this is not certain, and, even if it were, the chequer work might, like the quatrefoil band, be a later alteration. The masonry part of the diagonal work on the wall of the Rere Dorter is certainly original. A similar band of diagonal work is recorded as having existed at Westminster Hall, and chequered masonry occurs in the tympana of the " Norman " triforium arches at Chichester Cathedral. The stone and tile facing of the wall in the Deanery is certainly an interesting and beautiful type of work, and the wall itself must be the west end of the Refectory range.

The old Chapter House must have been on the east side of the Cloister ; it is described in a thirteenth-century poem as " a Chapter, in front towards the east vaulted and round." That is, it probably had, as Micklethwaite thought, an apsidal end to the east. Micklethwaite assigned it a position opposite the middle of the Cloister, in part, on the site of the present Chapter House entry, but he gave the Confessor's Church a transept extending much farther to the south than there is reason to suppose it actually did. In the upper floor, too, the " Norman " walls of the Dorter run on northwards of the position thus allotted to the Chapter House, which must, consequently, have been farther north, thus lengthening the vaulted cellar by one or two bays.

The " Norman " doorway near the south-west angle of the Dorter, and already mentioned, was thought by Micklethwaite to have given access to a chamber, but it really opened to a spiral staircase, and several of the upper steps still remain in place, although it has been destroyed below. Mr. Westlake suggests that it may have led to the cellar beneath, which was possibly a prison. It was built of fair masonry and was about 5 ft. in diameter. A flight of steps only 2 ft. 2 in. wide and a doorway not any wider would seem to be very narrow for the day stair to the Dorter.

On the other hand, the wall had to be considerably thickened to take it. Fig. 8 is a rough sketch-plan of this. When some chambers against the outer side of this wall were destroyed, the stair was broken into, and a photograph shows that it must have projected considerably on the outside. I have little doubt that a stair of this importance opened from the ground-floor passage. Micklethwaite thought that the Abbey prison was in another cellar near by ; the day stair, he suggested, might have been in the entry to the Little Cloister, occupying a central strip and only leaving narrow passageways on either hand.

Describing the entry to the Little Cloister, Micklethwaite said : " The roof is barrel-vaulted, and there is a large

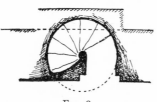

FIG. 8.

oblong opening in it [it is now closed up] which has been made or left for some purpose, which may be recent, but it is possible this is the site of the eleventh-century stairs to the Dorter. The stair would be carried on two walls and pass up a ' well-hole ' in the Dorter floor. If the original stair was not here, it is not clear where it was." On the whole, I am inclined to think that the spiral stair, just described, was the day stair.

Infirmary.—To the east of the Dorter range, reached by the passageway through its lower story, are the ruins of St. Katherine's, the Chapel of the Infirmary.

Micklethwaite says : " It consists of a nave of five bays, with aisles and a chancel. It has been suggested that the nave may have been longer and have been shortened when the courtyard [now Little Cloister] was built, but the arcades [between nave and aisles] end with responds at the west end, so that the additional length must have formed quite a separate hall, as it did at Canterbury."

When I described the chapel in 1906, I had not noticed

the fact that the western responds are bonded into the west wall in such a way as to show that this wall was of the twelfth-century work. I wrote : " The considerable remains of St. Katherine's, the chapel to the east of the Little Cloister, are of delicate late Norman work, almost transitional in character, which I should date about 1165– 70. . . . The nave and aisles of this building were almost certainly continued westward, over part of the present Little Cloister, and included the Infirmary hall. (An infirmary cloister is mentioned in the thirteenth century.) . . . That the chapel of St. Katherine was the work of Abbot Lawrence seems to be shown by the fact that his anniversary was celebrated here, and one of the altars of the chapel was dedicated in honour of St. Lawrence. St. Katherine's was destroyed in the year 1571." I suggested that the building master was probably Alnoth, Henry II.'s master of the works at the Tower, the Palace, and Windsor. He was working at the Palace from 9 to 24, Hen. II. According to Flete, Henry II. was a particular benefactor to Westminster, and the new works there, in the repair of the offices of the monastery and roofing them with lead, which for the most part had been burnt and ruined. In the Pipe Roll 21, Hen. II., is recorded the payment of 40 shillings to Alnoth for works at the Refectory. Certain work to the King's great chamber in the Palace, which had chevron mouldings around the windows, must have been done in Alnoth's time. The New Hall and Queen's Chamber are mentioned in the Pipe Rolls of 13, Henry II., and in the twenty-third year the chapel at Westminster is named, but this may be the Palace Chapel. Alnoth was called the King's *Ingeniator*, and later, in 1199, Elyas, working at the Tower, was *Ingeniator* to Richard I. We know from the book of Villars de Honnecourt how architects were concerned with " engines." I am drawn to think that the experts in war engines may have been the first lay masters.*

* Two building masters working about this time at Durham were also designated *Ingeniators*.

The date of the chapel, as given in *Gleanings*, is *c.* 1160. Mr. Westlake also suggests " between the years 1154 and 1161." There is a record that Abbot Lawrence (1158–73) made a speech in St. Katherine's Chapel, in Lent, 1163 (*St. Albans, Gest. Abb.*, p. 150). When I wrote before, I spoke of its " almost transitional character, which I should date about 1165–70." I am still impressed by the advanced

FIG. 9.

character of the work and find it difficult to think it can be earlier than 1160.

Enough of the chapel remains to allow of a paper restoration (Fig. 9). The columns were 2 ft. in diameter and about 12 ft. high. They were alternately octagonal and round, corresponding on each side of the " nave." The capitals were scalloped and varied slightly; the arches had various forms of chevron decoration. The western responds are fully bonded to the wall, and there was fair bonding masonry also at the angles of the structure (See Fig. 9).* The chancel arch had small attached shafts. The window jambs had round mouldings with small scalloped capitals at the angles (Fig. 10b). The wrought masonry of the jambs and arches showed, while the wall surfaces of rubble were covered with plaster, which was finished to a line against the windows (+). The splays were also plastered in a similar way, leaving a margin against the outer stonework. The soffits of the " nave " arches also had strips of thin plastering, finished with zig-zag edges against the margins (Fig. 10a).

Over the arcades were stone wall courses, carved with a zig-zag, of which only a few hardly recognisable fragments remain. Under the window sills is a half-round string moulding. The roof was evidently of the hall type, that is, in one span over the whole width. I have a note that traces of the "lining out" of the interior

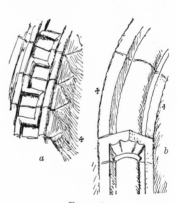

Fig. 10.

wall surfaces in red were found, being the ordinary "masonry pattern," with a segment (quadrant ?) in the lower left-hand angle of each rectangle. Altogether, this chapel is a very refined example of transitional work. The fourteenth-century doorway in the west wall is at a higher level than the chapel floor, and I have little doubt that the jambs of the earlier door would be found beneath, if searched for.

* I have recently found that the floor was at a lower level than that indicated on the sketch (Fig. 9), and that there were chamfered plinths below the bases shown. The details should be compared with those of Ely. In the sketch the columns appear more slender than they are.

EARLY ABBEY BUILDINGS

According to Scott, in *Gleanings*, " The Infirmary proper [the Hall] is gone and may have been destroyed when the small cloister was built. If so, it no doubt extended westward to the wall of the dormitory. This, however, would be disproved if the small cloister can be proved to be earlier, which Widmore imagines it to be. In that case, I should imagine the infirmary surrounded it."

Mr. Westlake gives some further evidence to show that the hall for the sick was to the west of the chapel, and he suggests a restoration, in which it covers the whole of the present Little Cloister, and is several feet wider than it. This would be a very large hall for the Westminster monks. Moreover, there seem to have been separate houses or chambers as well. The south-west angle, as suggested, abuts on the early " Norman " masonry of the Rere Dorter, and I do not think that there has ever been the attachment of a wall here. The mention of the Infirmary cloister, Mr. Westlake would apply to the vaulted entry.

Such record as there is of the Hall suggests that it was an inferior work to the Chapel and possibly of earlier date. We have seen that the Chapel was entirely separated from it by a west wall. Altogether, I would accept the " Infirmary Cloister " as meaning a court, and suppose that the Hall was much inferior to that planned by Mr. Westlake.

Mr. Westlake quotes an order issued about 1268 that the Prior should no longer occupy the chamber " before the door of the infirmary next the infirmary cloister," except in sickness (p. 443). " Whether the structure of the sick-room was of the same solid character as that of the chapel itself may well be doubted. The infirmarer was evidently much gratified to record that the pulling down of the old apartment provided sufficient fuel to save him from purchases for two years." A chamber in the Infirmary Cloister is referred to again as late as about 1350 (*The Church of St. Peter*, p. 113).

30

On the plan (Fig. 11) is shown how a hall of a smaller, but seemingly reasonable, size, indeed, as wide and nearly as long as the "nave" of the chapel, would leave room for an infirmary cloister. A is the chapel with known buildings projecting from it; B is the infirmary hall as suggested; C is the little cloister

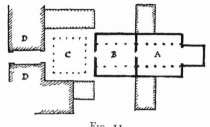

Fɪɢ. 11.

with "chambers" and "houses" accessible from it, and DD shows the dormitory range of buildings. The projection shown to the south of the Chapel is a later, and still existing, residential hall, probably the Infirmarer's. The projection opposite, on the north side, is only represented by some fragmentary ruins; one is a carved corbel of the fourteenth century.

Fɪɢ. 12.

Among a great number of "Norman" carved stones preserved in the museum, there is one which, from its style, may have belonged to St. Katherine's Chapel. This is a voussoir of an arch order or label moulding, carved with what must have been a repeating unit (Fig. 12). It came from an arch of considerable width, probably the Chancel arch of the Chapel which, as we see, is of such a plan that the arch must have been in several orders (Fig. 12). The style of this nearly approaches the work of the west door of the Temple church. Diagrams of the forms of the main

31

FIG. 13.

capitals are also given on Fig. 12. In the store of fragments is a stone from an interlacing arcade of remarkable character, which looks as if it might have come from St. Katherine's (Fig. 13). The chevrons project so much from the ground that they seem undercut.

It may also be mentioned that in the museum is preserved the half of a large late "Norman" carved capital for a shaft of 2 ft. 4 in. diameter. From a sketch of it given me by Mr. S. Weatherley, it appears that it was found in the Chapter House (works) in 1868. I give, in Fig. 14, a sketch of an elaborate and beautifully worked shaft, probably from a door jamb; the spiral roll-moulding is coloured red. In *Gleanings*, an illustration is given of an elaborate diapered stone found under the nave in 1848. Fig. 15 is from another stone of the same kind, but with a different and beautiful pattern. These seem to be much of the same date and style as the work in St. Katherine's Chapel.

The Cloister.—Many Norman capitals, about one foot cube in size, are preserved among the fragments, and some have been fitted into the short length of Cloister arcade which has been set up

FIG. 14.

in the museum. Some of these capitals have sculptured figures, some are carved with scrolls, and interlaces of foliage, and others are a developed variety of the cushion capital. Many of these were found when Scott practically rebuilt the outer walls of the west and south cloister walks, and, as he saw, they must have belonged to the ancient clois-

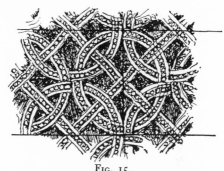

Fig. 15.

ter. There are also some early bases, 16 in. square, which bore a shaft nearly 8 in. in diameter, a size which exactly suits the capitals. Other bases of the same scale were finished for shafts of quatrefoil form shown in Fig. 16.

Fig. 16.

Now some of the capitals are also of quatrefoil form above the necking (Fig. 17a). About 1909, I looked for shafts of the form required and found one which seems to have been of the full original length. Again, in 1911, another piece was found in the later masonry of the south cloister. A little later, the dwarf wall of the arcade of the western walk was found beneath the grass nearly parallel with the present cloister: the capping slabs were 1½ ft. wide and on them were traces

D

of the bases of the old arcade of narrow arches. (Some half-bases and capitals suggest that the arcade was broken into groups between piers.)

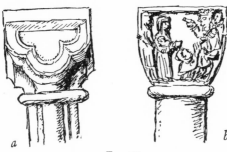

FIG. 17.

Later again, in removing accumulated earth and stones from the Dorter cellars, a large number of stones from narrow arches, decorated with chevron work, were found, and with these we were able to complete a short length of arcade. The manner of work is rich and the elaborate cushion capitals are similar to many in the Reading Museum, found in the Abbey ruins of that town. We might date these capitals about the middle of the twelfth century. A capital of the same type, how-

FIG. 18.

34

ever, found at Westminster, outside the Abbey, which obviously belonged to the sculptured series, had a carving of an Abbot receiving a charter, together with an inscription, naming William II. and Abbot Gilbert. This would seem to date the work between 1087 and 1100, which is impossible; the inscription must have been retrospective in its character. Possibly there was a series of capitals recording gifts. The King does not seem to have been shown as crowned, but he is seated on an X-shaped throne, having beasts' heads and feet, a royal fashion, of which not many records are preserved in England (Fig. 18). For this capital, see Dr. Armitage Robinson's *Gilbert Crispin*, p. 35. This capital was sold to a collector and has been entirely lost.

FIG. 19.

Of the other sculptured capitals which are preserved, one is carved with the Judgment of Solomon (Fig. 17*b*), another has devils and the Jaws of Hell, while a fragment represents two dragons biting at a woman's breasts. This is the symbol of one of the Vices (*Luxuria*) and suggests that a series of the virtues and vices were represented. Fig. 19 is a partial restoration of this interesting fragment. So far as I know, no other figure of the kind exists in England. On the return side, there seems to have been a devil seizing a person. Fig. 20 is one of the foliage capitals, and a magnificent work of art. It is an example of late Romanesque, which was being influenced by Saracenic art, through ivory carvings, I believe.

Refectory.—The north wall of the Frater stands its full

length and height. In the upper part, fourteenth-century windows have been inserted in the place of the old ones, which, doubtless, were originally similar to those of the Dorter. A " Norman " string mould of rounded profile still remains beneath the windows. Below ran a continuous wall arcade ; the ground on the site had accumulated so that, in the excellent engraving given of the wall in *Gleanings*, it looks as if the base of the arcade were at seat level. It has

Fig. 20.

been further exposed since, and even now the original floor level is about 1½ ft. below the grass. The base of the arcade was originally about 7 ft. above the floor. The capitals are of simple block type, square above and rounded below, and the bases are plain splays.

A further portion of the arcade was also found on the south side, in the present Song-school, about 1912. On the soffites of arches was some thin plastering, which left 2 in. of the stone exposed at the margins ; there were traces of red, and, doubtless, the whole was originally washed and lined into blocks. When fresh and fair, it must have been a noble barn-like structure—as barns were in the Middle Ages.

The exterior of the wall appears over the south walk of the cloister, and in repairing it, about 1912, some sound masonry was found, many of the stones of which still

36

retained their original masons' marks. These were similar to others on the west wall of the Dorter, by the entrance to the Pyx Chapel, and one seems to occur in both places. The external walls of Westminster Hall were also plentifully scored with these marks. From the character of the work and these marks, and the fact that the little arches of the wall arcade had alternate voussoirs of two kinds of stone, it must have followed on the Dorter at once, and, doubtless, was an eleventh-century work. The two stones used in the arches were a deep yellow sandstone and chalk, the latter, where exposed, becoming as soft as a packet of flour. From the inscription on the capital mentioned above, it seems possible that the Refectory was built at the cost of William Rufus. Probably the same building master was employed at both the Palace and the Abbey. A full and clearly illustrated account of eleventh and twelfth-century Westminster would be a romantic contribution to English history.

CHAPTER III

FIRST AND SECOND WORKS OF HENRY III.

Lady Chapel and Belfry.—By the two works of the King is meant the building of the transepts, crossing, and the whole of the church to the east of these, including the Chapter House, in one effort; and then the extension towards the west in a second building period. Before the first work of the King was begun in 1245, a Lady Chapel had been built by the Abbots, and the foundation of this was laid in 1220 by the young King.

The problems in connection with this chapel are well discussed by Mr. Westlake. I find it very difficult, however, to think that if, as is supposed, this Lady Chapel occupied what is now the central area of the Chapel of Henry VII., it could have been built in exactly this position before the work of 1245 was set out on the ground. The setting out of work was hardly ever accomplished accurately, and that the position, level, axis, and scale of plan of the old chapel, should all have been perfectly suitable for incorporation in the new work seems to me next to impossible, while the junction in regard to heights must have been as difficult. The only material evidence for the exact situation of the chapel is a foundation which was exposed under the apsidal end of the main span of Henry VII.'s Chapel. On inquiring whether any memories were still held as to what was discovered, Mr. G. E. Wright (brother of the present Clerk of Works), tells me that he was present forty-eight years ago (from April 1923), when the excavation for a grave was made. " In front of the Sheffield monument (in the N.E. chapel), when we took up the paving, we came on a stone wall nearly 3 ft. wide, 9 or 10 in. under

38

it. They said it must have been the bottom of the wall of the early Lady Chapel. It was decided to try the other bay (the S.E. chapel), where we found the wall had been cleared away. I have no remembrance of bases or anything of that sort ; the stones were roughly laid and rough axed, like the Norman work, and they came to the conclusion that the stones were of the Confessor's Church, re-used by Henry III. It showed that the old Lady Chapel had an octagon end,

FIG. 21.

but there was not enough to give full width of the chapel."

A sketch shows the wall between the two piers at the entry of the N.E. chapel.

FIG. 22.

It would be easy to search this position again, but, in the meantime, it is not safe to assume that what was found was part of an apse of the old Lady Chapel. It might be a foundation wall of Henry VII.'s work, or part of a rebuilding by Henry III. A difficulty at once occurs as to the level, for the floor of Henry VII.'s Chapel is some 5 ft. above the level of Henry III.'s Church, and more still above the floor of the Confessor's Church. There is some evidence which suggests that the old Lady Chapel was rebuilt with the church, but until the foundation, above described, is re-examined, and all possible evidence obtained, further argument is premature (see *Inventory*, p. 18).

Among the fragments are a few of thirteenth-century

date, which seem to differ in character from the details of the church, and these may be remnants of the old Chapter House (Figs. 21 and 22).

The great isolated Bell Tower, which stood free on the north side of the nave, seems to have been built before the work on the church was undertaken. The foundation was exposed when the new public buildings were recently erected, and I saw here a large number of piles which had covered a wide area. In the Virtue MSS. at the British Museum (23096) is the following note : " At Westminster, in the Sanctuary [the precincts], the Tower pulled down in 1750. In the foundation a stone found at the bottom, this date, thus, MCCXXIV. This stone building, called the Belfry, built before the present Abbey, refounded by King Henry III., but how much earlier unknown, I lately took the measures of it, was a castellated tower, square about 70 ft., and at one corner was great bells for the use of the Abbey Church." (See *Craftsmen*, p. 58.)

It appears from the fabric rolls that a timber, lead-covered steeple was erected on the masonry tower while the first work of the church was in progress. An entry on the rolls for the fourth year of the works (1249) records a payment to *Mag'ro Alex. ad pilos Be'fridi*—that is to Master Alexander, the carpenter, working on the spire of the Belfry. William and Roger, plumbers, were engaged on it in 1253.[*]

.   .   .   .   .

[*] In modern times it became confused with the Westminster Sanctuary or precinct in which it stood. In the transition time, it was still known for what it was. In the Abbey records, a lease of tenements, in the south part of the Great Belfry, was entered in 1574. In 1578, the Sanctuary gate, leading to King-street, is mentioned, that is, the gateway to the Close. I may mention here that I find it ordered that " the Convent Kitchen, the Misericorde and St. Catherine's Chapel be taken down by the advice of the surveyor," in 1570. In 1575, tenements " where a chapel, late called St. Ermylles hill did stand," are mentioned, and, in 1591, it was ordered " that the old Dorter and great room before be converted, one into a library, the other into a school."

Fig. 23.—Gable of North Transept, before Destruction, about 1890.

FIRST AND SECOND WORKS OF HENRY III

The Two Works.—It used to be thought that the whole work of Henry III. on the church extended only so far as the first bay to the west of the crossing, but Micklethwaite demonstrated that the building, dedicated in 1269, included the Choir, which occupies a large part of the western limb of the church. There is evidence, moreover, to suggest that it had been intended to consecrate the eastern part of the church before the building of the Choir westwards was undertaken. On November 7, 1254, Henry III. issued a mandate that funds should be provided " out of the money of the treasury or elsewhere to recall the workmen of the church of Westminster who have left as the King is informed " [a strike !] " so that the work may proceed, as the church must be consecrated at the latest on the Translation of St. Edward, the quinzaine of Michaelmas " (Patent Rolls).

This proposed date would be October 13, 1255, but, so far as we know, the King's intention was not accomplished. Possibly the difficulties were too great, or the King determined, in the meantime, to take up the extension and consecrate the whole together. In any case, it appears that the first work was so forward at the end of 1254 that it seemed possible that it should be dedicated in 1255.

It has been observed that the fabric roll of 1253 shows that a special effort was made in that year. At one time, no fewer than seventy-eight white-stone cutters were employed, and again forty-nine marblers, and parts of the work were also being done by task or special agreement. Much finishing work was in hand. Lozenges for paving are mentioned. Thirty-two carpenters were employed at one time and fourteen glaziers ; plumbers and painters were also engaged. Adam, the whitener, and his mate were working steadily. The King was away in France from August 1253 to January 1255, and he, doubtless, intended that the glorious new fabric should be ready for consecration on the Saint's day following his return. It may not be doubted that practically the whole of the first work, including the transepts and Chapter House, belongs to the period

FIG. 24.—South Transept in 1860 before "Restoration."

1245–55, and that all the details must have been settled by 1250. It is important to recognise that everything most

43

characteristic of Westminster was decided in the first half of the thirteenth century.

It was a great piece of work, but the energy with which it was done was not exceptional. Viollet-le-Duc, again and again, calls attention to the rapidity with which immense works were pressed forward in France. The character of Henry III., the records, and details of the structure agree in evidence that Westminster fully conformed to type in this respect. Yet we may wonder at the co-ordinating ability which could do so much in so little time. Even the unremembered foundation required vast labour. The outer walls stand on a great mass of concreted rubble wide enough for the projection of the buttresses ; it is some 10 ft. deep, 20 ft. wide at the top, and 30 ft. wide below.

After the practical completion of the first work, there was, the evidence suggests, a relaxation of effort for several years, during which other and minor works were undertaken. On the marriage of Prince Edward in 1254, the King had undertaken to provide an establishment of £10,000 a year, and money was hard to get. In 1255–56 the King ordered that the roof of the Lady Chapel should be taken down and that it should be vaulted in stone—an order which possibly implies complete rebuilding. The Sacristy was roofed about the same date and works, like paving in the church, were done. The times became increasingly difficult, politically, and very little building can have been done in what Sir James Ramsay calls " the critical epoch 1258–1261, a time of confusion hard to follow." In 1258, the King issued an order that the monks should throw down the walls of the old church, as far as the vestry by the King's seat, " so that it may be rebuilt as the work begun requires." The order must show an intention to resume the work, but this was " the memorable year " of the Oxford Parliament when, as Matthew Paris says, " were never known so many folk to die of hunger."

In 1260–61, John of Gloucester and Alexander, the King's

mason and carpenter of that date, were granted double wages when travelling to make provision for the church. This must mean gathering craftsmen and materials for the

Fig. 25.—Triforium (R. J. Johnson).

works. In this same year, the mason died, and it may be doubted if any of the second work, above ground, was done by him. This work can probably be assigned to the years

45

1260–69. It is not more than a quarter as much as the first work, but the period includes that of the Barons' war. Money was still a difficulty and, in 1267, the King had to pledge the golden images of the shrine for his immediate necessities.

There is a special freshness in the details of the second work; a subtle difference of spirit; and, as will be shown below, there are reasons which suggest that this new spirit was brought in by a master mason from the north.

. . . . .

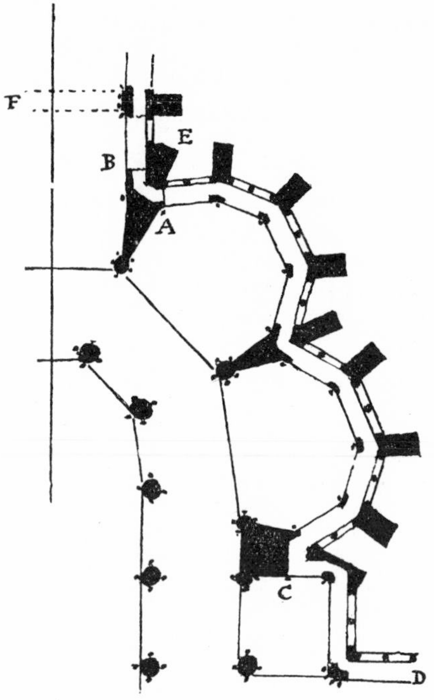

Origins.—When I considered the question of sources of design before, I concluded that Reims Cathedral was the chief prototype. Now I would substitute Amiens. The principal borrowings from Reims were the apsidal chapels with their pair-light windows and wall passage. The *planning* of the apse, with the surrounding chapels, was, however, modified by a study of more recent developments at Amiens. The setting out of the apse at Westminster is well analysed in *Gleanings*. The centre of the radiating system is half a bay to the east of the last normal bay (Fig. 26). This gives a slight drawing-in of the

Fig. 26.—Plan of Wall Passage.

46

bay next the normal one, making thus an easy transition to the fully canted bays of the apse. The system of setting-out the *apse* (not considering the chapels), is similar to that followed at Beauvais Cathedral (Viollet-le-Duc, vol. vii., p. 551), and also, I believe, at Amiens. Viollet-le-Duc proposed another system for Amiens, and this is accepted in *Gleanings* ; but the plan, given in Durand's great monograph, plainly shows the gradual drawing-in of the lines at the beginning of the apse. At Hailes Abbey was an apse which was suggested by Westminster, but its plan is half a regular decagon.* At Westminster, the forms and slender proportions of the interior piers, especially those at the crossing,

appear to be adapted from those at Amiens (Fig. 56) ; and, there also, a low lantern-tower seems to have existed, such as was projected at the Abbey.

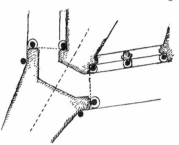

Fig. 27.—A. B. of Fig. 26 enlarged.

The " upright " unit bay of the interior was also adapted from the same Cathedral, as also were many details, as will be pointed out in regard to the Chapter House and the north transept with its portals.

Turning to this last, I would call attention to the manner in which, at Amiens, the triforium passage with its arcade passes across the end of the nave at the same level as an outer gallery. The same arrangement is found at the north front, Westminster. The wall arcade in the " blank porch " (like that in the Chapter House), is similar to an arcade just within the western portals at Amiens. What will be shown of the detailed resemblances between

* Hailes Abbey was founded in 1246, and details illustrated in Mr. St. Clair Baddeley's book show a close relation with Westminster. Possibly Master Henry, the Westminster mason, gave advice.

the sculptures of Amiens and those of the Chapter House
will reinforce what is said in the examination of the sculptures of the portals. In the carvings of the west aisle of
the north transept of the Abbey are deaf adders stopping
their ears with their tails; their parent is at Amiens.
Minor carvings, like the wall diaper and rose decoration,
were derived from Amiens. The dependence of Westminster on Amiens is so certain, that it becomes evidence
to turn back on the source. At Amiens, the west front
must have been well advanced, some bays of the interior
completed, and the chevet out of the ground by 1244.
The remarkable rose window of Westminster, set within
a square, may have been taken from one not now known,
but *designed* for a transept at Amiens. The western rose
at Amiens was of an earlier type, but there are blank
trefoils around it, filling out the square in which it was
set (derived from Notre Dame), which might well have
been the original suggestion for squaring the whole window
as at Westminster. Our Master Henry, the mason, would
have had some interesting conferences with the master at
Amiens, who, doubtless, explained how he " would do it,"
by sketches.

There are some striking correspondences between Westminster and the Ste. Chapelle at Paris, which, however,
does not seem to have been *begun* before our church. Enlart,
Durand, and Anthème St. Paul give the time of building as
1245-48. The chief resemblance between the two works
is in the sculptured censing angels in the spandrels of
arcades. The triangular windows of the triforium at
Westminster, and the four light windows of the Chapter
House, resemble windows at the Ste. Chapelle, but there
are windows of the same kind at Amiens. The Ste. Chapelle
itself resembles the east end of Amiens. Viollet-le-Duc
says : " The apsidal chapels at Amiens have the closest
resemblance to the Ste. Chapelle, even to the same moulding
profiles." The windows in these apsidal chapels have
uncontained trefoils, such as appear in the early bays of

the cloister at Westminster, and Durand states that these chapels were built *c.* 1240.

    .   .   .   .   .

Original forms.—What may be called modern repairs in the church began in 1600. (See B.M. Add. 34195, f. 14 and 16). Dean Andrews established a fabric repair fund. Hackett says of the next Dean, Williams, " he found the church in such decay that all who passed by shook their heads at the stones which dropped down from the pinnacles. Therefore he took care to strengthen it. He began at the south-east part, which looked the most deformed with decay, because of Henry VII.'s Chapel, which was tight and fresh ; the north-west part also, which looks to the great Sanctuary, was far gone in dilapidations. The great buttresses, which were almost crumbled to dust with the injuries of the weather, he re-edified with durable materials and beautified with elegant statues (among whom Abbot Islip had a place) so that 4,500 pounds were expended in a trice upon the workmanship."

Norden, writing about 1600, says of the pinnacles of the buttresses that " many through antiquity have lost their form." Hollar's print shows the buttresses of the chapels without pinnacles, and the whole east end looking very bald. (Compare the engraving by Collings, 1689.)

The exterior of the ring of eastern chapels has been so terribly pared down and put into a modern casing that it looks like a convict's garb, compared with what its ancient, graceful beauty must have been.* However, it is better than anything we could now substitute for it. A photograph of the chevet of Reims Cathedral will help us to make an imaginary restoration. The chapels at West-

---

* In the books of accounts for work done in Wren's time, from 1698, the renewal of the external masonry can be followed in detail in items like this : " Taking down 4 pyramids " (pinnacles). " 416 feet supl. of axing pointing and cleansing old Reigate ashlar at 4*d*. a foot." Wren's name last appears on the accounts in 1721, and no successor was appointed until after his death. Crull, writing of the exterior in 1713, says : " By way of renovation they have put a new outside upon it very lately."

minster so distinctly echo those of Reims, that we may be confident that parts, which have been superseded, also followed the great prototype (Fig. 26). At Reims, the big pinnacles of the buttresses contain statues of a choir of angels, in niches. The eastern buttresses at Westminster are utterly dry, drab, and dreary, but those to the west of the transept have niches for statues, which look as if they must have been derived from Reims, and, in that case, it would be through the buttresses of the first work.

Now, in Hatton's *New View* (1708), it is remarked of the Nave : " It was on the outside adorned with the statues of princes who contributed to this building. They were placed in niches in the said 18 buttresses between the cross aisle and the west end of which not above eight remain on both sides." The transept end is then described, and the author adds : " There were also several figures on the buttresses on the east side of the church, which buttresses in the reparation thereof are rebuilt plain ; but though that grand enemy of beauty Time has somewhat defaced her external features, yet there remains not a few marks of her outward gracefulness."

The windows of the apsidal chapels are obviously like those of Reims, and the buttresses are similar, in having their lowest slopes in continuation of the window sills. The buttress slopes were in smooth slanting planes at Reims, and this, as we shall see, seems to have been followed at Westminster. At Reims, the outer window arches are studded with foliage, and this, I doubt not, was so, also, at the Abbey ; we find such arch decoration inside the north transept doorways and elsewhere. The bare external hollow-mouldings of the chapel windows now existing suggest such carving.

The exterior of one of the original windows of the apsidal chapels has been preserved in a sheltered recess at the S.E., next to Henry VII.'s Chapel, together with its six-foil rose. It has been shorn of its mouldings outside, but, within, even the carved ends of the cusps remain. This window is a treasure; it assures us, what, indeed, is plain enough from the blank tracery within the chapels and from old prints, that the lower stage of windows in the first work really had these six-foiled roses. Remembering the insistence on rose decoration throughout the first work, we may not doubt that this tracery form was actually seen and understood as a rose. We shall find that exactly the same form, on a very small scale, was repeated in paint, on the walls, as a rose decoration. The jointing of the old window, which must have been one of the very first erected, looks a little uncertain and experimental. Some decayed pieces of carved ends of cusps remain among the collection of loose fragments.

FIG. 28.—From North-east Door.

The inner part of at least one of the triangular triforium windows still remains, except for the foiling; and the ancient ironwork of the foiled circles also, I believe, exists in several cases.

The clerestory windows of the first work have five-foiled circles and these are guaranteed in several cases by old iron-work. Some portions of what appears to have been the ancient cornice have been found (Fig. 48, G). Doubtless, it was of the typical French fashion, a deep course with hollow-moulding, studded with carving, and a shallower drip course above. Evidence for this has been carried on in the series of renewals. The wall plinth was a French form (Fig. 48, H).

One flyer of one of the ancient buttresses is preserved

on the S.E. part of the clerestory, an arch of two chamfered orders. The higher ends of the arches were supported by large capitals, and I was told, many years ago, that the ends of some of these, of Purbeck marble, had been found while recasing the apse. Fragments of the Purbeck shafts were also found in the walls.

FIG. 29. — From the northern jamb of South-east Door.

The doorway entering Poets' Corner, together with the walling about it, is the largest piece of ancient external work that remains. It is a companion to a similar door on the east side of the north transept, which is also largely ancient, although un-

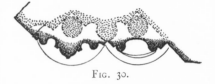

FIG. 30.

happily it went through the process of learned restoration, so that it is difficult to tell what is really old. Some of the carved caps —one of the French foliage type (Fig. 28)— remain, and enough of the carved arch to show that such carving existed. The Poets' Corner doorway has nearly lost its capitals by decay. My

FIG. 31.

sketch (Fig. 29), from one of them, is largely " made up," but it gives the style. The jambs of this doorway in Poets'

Corner have been altered by the putting of a central shaft between two others in each jamb. Originally, as may be seen at the companion doorway in the north transept, the central member was a roll, part of the coursed masonry. I had often looked at these jambs with doubt until, in some special light, the traces of an upright leaf above the roll moulding,

Fig. 32.—Jamb of Door to Cloister.

between the pairs of capitals, were visible. The southern door had a carved arched order, like the other, and a label moulding above. Accurate restored drawings of both doorways might be made. These two external doorways with their original carved capitals are most precious. Fig. 30 is the jamb of the south doorway; Fig. 31 is a sketch of the capitals of the south jamb.

Together with the evidence as to the great portals given later and the carved caps of the windows in the interior, these doorways show that the door and window capitals of the first work were carved and not moulded.

The south doorway into the east walk of the cloister decayed very rapidly until late years, when a coating of lime did some good. It has diapers of the Amiens fashion up the jambs, with roses studding the moulding, rounds of foliage in the arch, and crowned heads as label terminations. The carved capitals were of the foliage crocket type. Some notes of these details are in Collings' sketches (1842) at South Kensington (E 4086), and earlier records by Carter carry us back to 1795. The sketch, Fig. 32, was made in 1910. Fig. 33 is a vaulting capital near by, with one from the doorway also. The former is much decayed.

FIG. 33.—Capital by Door to Cloister.

Sep 14 1923

The vaults to the three northern bays of the east side of the cloister were the earliest built, and with their plastered cells and small bosses they are of an earlier type than others in the church.

The south transept, as recased in Wren's time, was "restored" into correct sham "Gothic" fashion in the upper part, about 1870, and a new south rose was inserted about twenty years later. Some old photographs show pleasant Elizabethan cappings to the turrets as still existing (Fig. 24). Repair of the lower part of the transept was undertaken about 1913. The casing—"flagging," as Wren called it—had become detached from the solid walls in big patches, but it was decided to repair the work as it was, making no vain attempts in sham Gothic. I have a note before me, dated July 5, 1916: "The repair of south transept has reached the buttress on the left of 'Wren's arch.' There were four plain weatherings to the buttress at the height of coping of cloister, the slope being continuous; the courses are 7 : 8 : 9 : 6 inches. There was another slope of two courses at level of springing of Wren's arch and another near the level of triforium windows. Some 30 ft. in height of the buttress face, which was 5 ft. 8 in. wide, was ex-

posed at one time. The work was very closely jointed in courses, varying from 6 to 11 inches. The face of the slanting wall of stair turret also exposed; original face still remains in the recess under Wren's arch, which was built to carry the casing of the buttresses."

"October 24, 1917: Repair of south transept still going on notwithstanding everything! The splay angle of stair turret

FIG. 34.—Naturalistic Foliage (Interior).

was exposed for a great height showing original, much decayed face. The courses are very narrow, some only 5 inches, and few more than 8 inches. The joints white lime putty and very thin. The stair windows had probably been narrow slits originally. [A sketch of one in the turret next to Poets' Corner, by Carter, shows it 6 inches wide, with a circular enlargement at bottom like a castle loop, which was possibly caused by decay.] We have now seen a large amount of the original face of this transept." The facing courses of Chapter House and those which remain by Poets' Corner entrance are equally narrow. The stone

55

was very white, and the new building must have been bright and fair even before it received the usual protective coat of wash.

A lantern-tower was designed as part of the first work and actually commenced. The squinch arches, across the re-entering angles of the cross, represent old ones, built to carry the parapet walks past the corners of the tower.

The ancient roof of the church still remains; some strengthening timbers were added later: these do not appear in a drawing of the roof by Carter, dated 1777, and now at the Abbey. Each great rafter has long raking braces crossing in X form and a collar above. This roof was the work of Master Alexander, the King's carpenter. Figs. 34, 35, and 36 are of internal capitals of the first work.

FIG. 35.—Falcon Capital (Interior).

Exterior : Second Work.—About 1905, a considerable work of recasing and re-editing Wren's restorations of the clerestory on the west of the north transept and of the choir adjoining was begun. On my first official visit I noted: "December 12, 1906: The clerestory of west side of transept is practically completed. First bay of north side of choir is stripped for recasing." (It was arranged that, after the choir bays, we should repair in detail, continuing what existed, without any attempt at making the details more sham " correct.") " In this first bay, traces of the blank arch, to the right of the window, has been found (the

56

left was, doubtless, part of the first work : compare *Gleanings*),
the face of the recess, weathered as it is, shows how very
finely jointed the original masonry was. Mortar about
$\frac{1}{8}$ in. (This blank arch was 2 ft. wide and no less than
9 ft. high and formed of an order 9 in. wide.) Original
thirteenth-century squinch work at angles by lantern
exposed." These were remnants of squinch arches which
allowed the parapet walk to pass the angles of the lantern-
tower. " Original cornice was in two courses like,
' Wren's.' " That is, it had a deep main course and a
narrow dripping course over :
only the backs of the stones
remained. Some fragments
which exist show a course
about 12 in. deep, with a big
hollow having projections
(carved ?) at intervals (Fig.
48, G).

In the second work, there
were many variations from the
first ; the blank arches by the
windows were clearly not con-
templated by the earliest
master, for on the south side,
as on the north, the *eastern*

FIG. 36.—Moulded Capitals.

jamb of the first window, which belongs to the first work, is
plain. Such blank arches show a return to English fashions.

On the south side, they exist with the aisle windows as
well as in the clerestory ; they do not occur on the north
aisle, because the buttresses are here of full width, and there
was no room for such blank arches. These arches, flanking
the windows, are very similar to examples at Fountains,
Beverley, and Lincoln. The last-named were, doubtless,
copied, with much else, from Westminster itself, but those at
the two others are earlier. As to the date of these, I consulted my friend, Mr. J. Bilson, who tells me : " There is
no precise date known for the thirteenth-century choir and

transept at Beverley—second quarter of century or *c.* 1225 to 1245. The new work had been dedicated before 1261. Beverley shows influence from Fountains." All this seems significant, for the second work at Westminster was largely done under the mastership of Robert de Beverley, who fully succeeded John of Gloucester on his death in 1260–61. Robert was already working under the older master in 1259, and I have little doubt that he was already in charge at the Abbey when the aisle windows were reached.

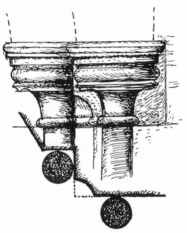

In the work of repair a few months later, one of the compound capitals, once under a window arch and on which a blank arch also fell, was found buried in the wall above the third clerestory window. This is of Purbeck marble *moulded*, and shows the type of detail of the second work (Fig. 37). The flying buttresses here had no marble shafts against the wall. We thus know the details of the Clerestory bays.

Fig. 37.—Caps between Window and Blind Arch.

The triangular triforium windows of this part have three-foiled circles instead of a single larger one. Essex, writing about 1780 (?), said : " The triangular windows at Westminster are of two sorts ; all that are of this form [sketch with three circles] are the original, but the others having been renewed of late years are not of true form " (MS. Notes at B.M.). Essex was mistaken as to the entire alteration of the renewed windows to the eastern part, but the others, when he wrote, were still *original*. There is a drawing of one of them, by Carter, now at the Abbey, and they seem to have lasted on till about 1835, when they and the aisle windows beneath were "restored" by Blore. The inner halves of some of these windows, except for the foiling, still remain.

The niches of the pinnacles of the buttresses appear in Wren's model of the church, and a sketch of them, by Carter, also exists; they must represent the original work with fair accuracy. The Cloister bays of this part are most elegant and share in the characteristics of the second work.

Fig. 38.

. . . . . .

Interior.—The setting out of the complicated plan is so exceptionally accurate that it is evident that the first work was begun, as a whole, on a cleared site. At the same time, there are small variations of detail, which show that the building was begun at the apsidal end. The bases of the apse pillars and those of the ambulatory are more delicate than elsewhere; some of them have hollows in their profiles and carved leafage filling the angles between the circular and octagonal forms. Apparently, the work was pushed forward so rapidly that much had to give way before the King's haste. The arches first turned must have been those which have wood ties, or rather props—the iron tie-bars were not ready in time. The diapering of spandrels of the main arches is smaller in greater part of the presbytery than at its north-west corner, and this earlier diaper is found on the east side of the south transept also. Capitals from one of the south-east apsidal chapels, vaulting shafts, and from a clerestory window are given in Figs. 38 and 39.

Fig. 39.

In the second work, the details of piers, wall arcade, triforium, clerestory, and vault were modified, but so sympathetically, that all is perfectly harmonious. The most

59

marked variation is in the additional ribs of the high vault. A part of the changes had been intended from the first. Thus the first pillar west of the crossing, although it is of the early work, is different in plan from those to the east (Fig. 48), but it has, like them, marble annulets, while those farther west have them of bronze—an English fashion. The vaulting shaft over the first pillar starts above a capital, while, beyond, it runs up from the floor without an intervening capital. The first bay of triforium here is also of the early pattern. In the second work, all the windows and the cloister openings have five foiled roses.

This second work does not show the signs of haste which are so apparent in the first effort. The details, such as the cloister tracery and the wall arcade of the aisle with its heraldic spandrels, are exquisite. Among the shields is that of Simon de Montfort, and, as Micklethwaite observed, this would hardly have been chosen after 1264.

. . . . . .

Planning.—The plan was closely conditioned by the then existing buildings and cloister. To the east was the Lady Chapel, perhaps to be rebuilt : connection with this may have been formed by a vestibule bay, or the chapel may have opened directly from the ambulatory, as at Amiens. A portion of the actual work against the ambulatory still exists (Fig. 26). This is a plan taken at the level of the wall-passage of the chapels. I formerly thought that this wall passage terminated with the existing polygonal chapels on the north-east and the south-east, but on October 5, 1909, I got into a continuation eastward of the passage from the south-east chapel, from A to B on the plan (Fig. 26). Beyond the point B, the passage is blocked by the work of Henry VII.'s Chapel ; what remains, however, is sufficient to show that there was a square bay here, rather than a polygonal chapel. At the triforium stage, it is evident that this space was floored at the level of the triforium which extends over the other chapels around the apse. There must either have been a transverse wall (Fig. 26, F), terminating this space to the east, or an upper story, at triforium level, extended over the whole chapel; the former is more probable. The surface of the wall passage still had its old whitening and rose decoration, and the marble shafts and bases still retained some polish. An inner base of the eastward continuation is on the level of window bases and falls on a sill similar to the window sills (Fig. 27). There was certainly here a blank, like a window light, similar to those in other chapels; and, doubtless, it had a companion light to the east of it, where not blocked by the buttress. The " blank " and the light would have made up a normal two-light composition. There was also an inner lower base on the passage, which ran east, exactly similar to those under the shafts of the rere-arches of the windows. Further indications of moulded arches were found later under the leads which form the roof of the existing low vestibule between the church and Henry VII.'s Chapel. This part was exactly similar to the polygonal chapels, except that it was square. Two radiating buttresses next to this bay, with their fliers above, exist, but they have been renewed.

The doorway in the south transept, entering from the east, was the immediate way of access from the Palace, and it must have been the King's private entry. It might be called the Palace door. Close against this door, in the transept, is another, which opens to a spiral stair, which ascends to a wall passage across the transept end, leading to a beautiful chamber, which forms a gallery story, intermediate between the ground floor and the triforium, and occupying the space over three bays of the cloister. This chamber, now known as the Muniment Room, is open towards the church on two sides, overlooking the altar and the choir, and it may be suggested that it was originally the royal pew. Such a position agrees with the tradition in palaces and castles of having gallery pews in their chapels. This fine chamber, moreover, has specially beautiful sculptured bosses in the vault. There are also several carved royal heads among the elaborate decorations and also traces of painting on the window jambs. One of the capitals has hawks perched on the foliage (Fig. 35).

There was a second way of access to this chamber from the cloister, and the series of radiating chapels around the apse might be reached from the chamber or pew by the wall passage without descending to the ground floor. All this may have been specially contrived for the King.

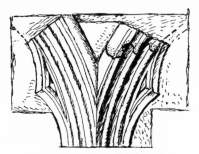

FIG. 40.—From Pulpitum ?

The chamber was altered in the time of Richard II., when an immense white hart, the King's badge, was painted here over a wooden partition which was set up to divide the chamber into two parts.

Over the " crossing " of the church, as before mentioned, a lantern-tower was to have been erected, and evidence of this intention is to be found within, as well as on the exterior. The great arches around the square space have label mouldings above them and, from the points where these intersect at the angles, rose vaulting shafts, the bases of which remain—sure indications that the work was to have been carried higher.

FIG. 41.—Piscina.

The choir terminated to the west with a stone screen or pulpitum. There are in the north triforium two fragments of trefoil blank arches, much like the wall arcade, but different from it. I have wondered whether these did not form part of the western front of the pulpitum, date *c.* 1270 (Fig. 40). Parts of the original marble pavement, consisting of squares set diagonally between longitudinal strips laid square, may still be found in the ambulatory, transepts, and aisles. Several years ago, in repairing a part of the wall on the east side of the north transept, the remains of a piscina were found behind a wall tablet. Of this Fig. 41 is a rough restored sketch.

CHAPTER IV

THE TRANSEPT FRONT AND GREAT PORTALS

" I was carving in the central porch. Now the porch was carved with a bas-relief of the Last Judgment. In the lowest division just over the doors was carved the Rising of the Dead ; above were angels blowing long trumpets and Michael the Archangel weighing souls, and the blessed led into heaven by angels and the lost into hell by the devil ; and in the topmost division was the Judge of the World."

W. MORRIS, *Story of an Unknown Church.*

North Transept Front.—This was the principal façade of the church as rebuilt by Henry III., and here—because it fell within the limits of the first work, and from its position in regard to the Palace and the chief approach by King Street—were placed the great portals. While mentioning King Street, I may recall that it was only recently destroyed, in widening the south end of Whitehall, well within " my time."

The transept front, it cannot be doubted, was pushed on with the earliest work undertaken—that is, it was begun in 1245. The King would have been specially interested in these splendid doorways. As will be explained, they show close study of the portals of Amiens Cathedral, and the first master mason evidently knew that great work as well as Reims Cathedral.

From what is known of it, and as an important work built in the middle of the thirteenth century by the connoisseur king, this front may be regarded as the supreme example of our mediæval art. A student who would make a trustworthy drawing of the front, by carefully bringing together all the evidence that can be gathered with the least possible amount of conjecture, would make a valuable contribution to the history of English building.

64

NORTH TRANSEPT FRONT

In 1906, I sought to show, by an examination of old prints and other evidence, what the main details of the north front were like before it was partly recased in Wren's time, and again almost totally renewed at the end of the nineteenth century. The conclusion was arrived at, that the north transept end, with its great sculptured portals, was modelled on the west front of Amiens Cathedral, which could hardly have been completed when the Abbey was begun. The central doorway contained a sculptured tympanum, representing the Doom, and there were large statues of the Apostles in the jambs below. The windows in the recesses, above the lateral porches, were originally of the form in which they remained when I drew them in 1875; the design of the original tracery, filling the transept gable, had also been preserved when I drew it at the same time; the form of the rose window might be established by a comparison of authorities; a passage-way arcade below it had eight pairs of openings, distributed in the side and central compartments, thus | 2 | 4 | 2 | , and not eleven, as in the present " restored " front, thus | 3 | 5 | 3 | .

The authorities were gone over again in the *Journal of the R.I.B.A.*, in 1920, and several of the prints referred to were reproduced in a way useful for reference. The conclusions which I had freely arrived at in 1906, without preconceptions, but merely by an examination of the evidence, were here contradicted. It must, however, be recorded, that I remain of the same opinion still. It is dreary work arguing again over conclusions which are denied, but new evidence is provided by a representation of the north front of the Abbey, on a seal of Westminster School, which was almost unknown in 1906; at least, I did not know of it. This seal is an amazingly delicate piece of work, engraved by Simon, who was, probably, the most remarkable English artist working in the Commonwealth period. Thomas Simon was chief graver to the Mint, and he walked at the funeral of Oliver Cromwell with the master carpenter, master joiner, master carver, and master mason,

TRANSEPT FRONT AND GREAT PORTALS

Mr. Philips. (No architect !) I owe to Mr. L. E. Tanner, of Westminster School, the following note on the date of this remarkable seal : " Westminster Abbey Muniments, 43166 is an order of the School and Almshouses dated 11th Feb. 1649 to pay 'Mr. Symons the goldsmith' £25 for making the new seal for the school and Almshouses. At the bottom is a receipt signed 'Tho. Simon.' It is reproduced as an illustration in Barber's *Richard Busby* (1895)."

The view of the Abbey given on the seal is in elevation, and nothing is hidden by projecting buttresses. It shows the later porch, which was erected against the central portal in the fourteenth century, as still existing. This porch was pierced with such large openings, that it must have been quite a glass-house. The gables of the side porches appear, also circles in the arch-tympana, and sculpture seems to be indicated in these. Large sculptured figures are on the buttresses and on each side of the lateral windows. There are shields in the spandrels of the arches over these windows and of the arches ranging with them in the central bay. The wall arcade between these arches and the rose window has four pairs of openings in the central space and two at the sides, | 2 | 4 | 2 |, as before described. Fig. 42 is a rough sketch enlarged from the minute detail of the seal. This part is very clearly rendered ; there were cinquefoils in a circle above the pairs of openings. The seal impression is injured at the Rose, but enough remains to indicate the general character of the tracery and the pierced spandrels. Because of the small scale, only about half the number of divisions were given in the tracery. I give a general rendering, of what I suppose the Rose was like on the seal, in Fig. 43, which may be compared with the results

FIG. 42.—Seal Enlarged.

reached before (see *Craftsmen*). The difference between the triforium windows to the east and to the west of the transept is accurately indicated on the seal. The main gable of the transept was obliterated. The testimony of this seal is of greater value, because of the fact that it was made many years before Hollar's view appeared in the *Monasticon*, the first volume of which was published in 1655. The wall arcade was rebuilt in a " Roman " manner, about 1670–80, but the old spacing, | 2 | 4 | 2 | , was still maintained. The alteration to | 3 | 5 | 3 | was made in Wren's time, but there was difficulty in squeezing three arches into the side divisions.

FIG. 43.—Seal Restored.

We know that the tracery filling the gable had three circles containing cinquefoils above a blank arcade; two of the circles were pierced as windows, but the central upper one was blank (Fig. 23). It must, I think, have contained a figure of the Majesty. Such gable figures existed at Wells, Lincoln, Salisbury, Crowland, and Lichfield. The actual figure from the gable at Crowland is the battered image now at the triangular bridge, and usually called St. Ethelbert. The gable figure from Lichfield is, I believe, at a little village not far away from the city. The blank arcade beneath the three circles was probably intended for standing figures.

Great Portals.—In my former study of the north front, I pointed out that its design was based on the noble west front of Amiens Cathedral, and I gave a diagram of the scheme of the latter. I have now re-examined the evidence, and there cannot be a doubt of the facts, as even the sketch plan of the Amiens porches is sufficient to show (Fig. 44).

The front at Amiens seems to have reached a final solution and it was again and again copied and adapted at Bourges, Reims, Poitiers, etc., as well as at Westminster. The influence of the west front of Amiens on the north front of Westminster is so marked that it becomes highly probable that the sculptures of the portals were also similar, and that the Last Judgment was the subject assigned to the central porch at Westminster.

This supposition is confirmed by the fact that the jamb statues at Amiens were of the Apostles, and there is a record that at Westminster there were statues of the Apostles of full size by the central door.

The magnificent south porch at Lincoln, part of a work just subsequent to Westminster, and obviously inspired by it, is sculptured with the Last Judgment. Christ appears in a quatrefoil, together with cross- and spear-bearing angels, in the upper part of the tympanum, and the rising dead are below.

Fig. 44.—Amiens.

The little figure sculptures and open-work foliage in the arch-orders are so like those of the Chapter House at Westminster that a close relation between the two works at Westminster and Lincoln is obvious. (The slightly later but much inferior west porch at Lichfield follows the same general type.)

Old drawings and engravings of the central porch at Westminster show a large quatrefoil in the tympanum, and Scott found evidence for it and followed it in his " restoration."

At Amiens, the top of the central tympanum is occupied by Christ on a throne, with hands upraised, exhibiting His wounds. On each hand is the Virgin and St. John ; also, on one side, an angel bearing the cross ; and, on the other, an angel with the spear and nails. Above is a group of angels carrying sun, moon, etc. Below is the separation of the just and unjust—a yawning beast's head represents the jaws of Hell. Still lower, little bare bodies scramble out of long box-like tombs ; while angels blow trumpets. Around the arch-orders are a crowd of lovely worshipping angels. On the central pier of the doorway is a standing figure of the teaching Christ ; the side door-posts have reliefs of the Wise and Foolish Virgins. To right and left, on the deep splayed jambs, are the Apostles, supported on corbels projecting from the jamb columns. The lower part of each jamb is covered by a series of reliefs in medallions, arranged so as to touch one another like rows of coins. Higher on the jambs, small shafts are placed between the larger ones, which bear the statues. Over the larger shafts are sculptured arch-orders, while over the lesser shafts they are moulded. This alternation of arch-orders is followed at West-

Fig. 45.—Eastern Recess in 1818 : (× × Sculpture Cut Away).

minster and at Lincoln. Some statue corbels, which remain at Westminster, are at a similar height to those at Amiens, and, it may not be doubted, that some of the standing figures at Westminster were set against the jamb columns. The jamb figures at Lichfield are placed in this way. The medallions, just mentioned, at Amiens were followed in the filling of the tympana of the lateral porches at Westminster (Fig. 45). Again, at Amiens, the door jambs were enriched by square diapering of a type which is found on the door to the Cloister at Westminster, and it, doubtless, existed at the north porches as well.

It seems probable that the right-hand lateral porch at Westminster, like that at Amiens, would be devoted to the Virgin. The keystone of the vault of the recess, which is one of the very few original external stones which remain, is carved with an angel which had outstretched arms, and hands which probably held a crown. This would be especially appropriate above some sculptures of the life of the Virgin. The bosses of the vault of the aisle *within* this door are of figure sculpture, differing in this respect from others which are of foliage, and these sculptures, David with his harp, the Coronation of the Virgin, etc., seem specially appropriate to this position. So, again, do the carvings in the spandrels of the wall arcade—a palm branch, St. Margaret the virgin, etc. Further, there is a record that, in 1644 and 1645, when the Abbey suffered from the process called " cleansing out pictures," Thomas Gastaway was paid £3 3s. " for work done on the outside of the north side of Westminster, including the hire of scaffolding for taking down statues of the Virgin Mary and other saints " (May 13, 1645). Mr. Westlake has printed some extracts from the Sacrists' Rolls, mentioning, in 1338 " Offerings at the Image of the Blessed Virgin outside the door of the church "; in 1363–65 " St. Mary at the north door," and in 1428 the " image of St. Peter outside the north door " (*Church of St. Peter*, pp. 19–20). At Amiens, the left-hand lateral doorway is devoted to the story of the local saint, and at Westminster the sculptures in this position *may* have referred to St. Peter and the Confessor, but of this there is no other evidence.

That the central portal contained the Majesty in a quatrefoil on the tympanum, with cross- and spear-bearing angels on either hand, and others with trumpets, and the rising dead below, is as certain as circumstantial evidence can make it. Scott's original drawings for restoring these porches are in the Print Room at the Victoria and Albert Museum. He proposed, from the first, to put a quatrefoil in the tympanum, but it was comparatively small and had a major vertical axis. When the work was begun and Wren's casing of the tympanum was stripped off, evidence for the position, form, and size of the original panel was found. (My authority for this is some paper by the late Mr. John O. Scott, to which I have mislaid the reference.)

The panel, containing the Majesty as executed, is of great size, and the form is that of a quatrefoil with square angles projecting between the curves. Now, in the little church of East Bedfont, Middlesex, there is a remarkable wall painting of " The Doom," which may be dated about 1260–70. In September 1923, I made a pilgrimage to examine this painting, of which good copies are preserved in the Victoria and Albert Museum.

There are two paintings in recesses which adjoin at the north-west angle of the chancel arch ; " The Doom " is in the northern recess and " The Crucifixion " in the eastern. The paintings are in the form of the tympanum of an arch about 4 ft. wide and as much in height. They are of fine style,

Fig. 46.—Central Porch.

simply executed in red, grey, and white, the background red, and they must be the work of a London or Westminster painter. " The Doom " picture has a solemn figure of Christ seated, in a large panel of exactly the form of the new panel at Westminster ; He throws up His hands to expose the wounds, which also appear on the feet and side. In the lateral lobes of the quatrefoil are angels, the one on Christ's right supports the Cross and the opposite one holds the spear and a nail. Directly below the quatrefoil are three or four small figures pushing up the long covering slabs of their graves, while right and left, in the lower corners of the arch-form, are larger figures of two angels blowing trumpets. This remarkable painting, it would appear,

71

must be based on the design of what, when it was painted, was the most splendid new sculpture of the Doom in the portal of Westminster Abbey. It is so similar to the Doom sculpture at Lincoln, which almost certainly followed Westminster, that it furnishes strong confirming evidence as to the portal sculpture at the latter.

Again, there is another strange piece of constructive evidence. Stone church, in Kent, has long been acknowledged to resemble the work at the Abbey very closely, and Street thought the details were even superior at the village church. Now, on the south side of the church is built-in a beautiful early piece of sculpture of V form, representing small figures pushing away the lids of their long, box-like coffins. Street, who illustrated it, in his little book on the church, describes it as : " A spandrel of an arcade, sculptured with a portion of the Resurrection of the Dead. It very nearly fits the spandrel of the arcade discovered in the south wall, and, in order that it may be preserved, I have had it placed there. The treatment of the bodies coming out of the coffins is good, and the work is about the date of the church." Again, of the fragments actually found in the south wall, he writes : " A portion of an arcade ; this seems never to have been completed, for whilst the lower stone has the dog-tooth enrichment of the arch finished, the upper stone has it simply blocked out. . . . We found a corresponding fragment of arcading built into the upper part of the chancel wall. . . . The conclusion at which I arrived is, that these are fragments abandoned at the very time the work was going on." Street also found " A portion of a sitting figure of our Lord of about 4 feet 6 inches in height. The feet are naked and pierced with wounds. There is no sign of any place from which it can have been removed. Its date is about that of the church." The west end of the Nave was altered at a later date, but there is some evidence that there was a " groined porch."

I believe that the sculptures were parts of the middle

of a tympanum sculptured with the Doom copied from the Westminster doorway.

Mr. Westlake, in his big new history of the Abbey, mentions Master Ralph of Dartford, mason, who was living at Westminster in the time of Henry III., and suggests that he may have been the master of the Lady Chapel, begun in 1220. Stone is close to Dartford, and it seems possible that the link between the village church and the great Abbey was this Master Ralph. I have found another reference to him, that is, he signed the document, 17498 in the Abbey Muniments, together with Odo the King's goldsmith, an important person of the earlier part of the King's reign. It really does look as if he might have been the master for the Lady Chapel. Possibly he built the nave at Stone, which looks earlier than the chancel, which is in the mature Westminster style.

Mr. Westlake is now kind enough to give me the full reference. It is the lease of a house " opposite the Almonry near the messuage of Master Ralph de Derteford cementarius." The date is that of Abbot Richard [de Berkyng], i.e. 1222–46 (Westminster Abbey Muniments, 17342.)

The following notes, from Mr. John O. Scott's report in 1880 on the work to the porches, are worth reprinting : " Very careful investigations were made in 1871, and these led to the discovery of much of the antient design, including portions of the *stone roofs* or gables over the portals, also of the long *stone splays* below the transept windows [i.e. the slopes] against which the gables abut. . . . The antient stone being much decayed could not be wholly retained, but some portions are still performing their office as they did 600 years ago. . . . Nearly the whole of the *mouldings*, except those on the actual face of the gables, have been traced more or less completely, together with the *foliage* and *sculptured* orders of the arches—not the actual carving, indeed, but its position and size and heights of its main divisions, as also the mode in which *marble* was introduced." The italics are mine, the reference to sculptured orders is

73

especially valuable. I believe that the old porches were still unrestored, in 1875, when I saw them. In a letter of 1910, the late Mr. S. Weatherley told me that " there was a long interval between the measurements and my perspective [1878] and the work being carried out."

Many years ago, in a special study of the Doom door, at Lincoln, I identified two most beautiful female figures on the jambs as impersonations of the Church and the Synagogue. These are much in the style of Westminster sculpture, and I have little doubt that the Lincoln statues were imitated from some once at Westminster. Similar pairs of figures are found at Reims and Notre Dame, Paris. They were, Viollet-le-Duc says, specially set up in cities where many Jews resided. Again, at Lincoln, one of the sculptured arch-orders has a series of the Wise and Foolish Virgins. As we saw above, these figures are sculptured on the door jambs at Amiens, and it may not be doubted that what is found at Amiens and Lincoln was also at Westminster. A second arch-order at Lincoln has figures of kings and ladies under canopies, and they probably follow the form of a Westminster arch. Comparison of Amiens, the painting at East Bedfont, etc., shows that the Christ at Lincoln (and at Westminster) raised his Hands; this noble figure and the angels on either side have been unhappily restored. The portals at Amiens have cusping around the main outer arches, and the western doorways at Lichfield have somewhat similar cusping. This raises the question whether the cusping of Amiens was imitated at Westminster, and I think it probably was. At Lichfield there were little figures under canopies in the arch-orders as at Lincoln.

The drawing of Wren's time indicates the general design of the Doom portal at Westminster. It had a large quatrefoil at the top and sub-arches divided into tracery beneath, the tracery rising from level lintels. How the tracery sprang from the marble lintels is explained by a contemporary doorway in the Cloister, which opens to the Library stair. There are here little corbels wrought on

74

the lintel, from which the tracery of the tympanum springs ; moreover, the tracery is filled with carving, although it is of foliage and not of figure work, as would have been the case at the Doom door. Putting together all we know, I suggest that Fig. 46 indicates a possible arrangement of the tympanum, but the similarity of representation in Colling's engraving (1689) and in the elevation of Wren's time is in favour of the disposition shown in *Craftsmen*. A is the Majesty with two angels ; B B trumpeting angels ; C C the rising dead ; D hell-mouth, as at Lincoln (see also Amiens above). We have seen that Scott found evidence for sculptures in the arch-mouldings of the north doors. Cottingham had a scroll of foliage of finest style " completely undercut with lions and birds at intervals," and described as from " the Door of north aisle of Nave." Lions and pairs of birds are found, not infrequently, in early mediæval art as symbols of Fortitude and Concord. Keepe (1683) described the central porch as " adorned with several intaglio's, devices, and fretworks that helped to the beauty thereof."

It appears from a description of the transept front in *Hatton's New View of London*, 1708, that the sculptured reliefs of the central porch must have been defaced before that time, although those of the lateral recesses remained. " The north end was adorned with the figures of the 12 Apostles and some others (as 8 more) to be seen higher, as big as the life and placed in Gothic niches, of which there remains 6 below and 4 above, besides a prodigious number of small figures carved in *relievo* within the east and west porticoes of 3 at this north end." These small reliefs would have been in the medallions of the tympana of side archways as well as in the central portal. A beautiful sculptured doorway at Higham Ferrars has the life of Christ sculptured in such medallions, which touch one another like those at Westminster ; moreover the Westminster diaper is copied in another part of the same doorway, so that it is almost certain that Westminster was imitated here also.

75

In examining the Chapter House, we shall see that the influence of Amiens Cathedral is plainly evident there also, especially in the sculpture. If we could see the Westminster portals, there is no doubt that we should find the Apostles on the jambs, directly imitated from those at Amiens, each with his significant emblem. Even in late reports of them, they were recognised as Apostles. (Fig. 47 is from Mr. Weatherley's drawing of Sir G. Scott's proposed restoration.) We have a record of the mouldings of the great central doorway in a sketch by Carter, now at Westminster (Fig. 48

FIG. 47.—Details of the North Front (S. Weatherley).

F). Scott followed the evidence, in the main correctly, from the decayed *original* work, but made some modifications. On comparing the "restoration" with Carter's sketch, we can arrive at the original form. One of the arch-orders had a great hollow for carved work, doubtless, of figures under canopies, like those at Lincoln and the figures of Virtues and Vices of the Chapter House door at Salisbury. From the jointing Scott thought that there were such figures and those at Lincoln and Salisbury probably derived from this source. The resemblances between the Westminster and Lincoln portals are many and minute. At Lincoln, each jamb had six columns, three of which projected more than the alternate ones, the more prominent supposed sculptured orders, the others moulded arches of similar profile to those at Westminster; one of the carved orders was of whorls of foliage of the Westminster type, the second was like the carved order of the Chapter House doorway, and the other had the little figures under canopies. I give an extract from a

76

letter of Mr. Baker King, who worked for Sir G. Scott, as every morsel of evidence on these wonderful porches is valuable. " I have in my note book some sketches and dimensions giving the sizes of voussoirs of the arches which were carefully followed in the new work. Much of the old work, where it had partly perished, had been reworked in the eighteenth century. The orders of the arches which had had carving were reduced to this form (A, Fig. 48), the carving having been cut away. The Purbeck marble abaci of the caps, which had been something like this (B), were reduced to (C). The neckings of the capitals also extended along the jamb splays thus (D) not dying against the splays. If you have been up to the stone roofs of the portals you will have seen that a considerable portion of the ancient stone slopes remains. The pitch of the gables was given by several of the stones which had the in-

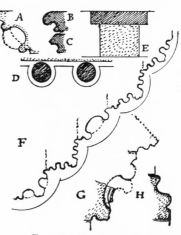

Fig. 48.—North Portal.

tersection of the two slopes. I do not think that any of the Purbeck marble shafts remained. The jointing of the corbels for sculptured figures inside the porches gave the dimension for these features, but all had been worked off flush [E, but part of one old corbel remains]. The sunk panels in the tympana of the inner arches had all been pared down " (September 2, 1907).

The " sunk panels in the tympana," just mentioned, must mean the series of cinquefoils in circles which form a series of medallions. That these had been reworked is confirmed by a sketch of Carter's, which shows them thin and poor. I have no doubt that these circles originally contained little sculptures, as at Amiens, and that there is an echo of them in the doorway at Higham Ferrars.

Even small details like the continuous base mouldings and neckings (Fig. 48, D) were taken from the portals at Amiens, and they are found again at Lincoln, which was derived from Westminster. Further, the record that the abacuses of the capitals only were of marble shows that the capitals themselves were carved, for all moulded capitals were wholly in marble. The late Mr. William Brindley informed me that fragments of the Purbeck marble shafts had been found, and these were of a scarce reddish tint, as if they had been specially selected.

Some slight notes of mouldings and details were made by John Carter. A drawing of the eastern recess made in 1818, by Ambrose Poynter, was shown to me by his grandson (Fig. 45). Important drawings of Wren's time, companions to the elevation published in the *Building News* (October 26, 1888), were also in the possession of Mr. Lee. These were most valuable sources, and, I am sorry to say, I cannot tell where they are now. The scale of the work is not likely to be recognised without some dimensions; it is 14 ft. to the soffit of lintel of central doorway and 37 ft. to the vault of porch; the central arch is 35 ft. high; and the side arches over 25 ft. high, and it is 50 ft. to the socket of the central gable-cross.

When the repairs of Wren's time were done, older wooden doors were new cased. In the accounts of Wren's works at the church is an item, under 1700, for "mending Solomon's Porch doors." These were broken up and thrown aside in the more thorough restoration of later days. A considerable fragment of one, which remained, has recently been adapted as a door to the stair of the Octagonal Crypt. It has diagonal framing covered with plain boarding, and such doors are shown at the North Transept in one of the seventeenth-century views of the interior.

Fig. 47 shows what Sir G. Scott thought the details of the windows above the porches would have been ; the suggestions I made, in 1906, agree entirely, except that Scott rightly put carved capitals instead of moulded. In the actual " restoration," as carried out, the forms which had come down to our time were altered. The remarkable gable tracery (Fig. 23) was destroyed about 1890. An original sketch by Hollar, in the Pepys collection, Cambridge, shows the pinnacles in better proportion than his etching.

.　　　.　　　.　　　.　　　.

Colouring, etc.—This wonderful work would have been completed by the usual vesture of whitening, colour, and gilding. Our modern way of setting up costly structures in friable stone entirely, without surface protection, is a modern heresy which, I can only suppose, rests on an unconfessed and, indeed, unrealised idea that decay is good for trade. The arcade and sculptures of the west front of Wells Cathedral still show such extensive remnants of a general coating, and traces of painting and gilding, that it is certain that the whole front was brightly illuminated. Stains of colour—red and fair copper-green—are preserved in the west porches of Salisbury and in the great open north porch; here and there on the walls are patches of the general wash, and the wooden doors were painted. High up under the great open arches of the west front of Peterborough Cathedral, I observed, nearly thirty years ago, whitening, with much original thirteenth-century lining-out in red. Stukeley noted that the sculptured west front of Crowland Abbey—which may be counted as one of the derivatives of the north front of Westminster—was coloured. Oliver recorded the colouring of the sculptured front of Exeter Cathedral, and slight traces here and at the north porch are still visible. The wooden doors were bright red. Britton also noticed remnants of colour on the great Judgment portal of Lincoln, which, as we have seen, was practically a copy of the Westminster portal.

The reliefs of the doorway at Higham Ferrars were also
" emblazoned in colour."*

At Westminster itself, it is known that the sculptured
doorway from the Cloister to the Chapter House was
brilliantly coloured and gilt. Similar evidence is to be
found for the great foreign churches. I have observed
traces of chevron patterns on the shafts of the west front
of Reims ; and there is record that the west portals of
Notre Dame were largely gilt. The second half of the
thirteenth century was indeed the special age of gilding, and
the sculptured north porches would have been gay and
glistening beyond our power to imagine. The rest of the
exterior, except the marble shafts, capitals, and bases, which
were polished, would have been whitened and " picked
out " with red. In the accounts of Henry III.'s works,
whiteners appear, but we are not told if they were engaged
on the exterior. In the orders for Henry VII.'s Chapel,
however, it is provided that the sculptures within and
without should be coloured.

When the church was consecrated and the golden shrine
of the Confessor was carried through the great central
portal (in 1269), its fair shining beauty must have been
entrancing.

Putting aside the preliminary discussion of evidence, I
should like to write an entirely new description of the
great church, in its first freshness, as it was revealed when the
scaffolding was struck and while the stone dust still whitened
the ground, but I must leave readers to form this final
impression for themselves.

* See Note 1 at end.

CHAPTER V

THE ARCHITECTS OF WESTMINSTER ABBEY

In thys maner throgh good wytte of gemetry
Begun first the craft of masonry.
HALLIWELL, *History of Freemasonry.*

In *Westminster Abbey and the King's Craftsmen,* 1906, I
discussed more fully than can be done here the story of
the masons and carpenters who were engaged on the work.
What follows in this chapter is, for the most part, supple-
mentary. It was shown that the first Master Mason was
Master Henry. In his fine new book on Westminster
Abbey, Mr. Westlake, by fresh study of the documents
preserved at the church, has shown that Master Henry, the
mason, who was what we should call the " architect " of
Henry III.'s great work, was almost certainly the same as
" Master Henry de Reyns, Mason," mentioned in 1256,
in a deed, by which Hugh, the son of this Henry, assigned
to the Abbey a rent of five shillings a year from a messuage
in Westminster, which had been given to him by his father.
Mr. Westlake also quotes a record of the purchase of houses
at Westminster by the King for Master Henry, on July 6,
1245. This is exactly the date when the building was begun;
in the Close Roll, the purchase is said to have been " for
the work of Master Henry."

Now, it has long been acknowledged that many characteristics in our church are derived from the Cathedral at
Reims, and this fact, together with the name Reyns, makes
a strong case for arguing that the architect at Westminster
was a Frenchman, who had been employed on the French
Coronation Church, and was brought here by Henry III.
to build the English Coronation Church. On the other
hand, the general view, in regard to the architectural

G

character of the church, has been that it is specifically English, but shows study of contemporary French art. Sir Gilbert Scott put it thus :

" Judging from internal evidence, which is all we have to go upon till the documents are thoroughly searched, I should imagine that an English architect, or master of the works, was commissioned to visit the great cathedrals then in progress in France, with a view of making his design on the general idea suggested by them. The result is precisely what might have been expected from such a course. Had a French architect been sent for, we should have had a plan really like some French cathedral, and it would have been carried out, as was the case with William of Sens' work at Canterbury, with French details. As it is, however, the plan, though founded on that common in France, differs greatly from any existing church, and contains no French detail whatever, excepting the work of apparently one carver. The church is remarkable as marking the introduction of the French arrangement of chapels, which, however, failed to take root here ; and the completed type of bar-tracery, which was no sooner grafted on an English stock than it began to shoot forth in most vigorous and luxuriant growth."

Our being able to accept a French architect for our famous church depends on whether we can allow a predominantly French character to its architecture. This is a question of style criticism, and it is as difficult of proof as it would be to prove whether an unsigned picture was by Raphael or Titian. Certain students will be quite sure for themselves, without being able to demonstrate their view. It happens that my days of studentship were in the time when there was a special enthusiasm for French cathedrals, and I must have been one of the last of those who concentrated on the " professional " study of these masterpieces of structural art. I have worked, measuring and drawing, at all the great monuments of Northern Gothic art, at some of them again and again, and I may set down three dozen as they occur to me, partly for the sound of the delightful names : Amiens, Reims, Paris, Beauvais, Chartres, Bourges, Vézelay, Tours, Nevers, Autun, Auxerre, Clermont-Ferrand, Lyons, Mantes, Laon, St. Quentin, Noyon, Soissons, Senlis, Meaux, Châlons-sur-Marne, Langres, Strasbourg, Rouen, Coutances, Bayeux, Le Mans, Troyes, Sens, Angers, Poitiers, St. Omer, Abbeville, Tournay, Geneva, and Lausanne.

I vote for an English master without bias, for it would be a romantic thing to have a great French church in London. All English architects, so far as I know, have taken the same view, so also have American students, and no Frenchman has wished to claim Westminster as an example of great " ogival " art. It has been studied by Count Paul Biver, M. C. Enlart and Viollet-le-Duc— the last-named, significantly dated the South Transept at Westminster as 1230—that is, he thought it not nearly so advanced as French work would have been *c.* 1250.

Mr. Westlake supports his theory by a reference to the late Mr. F. Bond's *Westminster Abbey*, 1909. However, it was not Bond's view that a French master conducted the actual works at Westminster. His was an intermediate position. He pointed out French characteristics, such as the radiating chapels ; the proportions of the interior and the tracery of the windows ; the buttress system ; the North Transept front with its porches. Then he considered how far English ways prevailed. But, he then argued : " Practically in all essentials it is a French church and had little influence on English architecture." However, he goes on : " If the church was designed by a Frenchman it was certainly not carried out by him." . . . " It was designed by a Frenchman, but built by an Englishman." He did not know that the Henry who was the first master probably had the name of Reyns, and he might have gone further in his claim if he had ; but his recorded view was that a French master sent some drawings and " may never have come near the work." This scheme would have allowed of the large English contributions in the work which Bond himself admitted, whereas, under a resident first master who was a Frenchman, these could not be explained. Even this view, however, does not sufficiently recognise the English "feeling" which penetrates the entire work done from 1245 to 1270.

Mr. Westlake says: "When so much of the skeleton fabric is French and nearly all the subsequently added detail English, is it too much to suppose that he who had to do with the former was a Frenchman?" It is not possible to divide skeleton and detail in this way. Much of the skeleton is of English type, and the detail is subsequent only to the making of plans, not to the building of the skeleton. Again, it is further suggested that the English character of our church may be explained by the fact that the works were not very forward when Master Henry died, about 1253. Now, there are two important Fabric Rolls of this year, which have been printed and analysed by the late Professor Willis (G. G. Scott's *Gleanings*, p. 231), and from these and other references we can determine, within fairly narrow limits, the progress of the works up to this time.

The eastern part of the Confessor's Church was destroyed in July 1245, and actual building from this time was pressed on by the eager King. The Crypt of the Chapter House must have been the first part of the whole church which was entirely completed (say 1246), and this is English in every respect. The three bays of the Cloister, between the Transept and the Chapter House entry, have the next earliest vaults, and these may be dated about 1248–50; they are of an earlier character than the vaults in the church, but, like them, they are typically English. The first part of the superstructure to be finished was the Chapter House, and this everybody admits is in the English tradition. As early as 1248–49, "task work" (special agreement) for the masonry in the Cloister (under the west aisle of the South Transept) is recorded.

84

In 1252–53, the King ordered that timber should be obtained for the roof of the new work of the church and for the stalls of the monks in the same. In the Fabric Roll of 1253, we find references to great marble columns (doubtless those of the interior); window tracery; voussoirs (of the arches); bosses, and chalk for the filling of the vaults; also a large quantity of iron from Gloucestershire (for the tie bars of the arches and stanchions of windows). Still more significant of the completion of some parts, we find lozenges (marble squares for paving) mentioned; and glass, white and coloured, which was issued for the use of several glaziers. Plumbers were also employed and limewashers and painters. The entry to the Chapter House from the Cloister was being built, and canvas for the windows of the former was obtained.

On this last item, Professor Willis remarked: " The mention of canvas for the windows of the Chapter House shows that these windows were so far completed in 1253 as to require to be closed with canvas until the glass was ready for them." Two sculptured figures for the Chapter House (probably a beautiful " Annunciation " group) are also mentioned at this time, and later, in 1258, it was directed that the residue of the tiles, used for paving the Chapter House, should be laid elsewhere.

As early as 1249, the King had ordered Master John of St. Omer, then painting the King's wardrobe, to make a great lectern for the " new Chapter " (Liberate Roll). Now Matthew Paris mentions the incomparable Chapter House at Westminster under the year 1250, and it may not be doubted that it was even then well advanced. The fine tiles, which are still on the floor, would have been put in hand about 1250–55. They contain the pattern of the great Rose windows of the transepts, which must thus have been designed before the tiles. These windows thus belonged to Master Henry's work. Indeed, this is shown by the fact that they were the most French of all the parts of the church, and they certainly belonged to the first Frenchcopying impulse. So do the fine sculptured angels in the spandrels just below them, which seem to have been inspired by angels at the Ste. Chapelle. It becomes clear that the first work, 1245–54, was settled wholly by Master Henry, and I am now disposed to think that the portrait head in the North Transept may be that of Master Henry rather than his successor.

There is no change of style in any part of the first work. Already, in the wall arcade of the Chapter House, which can hardly be later than 1247, diapered spandrels—the most differentiating characteristic of the internal work of the whole church—are found, and, in the upper part, is the most advanced tracery. Gilbert Scott, considering this question, said : " The church itself was by this time [1253]—indeed as early as 1249—in a state of rapid progression, so that the architecture must, in the main, have been settled at the time of its commencement."

Twenty years ago, I wrote : " Master Henry must be considered the architect of the building in all its parts." Then, after pointing out the debt to France, in detail, I added : " We may readily make the fullest allowance for French influence at Westminster, for so entirely is it translated into the terms of English detail, that the result is triumphantly English. It is a remarkable thing, indeed, that this church, which was so much influenced by French facts, should, *in spirit*, be one of the most English of buildings. This, perhaps, is only to be felt by those accustomed to read what is in buildings and cannot easily be demonstrated." I gave some details as to the character of the details in a notice of Mr. Bond's book in the *Journal of the Institute of Architects* (1910).

As was well said by an English architect—I think, Sir Gilbert Scott's son—" Westminster Abbey seems like a French thought in English idiom."

Now we will go back to what is known of Master Henry and consider whether he was necessarily a Frenchman if, as appears to have been the fact, his second name was Reyns. I have to make a little reservation even here, for if it could be proved that Henry de Reyns the mason must himself have come from Reims, then I should have to think that he could not have been the same Master Henry who began to build the church. I may remark that the name Henry was very popular in England at this moment ; and I cannot see, even if Reyns necessarily represents Reims, why the Henry of that name should himself be a Frenchman. Matthew Paris does not seem to have been a Frenchman ; William Torel, the artist, who made Queen Alianor's exquisite but very English bronze effigy, also bore a French name. If Master Henry had been specially brought from Reims to build the church, it would be difficult to understand why the name Reyns does not appear while he was working for his patron. It has further to be pointed out that the *Oxford Dictionary* gives Reynes as a form of the name Rennes ; and, as Mr. Westlake says, " it must not be forgotten that Rayne in Essex bears a name somewhat similar in sound."

The two successors of Master Henry at Westminster took their names from Gloucester and Beverley, and is it not probable that Henry was called from Rayne, otherwise Reynes ? Some entries in the Patent Rolls show that, at the time with which we are engaged, Reynes, in Essex, was a place well known to Henry III., who issued three mandates while staying there. In 1240, the King ordered that a tun of wine should be sent to " Resnes " (Liberate Roll). In the index to the charters at the British Museum, I find that " Reine " was said to have been granted to Westminster itself by the Confessor. There is a further charter of the time of Henry II., where it is called Reines, and in 1417 it is spelt Reygne.

In the London *Feet of Fines*, William de Reimes is mentioned, in 1198, in reference to land at Edgware ; and, in 1230, William de Reyne is named in connection with premises in Stanmore. The names, or forms of the same

name, Reymes, Raines, Roynes, are also found in the
Patent Rolls of the time of Henry III. In the Calendar
of St. Paul's Documents Great Reynes is mentioned. In
Buckinghamshire is Clifton Reynes with a church in which
are several fine tombs of members of the Reynes family.*

There is thus ample evidence to show that a mason
bearing the name of Reyns, and working in London, may not
himself have come from the city of Reims. There are
also reasons beyond the (to me convincing) architectural
evidence to show that Master Henry was, in fact, an
Englishman.

The first known reference to him is a mandate issued
December 10, 1243, that robes should be given to William
le Brun, and to Henry, Master of the King's masons. The
King had come to Windsor, on the day before, to keep
Christmas, and this is the first of several orders for robes
which were granted, once or twice a year, to persons in the
King's service. Now, William le Brun was a King's clerk
and Keeper of the Works at Windsor. Sir W. St. John
Hope tells us of certain works ordered in 1243, that " the
custodes operacionem at this time seem to have been Hugh
Giffard, William le Brun, and Simon the Carpenter, who
were *custodes* the following year." These robes of office
and the title " master of the King's masons," show that
Master Henry occupied the regular office of King's mason.
The association with William le Brun, and the place where
the order was issued, made it probable that the mason was
occupied at Windsor. And of this there is further evidence.

In 1243, a mandate was issued to the Sheriff of York that
the castle there should be strengthened according to the
advice of *Magistrum Simonem Carpentarium et Magistrum
Henricum Cementarium*, whom the King sent to confer
with " other masters expert in the science " (Close Roll,
wrongly indexed—p. 291 instead of 293). Such work was
part of the ordinary duties of the King's master masons

* Mr. Westlake allows me to say that he has found the spelling Reyns in
an English document.

and carpenters, and Simon at least had practice in castle work at Windsor. We have already seen that he was engaged at this time at Windsor.* Master Henry seems to have retained the office of King's master mason until his death about 1253.

We know that a son of Master Henry of Reyns was living in 1256, as shown by the record of his gift to the monastery. Forty years later, as appears in the accounts of the erection of the Eleanor crosses, a master mason named Nicholas Dyminge de Reyns built the Cross, which still exists at Waltham and is a typical piece of English work. The name Raine is still well known. Proceeding from my conviction, the result of all I know about mediæval architecture—that Westminster Abbey Church is English work, and allowing that the architect, Master Henry, probably bore the name of Reyns, I conclude that this was the name of a place in England or of some family settled in the country before the time of Master Henry.

. . . .

When I studied the work of Master Henry, some twenty years ago, I suggested that he was the architect of the King's Chapel at Windsor, built about 1240. Mr. Westlake's theory does not allow of this. His view is that Henry III. saw Reims Cathedral, when he was in France in 1243, and that he found his architect at Reims itself. After his return, Master Henry comes " suddenly into notice by receiving on Dec. 10, 1243, together with one William le Brun, a gown of office as Master of the King's Masons." The building of the Chapel at Windsor was in progress, but with it the mason " seems to have had no association." A reference to Sir W. Hope's big book on the Castle is

* From November 1236 onwards, Master Simon, the King's carpenter, was working at Windsor, and from 1243–44 to 1247–48 he was one of the keepers of the works. " He is last mentioned at Windsor in 1249. . . . In 1255 and for some years to come, the keepers of the important works then in progress were apparently Master John of Gloucester, the King's mason, and Alexander, the King's carpenter, who were also keepers of the King's works in Westminster Abbey " (Sir W. Hope, p. 70).

given, but there it is only said " very few names have been preserved of the craftsmen engaged for the period under notice."

No other King's mason than Henry is known at this time, and the work is likely, by reason of his office, to be his. Further, the existing part of the chapel so singularly resembles Westminster work that no one who will compare them will be able to doubt that they are by the same master. The Chapel was part of a large " work," which included new chambers for the King and Queen. Of the Chapel, Sir W. Hope says : " In 1239–40 the King issued a writ to Walter de Burgh for the making of a Chapel 70 feet long and 28 feet wide. . . . The north wall of this below the windows is actually a work of King Henry III." In 1244, another order directed that the works should " proceed winter and summer until the King's Chapel be finished." It was to have a high wooden roof, like that of the new work at Lichfield, " so that it may appear to be stonework." I take this from Hudson Turner. Sir W. Hope translated the last words (*appareat opus lapideum*) " so that the stonework appear," but the meaning was probably that it should have a wooden " vault." The Windsor Chapel had no buttresses and, therefore, no stone vault, and the north transept at Lichfield, which appears to have been the work mentioned, probably had a wooden roof.* The question arises, Was the latter the earliest of English " wooden vaults," and had the King's masters anything to do with it ? There are points about the Lichfield transept doorways which are closely akin to the style of the Westminster master, and I could suppose that he had worked at Lichfield before going to Windsor. The details at Winchester Castle should also be compared with the Abbey work. Stone church seems to be by some mason who had worked at Westminster.

I have made a special re-examination of the Windsor work, and I have no doubt whatever as to its near connection with Westminster. Not only was the master the same, but

* See a reference in *The Life of Sir G. Scott.*

the carver of some of the capitals also worked in both places. The Windsor work consists of an arcade of large blind arches, along the face of the external wall of the chapel, which formed the inner wall of a cloister. These arches resemble those of the Eastern Cloister walk at Westminster in function and in many details : in the sections of the arch mouldings ; in the fact that the arches have no drip-mouldings (compare the smaller arches next the Chapter House entry at Westminster) ; in the planning of the piers (two orders in one, three in the other), and the use of extra stout Purbeck shafts, about $7\frac{1}{2}$ in. in diameter ; the profile of the bases with the large roll overhanging the part below (Fig. 49) ; and the carved capitals. One of the arches at Windsor is much narrower than the others ; this was at the end and, doubtless, represents the width of a cloister walk ; the wider arches rise only to the same height, and are segmental, the centres being some 2 ft.

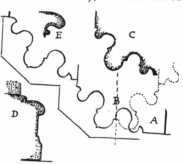

Fig. 49.—Windsor. A B C, Arch Mouldings ; D, Base ; E, Abacus.

below the springing line. A bold use of such arches is one of the singularities of Westminster ; we find it in the Chapter House entry, the diagonal vaulting ribs of the bays of the Cloister between it and the church door, the interior of the doors of the North Transept, the outer arches of the triforium windows, in a marked way over the Poets' Corner door, and above all in a big wall arcade in St. Faith's Chapel, which is remarkably like the Windsor arcade in scale and general character.*

* An interesting study might be made of the special characteristics of the great building masters. He of Salisbury seems to have experimented with half arches ; he of Lincoln with unsymmetry.

Sir Gilbert Scott illustrated, in *Gleanings* (p. 33), two capitals from the interior wall arcade at Westminster, which were of French character. He wrote: " Many of these are of the English type of the period, but among them are two kinds, both of which are, in their carving, distinctly French. The one is the *Crochet* capital the stalks of which are terminated, not as in English work with conventional, but with exquisite little tufts of natural foliage, such as may be seen in the wall

FIG. 50.—Windsor.

arcading of the Sainte Chapelle and many other French works of the period. In the other, natural foliage is in-

troduced, creeping up the bell and turning over at the top. In both the foliage is smaller and less bold than in French work, and the form of the capital is English." (See Figs. 33 and 34.) Now, among the capitals at Windsor, we find ordinary Early English foliage and both varieties of the French fashion, which so closely resemble those at West-minster that they must be by the same carver. In Figs. 50 to 53 I give some sketches from the Windsor capitals, and in Fig. 54 a tuft of foliage from Westminster.

FIG. 51.—Windsor.

One capital at Westminster, to the right of the tomb of

92

the Princess Katharine, has naturalistic oak leaves. In the Museum is a capital, of which the stalks of the "crockets" cross exactly like that sketched in Fig. 53. These were carved by the same man! The flat leaves (Fig. 51) may be compared with similar carving in the upper part of chamfer between the capitals in the East walk of Westminster Cloister, now much decayed. The lumps between the stalks on Fig. 52, now decayed, were birds, as I find from an old sketch, drawn about twenty-five years ago. Fig. 55 shows a capital at the doorway;

Fig. 52.—Windsor.

notice here the little corbel-like member which comes under the outer mould of the arch. At Westminster, these are similar, but more developed. They occur again at Stone, where there is carving, including a dragon in foliage, and a negro's head, which must be by a Westminster carver.

Fig. 53.—Windsor.

The Windsor Chapel was, in regard to the masonry details, the prototype of Westminster Abbey. This fact and the references to Master Henry, which are almost conclusive in themselves, show that he was the architect of Henry III.'s Chapel at Windsor. We thus carry back his tenure of the office of King's mason to 1239–40. He was not, therefore, first employed by the King on the great new church at Westminster, begun in 1245.

Master John of Gloucester succeeded Master Henry in the direction of the works about 1254. In 1255, he was

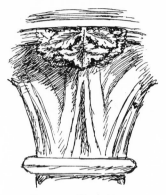

exempted from serving on juries, and the Sheriff of Oxford was to permit this exemption. He was also granted " for his service to the King at Gloucester, Woodstock, Westminster, and elsewhere two robes with furs of good squirrels yearly for life from the Wardrobe, such as Knights of the household receive." In 1256, Master John, the King's mason, was granted the serjeantry of Blechesdone. In 1257, he and

FIG. 54.—Westminster.

Alexander the carpenter were appointed chief masters of all works of castles, etc., this side of Trent.

" Master John, the King's mason (*cementarius*), is named in a grant *c.* 1250 in the possession of the Corporation of Gloucester as holding land" (*Notes and Queries*, 2nd S. vol. x.). I doubt if Master John did much more than carry on at Westminster in an interim period. Records of other works exist. 1258, Dec. 1: The King commanded Master John, the King's mason, to cause to be repaired the chimney of the King's chambers in the Priory of Merton, and the Gardrobe

FIG. 55.—Windsor.

and the King's Chancellor's chamber, and that the cost be charged to the King and allotted to the outgoings of the works at Westminster (Close Rolls, 42 Hen. III., Sharpe's Calendar).

MASTER JOHN OF GLOUCESTER

The great mason died in 1260–61, and, as Mr. Westlake has shown, he died poor. From *The Calendar of Inquisitions* (Misc. i., 298 : Jan. 3, 50 H. III.) it appears that " at the time of his death he was bound to the King in the sum of 80 marks by reason of arrears in the King's works. The debt was compounded for a yearly payment of 5 marks, but on inquisition being taken it was found that the income from his possessions was less than two marks a year." There was evidently trouble, and it looks as if the poor man was worried to death.

Master John was followed by Master Robert of Beverley, who brought Henry III.'s work to a conclusion. On the evidence of the fabric itself, I have come to think that all that is distinctive in the character of the second work must be ascribed to Master Robert. Although some of the changes in the Western extension of the Choir may have been intended from the first, there are

Fig. 56.—Plans of Piers.

many alterations of detail. French influence is much less apparent, and there are no new direct borrowings in this part. This work is most sweet and beautiful. Fig. 56 shows an intentional variation in the piers east and west of the crossing, both of the first work : the large pier is one of the four at the Crossing.

In 1264, Master Robert is named as one of the wardens at Westminster, receiving £100 for the works. The second work was thus proceeding at this time. The following year " Master Robert de Beverley, mason of the King's works of Westminster," was granted two robes a year from the Wardrobe, " so long as he be with the King in the said office in the same manner as Master John of Gloucester, sometime mason of the works, used to receive." In this year and the next, he and Alexander the carpenter are called keepers of the works (Patent Rolls). His name appears in 1272 as witnessing a charter, together with Edmund the Goldsmith and William le Verrer, who must have been glazing the church. Robert of Beverley was still the King's master of works in 1284; he thus occupied the position for about twenty-five years. Probably work of his could be identified at the Tower. He was a very great mason.

The best approximation to an English architect's drawing

known to me is one of tabernacle work surrounding a figure of Becket in the " Black Book of the Exchequer " (Fig. 57). It is so like the work of Villars de Honnecourt, that it must be very similar to the original drawings for the Abbey. In the sixteenth century, a house outside the north side of the nave was still called " Mason's Lodge."

. . . . .

Master Robert of Beverley was followed in the Office of King's Mason by Master Richard Crundale,

FIG. 57.—Thirteenth - Century Drawing.

who erected Charing Cross and made Queen Eleanor's tomb in the Abbey; he died about 1292–94. From mention of his appearing as a surety he is seen to have lived in the City (Letter Book B). He was succeeded by Master Michael of Canterbury, who built the Eleanor Cross in Cheapside (of which some remnants exist at the Guildhall) and commenced St. Stephen's Chapel in the Palace, 1292. Probably he made the tombs of Edmund Crouchback and his wife Aveline in the Abbey about 1296–1300. Two other import-

96

ant masons of this time were Master Richard de Wytham
(who succeeded Master Michael) and Simon de Pabenham.
These also lived in the city; they were " had up " before
the Mayor at the Guildhall, in 1298, because of a bitter
quarrel. (Mediæval craftsmen were very quarrelsome.)
In 1300, Richard de Wytham was sworn as a surveyor of
work proper to a mason in the City, and, in 1313, Master
Simon de Pabenham was likewise sworn as a " viewer "
together with Master Alexander of Canterbury. One of
these masons was probably the building master of the
choir of the Grey Friars' Church, which was begun, in
1306, by Queen Margaret, second wife of Edward I. (Stow).
Now, in a record recently published, it appears that, in 1306,
a jury of the venue round Cornhill and the House of the
Friars Minor was summoned to inquire whether John de
Offington, mason, had threatened the King's masons, who
had been brought into the City for the Queen's work, that
if they accepted less wages than the other masons of the
City they would be beaten, in consequence of which the
Queen's work was unfinished " (A. A. Thomas, *Early
Mayors' Court Rolls*, 1298–1307).*

* For a general account of mediæval masons see Dr. G. G. Coulton's
Social Life in Britain, 1916.

CHAPTER VI

THE CHAPTER HOUSE

" As the Rose is to other Flowers
So is this House among Buildings."

TILE INSCRIPTION.

THIS noble building is necessarily considered as an annex of the great church, but it deserves close, separate study.

The Chapter House can be securely dated as built about 1245–50. From the fabric rolls, it is clear that it must have been begun with the earliest work in 1245, and Matthew Paris mentions it, under the year 1250, as the incomparable Chapter House. In 1253, canvas was purchased as a temporary filling for the windows, in view, we may suppose, of some immediate use being made of the building.

The source for the octagonal type of plan, so far as is known, is the circular Chapter House vaulted in ten bays to a central pillar, built at Worcester in the first half of the twelfth century. A transition between the circle and the octagon is represented by the Chapter Houses of twelve sides at Margam and Dore, one formerly at Evesham, and that at Lincoln ; the last two had ten sides. Those of Beverley and Westminster are the earliest known which reached the octagonal type : the former was probably begun about 1230.

We will preface our examination of the building by condensing some descriptions of it, written before the great restoration of 1866. The first is by John Carter (1799) ; I call attention to some passages by putting them in italic.

" The entrance is from the Cloister through a double archway ; the work [here] is profuse and beautiful. How

Fig. 58.—Drawing by Mr. S. Weatherley, slightly altered.

99

is our just indignation raised at beholding the ravages of those savage hands which have destroyed *the statue of the Virgin* which stood on a bracket in the centre, and nearly so the accompanying angels. . . . We proceed along a double avenue ; a flight of steps brings us to the double archway entering the Chapter House itself. *This double archway has had its dividing column in the centre with nearly all its open tracery (in the manner of the Chapter Houses at Wells and Southwell) cut away.* We are now within, and find that five, of the eight, sides which were nearly open in one large window have had *their tracery* filled in with brickwork and small modern windows. The tracery in two of the remaining sides has been cut away ; the groins destroyed to a small portion which is yet springing from the delicate and delightful cluster of columns at the centre arched to the several angles of the structure, *where a few portions of their mouldings may be observed.* In all probability the stalls and decorations against the lower part of the walls may be remaining, but the presses block them up from the view of those few who may visit this once celebrated place. Here observers will find little but modern carpenter's work, vast rolls of parchment, dust and rubbish, and the famous Domesday Book. Among the reflections that occur is one for the danger that attends *the cluster of columns* in the centre by the modern false floor whose centrical part rests on *the remnant of the groins* springing from it " (*Gentleman's Magazine*, 1799). In his *Specimens of Architecture and Sculpture*, Carter gave a plate of the outer doorway, with a valuable account of it, in which the small sculptured figures of the archivolt were identified as the Ancestors of the Virgin.

The next account is that given by Neale and Brayley (1823) : " The present battlements are of brick with a stone coping. A small doorway, for official convenience [!] has been made through the wall adjoining Poets' Corner. [The filling of this may be seen in the north bay of the interior.] The great pointed arch across the [inner main entrance is sculptured and *the capitals display beautiful foliage*. The walls are surrounded by trefoil arches ; on the east side the wall behind is *beautifully gilt and painted* with a series of Angels who appear to be receiving the Faithful and rewarding them with crowns of glory ; the wings of the Angels are partly expanded, and the feathers are inscribed in black letter. The original pavement appears to consist of *figured tiles* wrought with lions, foliage, and other subjects."

About this time the valuable drawing of these paintings in the eastern bays, which is now placed near them, was made, apparently, by John Carter.

In 1842, Henry Cole (later Sir H.) wrote a popular guide to the Abbey, in which the Chapter House is again described: " The sculptures of the mouldings of the entrance arches will be found more perfect than those outside [in the Cloister], and *when cleaned of whitewash may possibly appear in all their original crispness and bright colour*. . . . Enormous windows : if we may judge from *a window now closed up*, their [lower] circles were quatrefoiled surmounting trefoiled arches. The ancient groins branch from *the exquisite capital* of the column of eight shafts which has been suffered to remain. The floor was paved with tiles, heraldic and otherwise ; portions are shown. Pillars on a stone basement support [wall] arcades. Sculptures above in *the capitals have been hewn away*. Behind the pillars all the walls seem to have been adorned with paintings executed on the stone. Enough in the paintings on the walls, *the colours and gildings of the arcades and the mural ornaments* [diapers] *above them*, exists to furnish authority for colours in Gothic architecture."

At this time, the sculptured Angel had been removed from its niche and was standing in the vestibule. The author says of the destruction of the vault : " In 1703 when it was proposed to make a gallery, Sir C. Wren absolutely refused." The old groined roof was standing as late as 1740. It was then reported by Thos. Ripley, Wm.

Kent [the chief architects of the time], and Wm. Gill to be so bad that it was necessary to take it down. " We have viewed the walls and buttresses and find them in a very ruinous condition. But the necessary repairs cannot be made to the buttresses without taking off the decayed roof " (October 4, 1744).

In *Gleanings* (1863), Sir Gilbert Scott gave an account of his examination of the building, which was to lead up to the " restoration." As this is so well known, I shall only make use of special points as we get further on.

In 1866, on the eve of the " restoration," it was also described in the *Ecclesiologist* by a writer who must, I think, from internal evidence, have been William Burges : " For loveliness there was probably no more conspicuous building in the kingdom when it was in its glory. What remains is so excellent—though, alas, sadly dilapidated—that we dread any attempt at restoration lest damage should be done to its precious fragments. The Chapter House which most resembles it is that at Salisbury, which was, in fact, to a great extent copied from it. . . . At Westminster we have tracery of a high order. These were *as fine specimens of four-light windows* as are to be found in any country. Over the portal the shortened window was of five lights, as may be seen from the sill which still remains. . . . Nothing can well be more shameful—every window blocked up ; the whole of the exterior so entirely defaced as scarcely to leave a vestige of its glory. Fortunately, *there is just enough to show that the exterior mouldings and ornaments* [of the windows] *were similar to the interior*, and so the task of restoring will be an easy matter. The interior has suffered less. The Government have simply let it go to decay. . . . A contemporary has actually recommended that nothing should be done but put the place in good repair [!]. It is urged that this fragment of art will serve the purpose of education better as it is than if placed beside twice its bulk of modern imitation. Though there is much good sense in all this, yet in the present instance [!] we

102

cannot agree with it. . . . It is by no means impossible that *some of the old work built up in the windows, etc., may be used again.* . . . Any attempt to make a smart new building will be worse than leaving the place alone, and the greatest possible care must be exercised in retaining every bit that exists. On no account must anything be done to the wall paintings except with a view to their *preservation.* It is to be hoped that there will be no hurry in deciding the execution of the stained glass ; the state of this manufacture—for at present it is no more—is not such as to warrant haste. As there is *so much valuable wall-painting* there can scarcely be a doubt that much of this *glass should be grisaille* so as not to exclude the light."

A useful record of the unrestored interior is given by a woodcut from one of the illustrated papers (May 1866), which stands in the Chapter House. A smaller woodcut is given in *Gleanings,* and Mr. Stacy Marks made a large water-colour drawing.

* * * * *

Vault and Tie-bars.—The slender central column is now a copy of that which remained until our own day, together with a part of the central springer of the vault. "The central pillar," Scott said in 1863, "*still exists* and is about thirty-five feet high. It is entirely of Purbeck marble and consists of a central shaft surrounded by eight subordinate shafts attached to it by three [two] moulded bands. The capital, though of marble, is most richly carved. On the top of the capital is *a systematically constructed set of eight hooks of iron* for as many cross-ties. The same was the case at Salisbury, and I have no doubt that the hooks on the columns in the church are many of them original and were intended for security during the progress of the works."

There is a measured drawing of the Chapter House made by R. J. Johnson, about 1859, and now at Westminster ; it shows the central shaft 13 in. and the eight others only about $4\frac{1}{4}$ in. in diameter. The whole pillar is so slender that we may wonder at the skill and daring which balanced so great a load on so slight a prop. There was certainly here a definite attempt to do the most that might be possible in playing with stonework.

The capital is now probably a copy of the original; it is deeply carved with crisp foliage. Above it appear the eight hooks mentioned by Scott. Both here and in the church the hooks and tie-rods were intended to give not only " security during the progress of the works," but to the completed work as well. It was the fashion in Scott's day, as of ours, not to see a certain class of mediæval facts, and he seems to imply that the ties—eight rods of forged iron, 30 ft. long, which must have been very costly—were only of the nature of temporary scaffolding (Fig. 58).

However, Scott had the hooks replaced or copied, and eight corresponding hooks may be seen in the springers of the vaults at the angles of the octagon. The whole conception of this octagonal structure depended, in a large degree, on the use of these tie-bars. The same system was copied at Salisbury, where the ties lasted on into the nineteenth century. That careful observer, John Carter, put it on record that more than a century ago it was proposed to remove them; and soon they were removed, it seems, for, forty or fifty years after he wrote, the building showed serious evidence of failure, and the architects then called in explained that the buttresses were insufficient, and added great lumps to them, while cutting out the locked system of iron hooks from the central springer, which may now be seen in the south-west angle of the Cloister.

At Westminster, Scott did not put back the iron tie-bars, but a visit to the roof above shows that he would not trust the construction without them. His engineer has hung up the vault to the iron roof.

At Salisbury, there were never any external flying buttresses to the Chapter House, and, as it is obviously almost a copy of Westminster, this raises the question whether the flying buttresses here are original, and I believe that they are not. The one immediately outside Poets' Corner was

104

built for the first time by Scott. The one next to it has a plinth of fourteenth-century form ; the three others differ in their spans, and their plinths do not range with the plinth of the main building. I conclude that the Chapter House was built without flying buttresses in entire dependence upon its " chainage " of iron bars. (It may be mentioned that the flying buttresses around the Chapter House at Lincoln seem also to be additions.) Possibly, some of the hooks drew away from the springers and made additional support necessary at an early time. Besides the eight ties mentioned above, the windows are threaded by three tiers of strong iron bars, which are still wholly or largely original. One may assume that they link up at the angles and form bands right around the octagon. Scott found, from the fact that the round bars were beaten square where they passed through the mullions, that the western window originally had four lights like the others. It seems to have had five lights substituted in the fourteenth century, following the fire of 1298. (Fig. 58.)

Not only did the springing courses of the vaulting remain in the angles as well as at the centre, but Scott found many voussoirs of the ribs, several of which seem to have been re-used. There is thus no question as to the forms of the vaulting. (See Note 2 at end.)

Windows, Arcade, and Floor.—It is clear from the old views that the central mullions and larger sub-arches remained in many of the windows, and probably some tracery was found other than that of the blank bay, which was, in a large degree, intact. From some report following the completion, I have noted : " The roof has been entirely rebuilt. The tracery of the windows has been restored after the model of the one which had been left uninjured on the N.W. side." Drawings by R. J. Johnson, made about 1859, now in the Abbey Collection, show the windows and vault practically as restored by Scott ; and there is, fortunately, no doubt as to the form and details of the noble four-light windows. This is all the more important, as they seem to have been the source for the " geometrical " tracery which spread over England. Themselves derived from Amiens or the Sainte Chapelle, they were copied and adapted in the Chapter House and Cloister at Salisbury, the east window at St. Albans, the side windows at Lincoln, and those in the transepts of St. Mary's, York; also at Netley, Bakewell, Grantham, and other places. Altogether, Westminster was a great milestone in the progress of English building. It is more than a mere truism to say that every other church in England was either earlier or later than Westminster.

FIG. 59.

The scale of the windows is greater than might be supposed; they are about 19½ ft. wide and 39 ft. high, the lights being 4¼ ft. wide and the large central circle 10 ft. in diameter. A pretty minor detail may be observed in the two quatrefoils of each window; the upper moulding conforms to the shape of the pointed containing arch, and only the " daylight " shape is rounded.

The wall arcade above the stone benches surrounding the walls is largely restored, but there is hardly anything conjectural except the carved heads, etc., above the end arches in each bay. That there were such carvings is shown by one almost shapeless little body which remains. Not only the heads, but parts of the arches, and in most cases the fronts of the capitals, had been cut away. The marble capitals of the eastern recesses are all sculptured, and they have long bonding attachments to the wall, which are also carved. Scott, describing these eastern recesses, said :

106

" Their capitals carved in Purbeck marble are of exquisite beauty " (Fig. 59). They have, however, been " restored " with a heavy hand. In the Gardner Collection was a set

Fig. 60.—About half-size. Drawn by J. C. Bartholomew.

of sketches of these capitals with the attachments at the back, which prove that they were badly broken, and the existing work shows that large parts have been skilfully spliced on.* They are, however, original in a secondary

* These drawings are now preserved at the Abbey.

degree, and the sides of the bondstones are largely un-
touched. One of these, carved with dragons, is of high
beauty, and, fortunately, it is guaranteed by one of the
sketches just mentioned. Capitals carved in Purbeck
marble are very scarce. Some at South Kensington, which
came from Chertsey Abbey, closely resemble them, especially one with dragons. As will be seen later, I think that
these also came from a work of Henry III.

Most of the other capitals of the wall arcade have been
more largely renewed,
but usually with full
evidence as to their
ancient forms. They
had puzzled me until
the late Mr. S.
Weatherley, who had
been Scott's assistant,
pointed out to me that
only an inch or so of
the inner part of most
of them was really old,
and that the rest had
been spliced on with
great accuracy. Mr.
Weatherley gave me a
sheet of profiles that

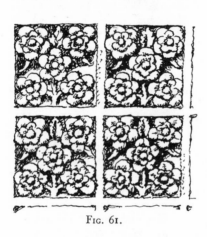

Fig. 61.

had been made in 1868 from the remaining parts by
the clerk of works, John Kaberry—" a more careful level-
headed Yorkshireman I never met." Mr. Weatherley
also wrote that " the detailing and superintendence " of
the work was confided to the younger Gilbert Scott by
Sir Gilbert. The work was executed by Poole & Son, the
Abbey masons.

There is a carved capital on the left of the north side of
the octagon which seems entirely original, and there are
some others—mostly next the angles—which look old. The
foiled heads of the wall arcade are halves of quatrefoils,

and a similar arcade is found at the inside of the west end of Amiens Cathedral ; the square diapering in the spandrels certainly was borrowed from Amiens. The large trefoils over the entrance doorway seem to have been imitated from those above the western rose at Amiens (Fig. 58). These correspondences make it more probable that the source for the four-light windows of the Chapter House was the same cathedral from which we shall find many other borrowings, rather than the Ste. Chapelle. The capitals and the carved spandrels over the arches furnish a striking instance of the old and natural delight in variation. The spandrels are of great beauty, several containing varieties of rose patterns. One, by the central eastern arch, has branches of roses on a trellis ; it almost looks as if it had suggested Morris's trellis-pattern wallpaper (Figs. 60 and 113). Others at the

Fig. 62.

north-east corner have repeated groups of five roses and there are other varieties (Figs. 61 and 62). A trail of roses is carved on the jamb of the entrance.

It was observed before that rose decoration was much used in the church, and roses were certainly in the minds of the builders of the Chapter House, as we shall see from an inscription. There was a cult of roses at this time, and rose decoration is found on the west front of Amiens Cathedral. Even at the end of the fourteenth century, when the panels formed by the wall arcade were painted, a margin at the beginning had a big rose pattern which can now hardly be traced.

The tiled floor laid down about 1255 is the finest existing pavement of the kind. There are six short inscriptions on the pavement, but they are so worn that little has been done in reading them. The best, indeed the only attempt, is that by Mr. Clayton (*Archæological Journal*, 1912). Four single lines are in the south-east sector, and two longer lines are associated with some " picture tiles " of a hunting scene on the south side. The second of the four short lines was read by Mr. Clayton :

[*Qua ?*] *Rex Henricus Sce Trinitatis Amicus.*

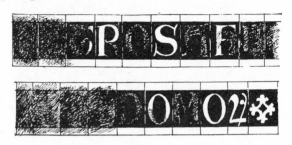

Fig. 63.—Beginning and end of line only.

The floor has recently been well cleaned, and that has allowed me to read enough of the first line to make out its meaning (Fig. 63). This first inscription is given by Mr. Clayton thus :

. . SPOS . F . . SI . . . SI . D . C . . . . . . O . . U +

(The U at the end represents a contraction mark.) Re-examining it in a good light I thought the first letters were rather . . TROSAF. At the end are letters which seemed to be OMO followed by the contraction mark, which I will represent by 4, and the same mark occurs near the middle. Fig. 63 gives the beginning and end of this inscription something as it appears.

WINDOWS, ARCADE, AND FLOOR

The well-known inscription written up in the Chapter House at York, likening it to a rose, now suggested itself.

In a guide book the York inscription is given thus: *Ut rosa flos florum sic est domus ista domorum.* On returning to verify, I found that there is no doubt as to the first five words or of the final word, and four places in front of that is a narrow space suitable for I, so *ista domorum* is also sure. I now give my reading of the Chapter House inscription,

Fig. 64.—All in one line.

the cross at the beginning being repeated from that at the end, and 4 being used as a contraction mark for *rum*.

+. TROSAF . . SFLO4SIC . . . . . ISTA DOMO4 +

It is quite evident that the saying told to every visitor of the York Chapter House was made for Henry III. to inscribe on the floor of the Chapter House at Westminster, and that it was only borrowed at York.

This, then, was the King's own claim, that his new Chapter House surpassed others as the rose surpasses other flowers. Matthew Paris, in calling it the " incomparable Chapter House," held the same view—possibly, indeed, he wrote the inscription.

THE CHAPTER HOUSE

The cleaning of the tiles makes it possible to confirm the general accuracy of Mr. Clayton's reading of the second verse :

. . A[?] REX HENRICS . . T . I . . T . TISAMI.

The word *Trinitatis* can now be read with certainty. At the end is another variety of contraction mark which I will represent by 2, and the same occurred, I think, in other places also.

. . . REX HENRI2 SCᴇ TRINITATIS AMI2

It would probably have had a cross at the beginning, which would allow room for only a word of two letters before Rex. I give, in Fig. 64, a sketch of this interesting and, one might have thought, important inscription.

The third of the verses is given by Mr. Clayton as below, and he pointed out that the last word must be *amavit*.

. RP . . . . B . . . T . V . . E . TE . . . . MAVIT

The beginning, I have no doubt, is + XPō. The mosaic floor of the Presbytery has an inscription beginning + XPI. All the letters cannot be filled in, but, I think, the following may be trusted (Fig. 65) :

+ XPō . . . . AVITQVISA . TE . I . AMAVIT

No word has yet been read of the fourth line, but the general meaning of the whole is pretty clear, and it could now probably be read by an expert : " This Chapter House as superior to others as the rose is among flowers : it King Henry friend of the Holy Trinity : to Christ dedicated who him loved." . . .

The other two inscriptions are in longer lines and appear to have referred to the hunting scene with which they were associated. The first began HIC RESONAN[T].

The tiles seem to be by the same craftsmen who executed a very remarkable floor once at Chertsey Abbey, where the tiles contained scenes from the "Romance of Tristram," which are of particular interest in furnishing a check on the early text of that romance. At the Chapter House, besides small figures of a King, Queen, and Abbot, one tile has figures of the Confessor and the pilgrim, another two musicians, and three others contain a hunting scene—a horseman and dog, a bowman, and a stag. Such tiles were called "painted tiles," and they must have been drawn by one of the ablest painters of the time. They were probably executed at Chertsey, where kilns have recently been found. Our kings had a special interest in the story of Tristram, and the version of the poet Thomas was, it is thought, written at the Court of Henry II. The pointless sword carried at the Coronations was said to have been the sword of Tristram. Now Chertsey is close to Windsor, and the Tristram floor at that Abbey must, I think, have been a gift of Henry III. The tiles seem to have paved the floor of a chapel which lay along the side of the choir aisle—

FIG. 65.—Beginning only.

a position in which a Lady Chapel is often found. From this chapel come the beautiful capitals carved in Purbeck marble mentioned above. I reach the conclusion that this chapel at Chertsey, with the Tristram tiles and marble capitals, was built by Henry III., and this finds some confirmation in the fact that, in the wardrobe account of his son, an item records the gift of a cross to the King's Chapel at Chertsey Abbey.

The picture tiles in both places are so alike that, I think, they must have been designed by the same artist. The ornament is also very similar, and there are one or two tiles at Westminster (not in the Chapter House) which are identical with others at Chertsey. The inscriptions at Chertsey are also very similar in style to those at Westminster ; some are on separate blocks, others are in longer

strips, and of one of these I give a sketch (Fig. 66).* The
style of all is very like that practised at St. Albans in the
middle of the thirteenth century. Apart from the figures,
a type of foliage occurs with a long, waving, pointed leaf and
cross bars on the
stalks (Figs. 67–69),
which I have only
found on a beautiful
St. Albans drawing
at the British
Museum (2 B, VI),
and in North French
MS. The same

FIG. 66.—Chertsey Abbey.

artist, who did the drawing, may have designed the tiles.
Fig. 68 is from the St. Albans drawing; Fig. 69 is from
one of the smaller tiles, which, I think, has never
been illustrated. The kind of leafage just mentioned
is most marked on some border
tiles.

The Annunciation Door.—
The doorway entering the
Chapter House from the vestibule is largely ancient. On
the left and right are two very
fine sculptures of Gabriel and
the Virgin. The arch has a
series of small figures in a trellis
of foliage. Attachments at the
springing and near the crown
of the inner order show that
there were sub-arches with a circle above. Some years
before the great " restoration " was undertaken, Scott wrote
thus : " The doorway was double, divided by a central pillar,

FIG. 67.

* The letters on the single blocks are still more like those at Westminster,
indeed, so much like, that they appear to be by the same artist, but slightly
more advanced.

114

and with a circle in the head; whether pierced or containing sculpture I have been unable to ascertain, as it is almost entirely destroyed. The jambs and arch are magnificent. The former contain on their outer side four large shafts of Purbeck marble. Their caps are of the same material, and most richly carved, and the spaces between the shafts are beautifully carved."

Fig. 68.

According to Carter's description given before, the doorway showed indications above it of " open tracery (in the manner of the Chapter Houses of Wells and Southwell) cut away." Scott's first design for " restoration," given in *Gleanings*, pierced the tracery, but set an isolated image of the Majesty in the centre of the foiled circle. As this showed the back of the figure to the

Fig. 69.

outside, it was, doubtless, thought awkward, and, in the executed work, two Christs were substituted, back to back, on a very thin solid filling. I have long been convinced that such a figure or figures would not have been here. The predominating importance of the Annunciation group, the Angel on one side and the Virgin on the other, negatives the existence of another figure, central, but an interference. An open foiled circle would have afforded an entrancing vision of the interior and its glorious windows. Moreover, the vestibule was required to be as light as possible, because the window of St. Faith's Chapel opens to it.

On approaching by the flight of steps, the solid circle, which now blocks the sight, comes almost exactly in the visual line to the foiled circle of the eastern window. The ancient stonework itself in no way suggests a solid circle ; what is left gives a tracery-bar profile similar to the general type found in the Church and the Chapter House itself (Fig. 70, B).

Finally and conclusively, the large trefoil panels in the spandrels of the arch have minor figures of angels censing the Virgin, who stands in the niche on the right. If there

was a central figure these spandrels must be seen in relation to it, and that such figures should be turning their backs on a Majesty, the centre not only of the composition but of the Universe, is unthinkable. Fig. 70 A, shows the angels in the trefoil on the right who turn away from the centre towards the Virgin (compare Fig. 71).

FIG. 70.

The figures of the Virgin and Angel are very noble sculptures, fully 6 ft. high. They are so strikingly similar to a pair at the Virgin's door of Amiens Cathedral that it may not be doubted that ours are imitated from the French figures, which were more or less copied at Reims, also, as, indeed, was the whole portal. The idea of the design is that the Virgin carries a book of the prophecies, and she lifts her right hand in surprise while the Angel expounds what was written. I have shown that the North Transept front, with its sculptured portals, was a modified copy of the west front at Amiens. The resemblance between the sculptures at Westminster and at Amiens suggests that not

116

only the mason at Westminster but the sculptor as well
studied French models.

The arch-order, which is carved in open-work of foliage

ELEVATION OF GREAT DOORWAY

Fig. 71.—Drawing by E. C. Shearman (altered).*

containing little figures, is largely old.   Many of the figures
carry scrolls and they are, doubtless, prophets.   The jambs
of this doorway have vertical strips of sculpture between the

* I wish to thank Mr. Shearman for allowing me to use this and Fig. 77.

columns, both inside and out ; but the north and south jambs are not similar. The two strips on the north have only foliage, while the two on the south have many little figures set one over the other in scrolls of foliage. At the top of the inner set of figures is Christ. The head is broken away, but the cruciform nimbus remains. The outer set has the Virgin at the summit—a very perfect and remarkable little figure. Over these two figures are pretty canopies, and there are others over the foliage strips of the north jamb, each of which has two birds perched under their shelter— symbols of concord. The little figures of the strips can better be studied from the admirable old casts, made about 1860, and now at South Kensington, than at the doorway itself. The foliage, which contains the series which is terminated above by the Virgin, is a rose branch (showing buds and flowers ?) None of the small figures can be identi- fied, with the exception of one about the middle, which has the horns of Moses. One next below is half clothed and is putting his hose off or on ; one near the bottom holds a square block ; one near the top is clothed like a friar, or possibly a pilgrim ; most are sleeping in a way that recalls the figure of Jesse in " Jesse-trees," to which the design is obviously allied.

The inner strip of the south jamb has, under the Christ figure, others of kings set in scrolls of formal foliage.

Now the arch-orders of the Virgin's Door at Amiens, from which the Annunciation Group was imitated, contains three sets of small images—angels, kings, and patriarchs(?). They are described by Durand as ten angels with censers and candlesticks ; twelve kings ; fourteen personages in the scrolls of a vine with no identifiable symbols—" evidently the [last] two together represent the genealogical tree of the Virgin Mary, but Jesse is not here." At Amiens and at Westminster, there were more regular trees of Jesse.

The general derivation of these jamb figures from Amiens appears to be certain. Even the crowd of censing angels in the trefoils above the arch seem to follow those of the third arch-order at Amiens. If the small figures of the jamb at Westminster are compared with those of the Jesse-tree proper at Amiens, illustrated by Viollet-le-Duc, it will be seen that, in each case, the figures have little patches of ground under their feet from which the scrolls and foliage spring out ; this is so alike in both cases that relation is certain. The small angels in the trefoils just spoken of are rather badly decayed, and, from below, give little idea of how beautiful they must have been. After close inspection, this may just be guessed and good photographs might bring it out.

The sculptures were certainly designed by one who had studied the Virgin's Porch at Amiens. It was specially thought of as the Annunciation Door, and it should be a comfort to us to be able to think away the intruded vain imaginings of the tympanum ; the doorway thus becomes a unity—it and the whole Chapter House stand in the " composition " for the House of the Virgin. The door-way at Salisbury, on which Scott probably based his treat-ment of the entrance to the Westminster Chapter House, has a central sculpture (originally the Virgin ?) but there were no side sculptures ; the whole tympanum is solid, and the sub-arches are not tracery bars.

With the data of the span, the curves at the springing, and the radius of the central circle, we may accept the general lines of the tracery. Possibly Scott found some indication which suggested the central quatrefoil in the circle (Fig. 71). The single central column is guaranteed by the tracery section and the size of the jamb columns. The capitals of the jamb columns are in marble elaborately sculptured—one of those on the south side has lions amongst the foliage. This capital is ancient and so, in the main, is its next neighbour. The imitative work is so clever or specious that it is difficult to be sure of anything without testimony, but the northern capitals may be copies of broken ones. I have a letter from Mr. C. Burgess (1909), who worked on " the restoration," in which he says : " The capital with the lions is old ; most of the others in arcade are modern, also the heads." There is a cast of the lion capital at South Kensington (Fig. 72).

This noble doorway is one of the most beautiful things in English art.

Jesse-tree Doorway.—The outer entrance from the Cloister

FIG. 72.

must have been equally beautiful, but it is now terribly decayed. " Over the entrance into the Chapter House was placed the statue of the blessed Virgin with our Saviour in her arms, and two Angels, one on each side, all richly enamelled and set forth with gold and blue, some vestigia or footsteps of all which are still remaining whereby to judge the former splendour and beauty thereof " (Keepe, 1683). When Keepe wrote, there was probably actual memory of the central figure. The two angels are ruins of most beautiful figures, apparently by the sculptor of the Annunciation. The field of the tympanum is covered with strong scrolls of formal foliage, now so much decayed that only the " shadows " of them may be seen. Old sketches, however, and the careful measured drawing by Mr. Knight at the Victoria and Albert Museum, have preserved some record. A sketch made by A. Poynter, about 1820, of part of the scrolls on the arch-space shows that they had doubled stems ; this is a point in development which is confirmed by Knight's drawing. An accurate-looking woodcut of this foliage in *Gleanings* is without much value, as it was done from a poor sketch now at Westminster.

Knight's drawing, just mentioned, shows some jointing in the form of a little gable over the central plain space against which the image of the Virgin was placed, and it is evident that there was a canopy here. This is confirmed by the existence of two minor corbels attached to the base on which the statue stood, for these must have supported small shafts under the canopy (Fig. 73). The figure of the Virgin, we may suppose, was like that of the Virgin's door at Amiens. The attitude of the angels on either hand suggests to me that they may have carried candlesticks ; the angels surrounding the Virgin at Amiens bear candlesticks and censers. One of our angel images is much injured ; the other is a very beautiful headless figure. These angels may be compared with some carrying candlesticks in a British Museum manuscript (Arundel 83, Fig. 73).

There is no doubt as to the doorway having been painted brilliantly and gilt. In the Victoria and Albert Museum, Burges collection, is a drawing which carefully recorded traces actually existing sixty or seventy years ago. The field of the tympanum was blue with gilt foliage, the hollows reinforced with vermilion. This explains the rather timid colouring on Carter's original drawing in the Gardner collection. The ground is tinted blue, there is red here and there in hollows, and some of the carving is yellow for gilding. Traces of colour have been seen in 1925.

One of the arch-orders is carved with the " Stem of Jesse," and this was certainly copied from the central portal at Amiens (see Viollet-le-Duc and Durand). There Jesse appeared twice over, being the bottom figure on each side, while the stem terminated at the apex in figures of the

121

Fig. 73.

Virgin and Christ. According to the text, with Carter's excellent plate of our doorway, " the three lowest figures are precisely the same on both sides of the arch. . . . It is probable it was intended that one side should represent the kings of Israel and the other those of Judah, both having had in common for ancestors Jesse, David, and Solomon." It is also said that in the centre of the top is the figure of the Virgin and Child ; this may have meant the central sculpture. Malcolm, however, wrote (1803) : " I recognised the Blessed Virgin and infant Jesus and King David. Frag-

FIG. 74.

ments of paint and gilding adhere in parts enough to show their former splendour." The foliage on the tympanum also showed traces of gild-ing, and the bosses of the vault outside were gilt. The foliage on the tympanum was considered to be part of the Jesse-tree. Fig. 75 is from a sketch of the arch made about 1910.

Larger sketches of the figures, by Carter from the Gardner collection, show that most of the figures had crowns and the second figure on each side had a harp—that on the left may still be seen. Carter's plate shows also the round, nest-like units of foliage which

FIG. 75.

decorated the other arch-order. The central part of each boss, which was undercut, has now disappeared. Many years ago I made a sketch, which is enough to show that it was almost identical with carving around the blank tracery at the end of the inner vestibule. Old descriptions gave details of the colouring and gilding of the Jesse arch. Some student should compile a restored drawing of this wonderful doorway, one of the most romantic things in English art. I wish we could interest ourselves in such drawings instead of destroying authentic antiquities and calling that "restoration."

The vault of the northern alley of the outer vestibule is modern work, the southern alley, with its fine bosses, is original.

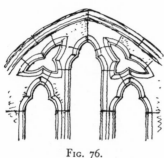

FIG. 76.

The work in the inner vestibule is largely authentic. The most doubtful major feature is the three-light window on the south side. Scott spoke of this as " a remarkable window now destroyed, but of which, by cutting into the walls, I have been able to gain some clue to the design." In his illustration, he shows a high central portion flanked by two lower lights which have curious long trefoils in the spandrels above. The window, as restored, is like this, except that the high central portion is of one light instead of two, as in the illustration. Mr. S. Weatherley told me that sufficient indications were found, when the work was done, to make the form certain. Indeed, it is clear·that there is not room for four lights. The upper cusps of the long trefoils are still old within, and the window may be accepted as of ancient form. The idea of the trefoils was probably taken from those over the Annunciation door, which were borrowed from those over the West Rose at Amiens. Fig. 76 is from the exterior of this window.

Fig. 77 is the end of the inner vestibule, mentioned above. (See Note 1 at end.)

.   .   .   .

Glass and Painting.—We have seen that Burges recommended grisaille glazing, but his advice was not followed. Since that time, remnants of such glass have been found in the apsidal chapels of the church. The companion or daughter Chapter House at Salisbury had grisaille windows with a bright shield of arms set in each light. That this was the arrangement, too, at Westminster, is further proved by what Sandford says of heraldic shields : The arms of Henry III. and Eleanor of Provence " are yet standing in several windows in the Abbey—the arms of Raymund, Earl of Provence, are painted in the Chapter House windows and several other windows ; the arms of Eleanor of Castile are in a glass window on the west side of the north cross." Three or four of these shields of arms still exist in the glazing of the apse windows. It is evident that the Chapter House of Westminster had similar glazing to that at Salisbury, and like that it must have been a vast vessel of light. At present, the windows are filled with double deep-dyed tints and the electric-light has been brought in. At Salisbury Chapter House, the centres of the large roses had pairs of figures, a King and an ecclesiastic, set on a grisaille ground. This, too, was probably taken over from Westminster.

The panels of the wall arcade contain paintings of " The Doom " and " The Apocalypse." These are of the fourteenth century, and I gave some description of them in the *Spectator*, July 7, 1923. The arches and diaper work, above the eastern bays only, show traces of colour and gilding, which may be of the original work. In Piers Plowman's *Crede* is a passage describing one of the great Friaries of London as having a Chapter House " painted all round like a Parliament house," and this allusion may have been suggested by the then recent decorations of what is known to have been the meeting place of Parliaments at

FIG. 77.—End of Inner Vestibule opposite doorway Fig. 71.

CRYPT

Westminster. The large provision of stone seats around the Great Octagon suggests that Henry III. had from the first intended to use it for such assemblies.

. . . . .

Crypt.—Under the Chapter House is a crypt, which is well described in *Gleanings*. It is very strong and was, doubtless, intended for a Treasury. The walls are nearly 18 ft. thick; three doors intervened between it and the South Transept; the stone stair stops about 4 ft. from the bottom and is continued by a short detachable wooden stair, which looks like a thief trap. In the central pillar of the crypt are some cavities once closed by thin stones.

It has been argued recently that this was the King's Treasury robbed in 1303—the most famous burglary in English history. The chief evidence is that the place robbed is said to have been " under the Chapter House." That seems conclusive, until we remember that " under " was often used in the sense of inferior and near, as under-hill, under-shaft. In the account of the affair given in *Gleanings* are two quotations from documents, one of which is translated, " the treasury below the Chapter House," and the other " near." Another Abbey treasury, the chapel of the Pyx, is under the Chapter House in the second sense. I should not enter on this much-disputed subject were it not that I may put on record some evidence from the structure which may be helpful.

I doubt whether the Crypt actually beneath the Chapter House was at an early time in regular use; for long it must have remained very damp. In 1909, it was cleaned out and then nothing more than a mortar floor was found. Scott says that earlier it had been " filled up some feet above its natural level with earth," and that he " lowered it to the original level." Such raising of the level with earth suggests flooding.

Mr. Hall, in *Antiquities of the Exchequer*, said that the King's great Treasury was the Chapel of the Pyx. " Here the King's four crowns and the other regalia were deposited with many jewels as late as the reign of Henry VI." He objects to the view that " the treasure of the Wardrobe was normally situated below the Chapter House," but he adds, " it was there undoubtedly in the nineteenth year and later " (1291, etc., *cf. Archæologia*, xliv.). There is a record that the Treasury " under the Chapter House " had a new floor of tiles laid in 1291. This entry is discussed by Mr. Clayton, in the *Archæological Journal* (1912), and he concluded that it probably refers to the Chapel of the Pyx, where a tile floor of about that date still exists.* Again, the violated Treasury is said to have been under " the Monks' Chapel," which those who accept the Crypt solution think may be another name for Chapter House, whereas the Monks' Chapel may have been St. Dunstan's, close by on the other side of the Pyx. In 1248–9 it was decided to keep proof pieces of money in the Treasury at Westminster. Now it was from keeping these standard pieces that the Pyx Chapel took its name, and there seems to be no doubt that at this time the Chapel was a Royal Treasurehouse.

The vault or walls of the Crypt have never been broken through, but Mr. Westlake suggests that the thief " cut through the iron bars " of one of the Crypt windows. The evidence, however, seems to point to a hole in a wall.

The burglary was effected from the Cemetery, between the Dormitory range and the palace. The chief thief was Richard de Podelicote, who was assisted by John, a mason, who made the " engines " or implements of iron used in

* Of this chapel Dr. Armitage Robinson wrote : " It has been argued that the Treasury, which was robbed, was the vault beneath the Chapter House. . . . But it remains certain that since the days of Edward III. royal treasures were kept in this chapel. Portions of the Regalia were also there, though others were in the Monastic Treasury in St. Faith's Chapel. Since the Restoration the Regalia have been in the Tower, but the old chapel was still used as a Treasury of Records." He suggests that it had been divided off from the undercroft about two centuries after building [*c.* 1270], but carvings on a capital in the dividing wall different on the two sides suggest a much earlier date. (W. A. in the *Seventeenth Century*, 1904.)

128

making a breach in the wall. Podelicote worked at it for months before he obtained entry. Professor Tout reproduced a nearly contemporary sketch of the thief at work, and it has been suggested that windows appear here. I only see an indication of a vaulted structure.

At the inquiry, it was asserted that four years previously an attempt had been made to break into the same Treasury from the Cloister side. It is obvious that this piece of evidence is strongly in favour of the Pyx site, although it has been said that it " need not necessarily be so, for it would be possible to attack the undercroft of the Chapter House from the Cloister side." I cannot see how, and, in any case, no window was accessible from this side. Again, Mr. F. Bond thought that the Poets' Corner door was an insertion made in order to give access from the Palace to the Crypt treasury, since it cuts into the arcading on the left. The doorway seems to me to have been foreseen and built-in with the work. Leaving the difficulties involved in the Crypt hypothesis, I wish to point out that there is some material evidence which suggests that the external wall of the Chapel of the Pyx against the Cemetery was at some time broken through. Directly inside the thirteenth-century north door, which Scott believed to be the original entrance to " the Pyx," is a patch of repaired walling low down, which looks, as was pointed out to me by Mr. Wright, as if it might have been the actual point where the thief entered. Outside is a blind corner, sheltered by a Chapter House buttress so completely, that it is easy to think that a man might long have worked here hidden. The north doorway, just mentioned, is that which has fragments of some skin (said to be human), which lined it within. The existing doorway into the Pyx from the Cloister is later than 1303 ; possibly, this door was formed and the old one walled off from the Pyx (as at present), in consequence of the robbery, as is suggested in *Gleanings*. An echo of the great scandal appears in the Close Roll of 1307 : " Order to deliver to the Convent of Westminster all the cups that were lately stolen from the Refectory by Richard de Pudlyngcote who was hanged for robberies committed by him."

Exterior.—The outside of the Chapter House has been almost entirely renewed. In the junction with old work near Poets' Corner, we see that the new masonry takes up with the old courses. Here and there on the sides towards the south, Scott left patches of the old face; he speaks, indeed, of having found a portion, which had been sheltered, as being so fresh that there were masons' marks on the stones. This is a point not otherwise known. In one bay, stones of most of the courses show (September, 1923) 5 to 9 in. high—notice how narrow, and this was characteristic of the exterior masonry generally. It is curious that the walling was different in each bay, the number of courses between plinth and window sill varying from about sixteen to twenty-two. Scott followed the old coursing throughout; he also, probably, had authority for making the buttress slopes in continuous planes. The drip at the bottom (one ancient fragment inserted) is of the typical French section. The plinth is also a French profile.

Old sketches show that the lines of the main subdivisions of the windows appeared here and there on the exterior parts. Of the flying buttresses, additional works of the fourteenth century, stones remain in some places. There is a record that in 1377 some boatloads of stone were employed on the " pinnacles of the Chapter House " (Rackham) ; probably this gives the actual date of the erection of new buttresses.

The Mason.—The entrance to the Chapter House, if not the whole of this work, as I now think probable, was executed by Master Alberic, working by sub-contract. The accounts show that much masonry work was done by " task," and this was, doubtless, a means of pressing it forward to meet the desires of the impatient King. In a fabric roll of 1248–49 at the Record Office, Master Alberic appears as

receiving the then large sum of £45 for "task work" on
the Cloister. As I observed before, " it is evident from the
large sum (worth, say, £1,000) that he must have had
several assistants, and that he was carrying out a contract
for the workmanship of those bays of the Cloister which
belong to the first work "—and, I would add, lead from the
Church to the Chapter House.

I also pointed out that Master Alberic was mentioned
three times on the " Long Roll " of 1253 (published in
Gleanings). " It is noted on the back of the Roll that at a
certain time he had begun three windows by task." (The
note says " with three companions," so it is clear he was
working with his staff.) In the shorter Roll of this year
(K.R. 466, 30), entitled : " Account of divers works at
the Church, Chapter House, Belfry and Palace," Alberic's
name also occurs, and " he is there said to have been engaged
on the entrance to the Chapter House. It seems that we
may definitely assign the bays of the Cloister leading to
the Chapter House and the entrance of the latter to Master
Alberic. We have seen that the system of task work was
largely made use of, and Master Alberic seems to have been
engaged in the execution of such work from the beginning."

The three windows mentioned above, I thought, might
refer to the traceried bays of the early part of the Cloister,
but, on the whole, this is unlikely. The windows may have
been in the Chapter House or in the entry. The traceried
openings of this part of the Cloister are now only copied
work, but old drawings by Carter show that they are
accurate copies. The original work even had the curious
pebble-like lumps filling up narrow gaps in the tracery.
Of the capitals I am less sure, but there is a sketch of one
like the new ones at South Kensington, which was made by
Collings in 1842 (E. 4086). It is certain that Master
Alberic was engaged for many years and, probably, from the
beginning of the works. I am drawn to think that he, with
his own men, probably executed the Chapter House
entirely under the general direction of the Chief Master.

The windows and the wall arcade were designed by a master who had studied French works, but there seems to be a distinct difference of feeling between the details of the Church and the Chapter House with the bays of the Cloister leading to it. This confirms the evidence of the documents.

I have no note of the sum, if any, mentioned on the Short Roll as paid to Alberic, but in the Long Roll of the same year appears : " for task at the entrance to Chapter House 50s." Such a small sum (say £50) could only have paid for small finishing work, but, as the year was 1253, when the windows were already erected, that is what we might expect, and finishing off would be done by the original artist.

In the Long Roll of 1253 is noted that Master Alberic was paid for 1,280 ft. of " voussoirs with fillets at 3d. a foot," for " 50 assises " (facing blocks) at 5d. each, and for " seven steps cut by task work." The seven steps may be those in the Chapter House vestibule.

The title given above of the Short Roll implies that the Chapter House was, to some extent, regarded as a separate work. This Roll includes an item for canvas used in closing the windows of the Chapter House ; a second payment was of 53s. 4d. for two images made by task works, which, Professor Prior has suggested, may be the lovely Annunciation group itself.

CHAPTER VII

LATER BUILDING MASTERS

Repairs.—In 1298, a fire, originating in the palace, spread to the monastic buildings, which suffered great injury. The Dormitory range was first repaired, and, as part of this work, pretty pair-light windows were inserted in the big simple " Norman " windows, before described.

The Refectory also needed serious repairs.* References to works appear from 1301, and in 1305–06 Master Edmund the Carpenter, with sixteen to nineteen other carpenters and several sawyers and labourers, were engaged on the works—doubtless, a new roof. An archway of very refined earliest fourteenth-century work near the south-west angle, which communicated with the kitchen and a low vaulted building to the south of it, of which shafts and bases (*c.* 1300) remain, are likely to be of this time. Master Robert Cementarius receiving 9*d.* a day, who is mentioned in connection with the repairs (Rackham), was probably the master mason of this work, and to him I would assign the pretty two-light windows in the " Norman " openings of the Dorter, which also followed on the fire. This work is very delicate and beautiful, and I am glad to make the acquaintance of Master Robert. A plan of the low vaulted building, just mentioned, is given by Mr. Westlake. The columns were 15 in. in diameter, and only 6 ft. high. The vault rose 4 ft. higher. It was very like the entry to the Chapter House.

Some considerable works in the Refectory must have been undertaken at a later time by Litlyngton, Prior and then Abbot (1350–85), whose arms are on some of the floor

* For the documents see Mr. Rackham's two essays named in the Preface.

tiles found here. The roof corbels are very like those in the Abbot's Hall. I have thought that the elegant two-light windows in the north wall were of an earlier period, about 1310–20, but I now think that they are Litlyngton's work. The rebuilding of the Cloister may have given occasion, by blocking the lower part of the "Norman" windows, for inserting new ones. There are several fragments of tracery in the triforium, from which I have been able to assemble

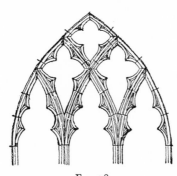

FIG. 78.

a three-light window of exactly the same style and scale as the others, which probably came from a gable end of the Refectory (Fig. 78). In this form the work looks later. There is also at the east end of the Refectory a wall arcade, which appears fully as late as, say, 1360 (Fig. 79). Again, the shafts of the inner jambs of the two-light windows are like those of the Refectory door, which it seems impossible to date before the middle of the century. This door resembles in feeling

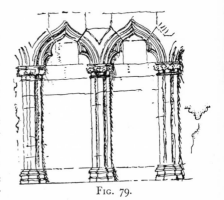

FIG. 79.

the doorway to the Chapel of St. Katherine. On the inside of the west wall of the Refectory (the chequered wall) remains the base of a window jamb at the height of

134

those in the north wall and probably the jamb of one of the three-light windows (Fig. 78). The quatrefoil band on the exterior of this wall above the chequers may have ranged with the parapet of the Refectory.

At the south end of the arcade (Fig. 79) is the springer of a door-like arch, which is, probably, part of the Reader's pulpit. The arcade ranges with the " Norman " arcade, and was obviously part of the general scheme of modernising the great hall. The " Norman " arcade is itself walled up flush, and the abacuses were cut down to the face of the wall ; evidently, it was obliterated, and the Refectory was *completely* transformed into a fourteenth-century work, of which the doorway and windows made part. The roof corbels are long, heavy stones, which pass through the whole thickness of the wall ; over the top of each there seems to have been an extra carved stone (see plate in *Gleanings*). From their position, it would seem that the roof cannot have been of the hammer-beam type ; it was fifteen bays long. We may now imagine the complete recasting of the " Norman " work, a precedent which was later to be followed at Westminster Hall.

Perhaps, we may assign all the masonry to John Palterton, who inserted the doorway into St. Katherine's Chapel. The masons of the fourteenth century who preceded him were, the Master Robert, mentioned above, say, about 1300–10, and Walter le Bole.

Other masons recorded about 1300 and soon after are Richard (1299), Maurice de Tothill (*c.* 1316), and Alexander de Tothill.

In 1342, Walter le Bole was Abbey mason, receiving dress and food. In 1349, his will was proved ; this was the year of the Plague, when the abbot and about half of the monks died. To Walter le Bole we, doubtless, owe the beautiful eastern bays of the Cloister. It was found by the late Mr. Rackham, in his examination of the fabric rolls at the Abbey, that John Palterton was master mason from 1349 to 1373–74. The south and west walks of the great

Cloister, begun about 1352, would thus appear to have been his work. In some special way, it was undertaken by Litlyngton while prior, for his initials are known to have been on the boss of the third bay from the entry, and in " Neale " it is said that the abbot's arms were also on a boss at the east end of the Cloister. Here there is still trace of an armorial boss. In 1352, stone was bought " for the work of the Prior in the cloister." The entry was built in 1362, and in this year a new cymbal for the Cloister was made;

FIG. 80.

this is now in the Museum. The Cloister was finished in 1365.

From 1364, the Infirmary buildings were rebuilt by Palterton. While engaged on this work, he was paid two shillings a week, with his daily commons of bread and beer, and received a fee of forty shillings in addition. The most significant part of the Infirmary building which remains is the doorway in the Little Cloister. It is a good deal like a door once in St. Stephen's Chapel, and is a very graceful work, having a row of quatrefoils up the jambs and around the arch. The capitals have little tufts of foliage set against the bells rather than springing from them. The drip-mould terminations are angels' heads—very pretty (Fig. 80). Mr. Westlake says : " In the roll for the year 1371–72, there is the record of taking down the older stone doorway and making the present beautiful entrance." This precise record is valuable, for the character of the work looks earlier than the great Cloister, and I am drawn to think that Henry Yevele, who is named as one of six chief masons of London in 1356, may have been concerned with the design of the Cloister. In any case, Yevele was the master of the work in building the new Nave, and the Cloister may well have been planned in connection with that. The south-east angle bay of the Cloister and the vaults of the two compartments north of it in the east walk might be by a different master than the rest. For plan of the Abbey buildings see the recently issued *Inventory*.

The Nave.—When Henry III. died in 1272, the old " Norman " nave remained attached to the new Choir (west of the crossing), transepts, and eastern limb. He must have had the intention of rebuilding the whole church, for in the bay of the Cloister, just west of the general termination of his work, may be seen (although I do not think its evidence has been considered) the beginning of another bay of the wall tracery of the Cloister. This tracery was afterwards cut away, but it shows that it had been intended to continue the thirteenth-century work. Almost certainly plans of the completed church had been made by the first master mason. The work executed before 1272 had been done in two separate portions, and King Henry would not have been content with an incomplete scheme. When, in the second half of the fourteenth century, the rebuilding of the Nave was undertaken, the general design of the thirteenth-century portion already built was maintained, and I have little doubt that the intention was to complete King Henry's plan. It is even probable that foundations had been put in for some distance beyond the point just mentioned, for when the Cloister was rebuilt (earlier than the Nave) it was very accurately planned in regard to the work which was to follow. The flank walls of the " Norman " nave were, I believe, far enough within the line of the new walls to allow of this ; in any case, the piers of the flying buttresses were entirely free. In the interior, the thirteenth-century

work terminates with ordinary piers and responds; ther
is nothing like a linking up with earlier work to the west
It was Scott's view that the " Norman " church consiste
of two parts, the Confessor's work to the east and a lat
" Norman " continuation to the west, and that Henry II]
rebuilt the Confessor's part. It seems more probabl
that the Confessor's work was continued until the whol
building was completed. The building itself is evidenc
that it was King Henry's intention to rebuild the whole.

After the King's death, however, the royal work ceasec
and minor works and repairs, except royal tombs, were don
by men on the Abbey staff. When the completion of th
church was undertaken, I have little doubt that it was o
the general lines of the plan of the original thirteenth
century master.

In 1375, the wall of the Norman nave next the Cloiste
was destroyed. Palterton's name does not appear afte
1373–74, and from about this time Yevele is likely to hav
been engaged in the important new work. He is known t
have made the tomb of Cardinal Langham, who died i
1376. It is not improbable, indeed, that he was chie
adviser at the church, from the time of his appointmen
as King's mason in 1360 or even earlier. Dean Robinso
thinks that it may not be doubted that Langham (abbot from
1349) determined to rebuild the Norman nave, and he lef
the Abbey in 1362. Now the western walk of the Cloiste
which was finished in 1365, is so accurately adjusted t
one of the Nave buttresses that its position must have bee
accurately known at that time; moreover, the west an
south walks of the Cloister seem to be in the style of the Nav
Compare especially the doorway from the west walk to th
Nave with the arch over the recess in the same west wall
Close scrutiny of the work has convinced me that, when i
the Roll it was stated that the Cloister was " finished " i
1365, it was indeed *complete*, including the three bays again
the Nave. The design of the west and south walks follow
from the north-west pier and that must have existed befor

138

they were undertaken. The vaulting of the three bays is of an early character, yet it has been supposed that this work followed on the taking down of the Norman wall of the Nave in 1375.

Five windows of the new Nave were ready for the ironwork in 1388–89. The earlier accounts of the work are missing, but one of the year before includes the " Fee of Master Yevele, chief mason, 100*s*. per annum, and for his dress and furs, 15*s*. ; Do. of Robert Kentbury, 13*s*. 4*d*. ; tunic of Thomas Padington, 10*s*." In 1375, Kentbury had a tenement in Westminster, and he was probably already Yevele's lieutenant. The account of 1388 includes a small item for breaking down the walls of the old church, and this appears, as Mr. Rackham remarks, to have been the last entry for taking down the old walls. All or most of the marble piers of the Nave were built by 1400 (Rackham). The Nave, except for the west front, is a continuation of the thirteenth-century building, but the west front was newly designed. It has been so much injured by Hawksmoor's changes and hidden in the interior by modern masonry that it has not been recognised for the fine fourteenth-century work which it essentially is. The window at the west end of the south aisle is still *original work*, although the similar windows along the flanks have been renewed, on the exterior at least. This precious window is of fourteenth-century form, and the large quatrefoil has the upper lobe larger than the rest, which gives it a touch of energy. Within narrow limits, it must be as early as any in the new work. The porch and the niches on either hand are still largely original. These niches have delicate " vaultings " to their canopies. The niches of the upper tier were dealt with by Hawksmoor, but they still represent what was there. They probably contained statues of kings ; over them were shields of arms. The porch and surrounding work is closely like Yevele's porch at Westminster Hall.

The great west window, as may still be seen in the interior, must have followed the first design of the front, although its execution was delayed; the mullions and transomes agree with the lines of the wall panelling, and this scheme of wall panelling starts from the plinth level. The window closely resembles the end windows of Westminster Hall and, like them, must have been designed by Yevele; it was not finished until Abbot Esteney's time (from 1474). There is a record, however, that lead was obtained for the chamber over the west porch in 1442 (Rackham), and the masonry must have been carried well above its level when this chamber was roofed.*

FIG. 81.

The exterior also has tiers of wall panelling following from the tracery of the west window, and I reach the conclusion that the whole front was carried on according to a design by Henry Yevele.

On examining the indications on the interior of the front, it will appear that it was conceived as panelled throughout with strong vertical strips rising from the plinth level, crossed by horizontal bands, knitting door, window, and wall together (Fig. 81). The inner arch over the door has the same moulding as the greater mullion strips which are continued below the west window. These greater mullion strips indeed framed in the doorway, which formed one large panel in the general " all-over " scheme of the interior. Above, on either side of the window, the heads of the wall tracery show exactly what the transomes of the lights were. Notice the inverted tracery arch directly over the inner arch of the door-

* John Pache was Abbey carpenter at this time, and he was followed by Robert Pache. The name " Pache's house " lasted till the Dissolution (Rackham).

140

way. The lower part of the interior is represented by an engraving in Warton's *Gothic Architecture*, and the old window is shown from within in Sandford's *Coronation of James II.*, while the exterior is given in Hollar's view. Now, the west front of Winchester Cathedral is conceived in the same way, inside and out, and its west porch is also very similar to that at Westminster. The front of Winchester appears to be the work of that William Wynford who was working with Yevele in 1370, and we probably see Yevele's influence throughout the Nave of the Cathedral.

The west front at Winchester was built by Bishop Edington in the last quarter of the fourteenth century. Willis says : " The design of the west window is singularly simple, reducing itself to the merest stone grating. Divided into three by principal monials, each of these is split into three by secondary monials. The arch can scarcely be said to be filled with tracery, so completely does the grating-like character pervade it ; in the central group of lights the grating extends to the very top." The work of the Nave was continued from the west end by Wykeham, who, in his will, dated 1403, wrote : " I will and ordain that the arrangement and conduct of the new work shall be entrusted to Master William Winford and such others, discreet, sufficient and approved in their art, as may be chosen if necessary." The description of the window might stand for that of Westminster Hall, and for that of the Abbey except that it had seven lights. At Winchester nave the front was built first and the rest proceeded eastward ; to some extent, this would have been the procedure also at Westminster.*

In Fig. 81, I give a rough diagram of the design of the

---

* Compare Bond's *Westminster Abbey*, where some suggestions are made amending Rackham's view as to the course of the works in the Nave. Micklethwaite, in his plan, marked the west porch as late work, and this is followed by more recent plans including *The Inventory*. Edington Church should also be compared with the works of Yevele and Wynford.

interior of the west front, from which it will be seen at once that it must have been completed from the scheme begun in the lowest courses. (The upper sill of the windows should probably be omitted as having been added by Hawksmoor.) Fig. 82 shows more or less what the window was like. Besides the engravings and parallels, just mentioned, the tracery of the porch, which is " Perpendicular "

in character, notwithstanding earlier survivals, is helpful in reconstructing the old window. For example, the transome bands in the tracery of the window were similar to those in the porch tracery. Another piece of evidence for the steady carrying out of the one scheme in the west front is to be found in the tower windows, which answer in position to those of the triforium and the clerestory. On the interior, there is a clerestory window in

FIG. 82.

the wall of each tower, and the original intention was, it seems, that these should receive light from the tower windows as in foreign cathedrals and at York.

Besides the advanced " Perpendicular " character of Yevele's work, an interesting technical point must be mentioned. He had a liking for big facing-stones, 16, 18, or even 24 in. high and 3 ft. and more long. These stones are set with fine flush joints of white lime. Workmen never raked out joints to prepare them for stone-rot until they

142

were instructed by architects of the sham Gothic " style."
The external walls of the Nave were finished above with
" battlements," as is shown by an entry in the accounts
quoted by Rackham. Some of the original Purbeck paving
of the Nave may be traced here and there, and the arrangement in strips is clearly indicated on the lithographed plans
of the graves made about 1860.

Considering the importance of the Abbot's House, the
date at which it was built, and the way in which its plan
interlocks with the west end of the church, so that the house
could not have been set out before the Nave, we may hardly
doubt that Yevele was the architect of both. In Dean
Robinson's account of *The Abbot's House* (1911), he has a
section entitled " An earlier building on the site of Jerusalem
chamber." Of this conjectured building, he thought, a
part had to be pulled down in order to make room for the
south-west tower of the church ; but the western half was
saved and renamed as the " *nova camera* of the Abbot." I
cannot agree with this view, for the adjustment of the walls
of the chamber with the west end of the Nave and its
right-hand buttress is so accurate that the chamber could
only have been built with or later than the foundation of the
west front. Moreover, the foundation of the south-west
tower must spread far under the chamber wall. The
suggested Abbot's chamber of Norman work requires that
the west walk of the Norman cloister would have been
about 20 ft. wide, that is much more than the present
Cloister ; further, the Eastern wall of the chamber could
hardly have been undermined by Litlyngton in the way
suggested. I will now quote from Dean Robinson the
historical facts regarding the Jerusalem chamber.

" From 1362 to 1365 work is going on above the entrance
to the cloister ; . . . the cloister was finished in 1365.
The roll for 1369 is missing, but for nine years after that
payments are made for what is called *novem edificium*. In
1371–72, canvas is bought for the windows of my lord's new

camera, and there is no doubt that Jerusalem chamber is here referred to. After this the Abbot's hall was built, and in 1375–76, it was so far finished that John Payable was putting in the glass, of which a fragment bearing the initials N. L. still remains. This work of reconstruction was completed some three years before the old [Norman] nave was pulled down ; and we may, perhaps, assume that the extent of the new Nave and its western towers had already been carefully calculated."

The windows of the Abbot's hall are original within, although they were completely refaced some thirty years ago ; those of the Chamber are new. The roof corbels of the hall are very fine indeed. They are of angels holding shields, two of which have the Despencer arms, two others have the same with the " difference " of a bordure set with mitres for Litlyngton, and the fifth and sixth bear the arms of the Confessor and the Abbey. (There are similar large corbels in the ruined Refectory, and the alteration of that great chamber may also be Yevele's work.) The Abbot's hall has a fine roof and screen, and these I would assign to Master Hugh Herland, who later made the roof of Westminster Hall. Some spandrel fillings in both are alike. Those of the tomb tester of Queen Philippa (1369) are also similar, and this being a royal work was, doubtless, done by the King's carpenter. The central trusses of the hall roof have been injured by having the arch and spandrel pieces removed (about Wren's time), but they remain against the walls, and the roof is original except for wall pieces and struts put in place of the removed tracery. In the combination of moulded arches and tracery spandrels, the roof is the prototype of that of Westminster Hall, and it may be that the great shield-carrying angels of the latter were suggested by the carved corbels of the Abbot's hall.

Of the glazing by John Payable four or five fragments remain. Two windows have the initials N. L. with a coronet above in the upper quatrefoils of the tracery. A third window retains the head of a little saint's figure in one of the other quatrefoils, and it is evident that initials and saints were in all the windows (Fig. 83).* Payable must have been the best-known glazier of his time, for, in 1362, he had reglazed the great South Rose of the church. Litlyngton liked to sign his good works. The first boss of the vault of the Cloister entry also has coroneted initials within a collar surrounded by a hunting scene (Fig. 84). The abbot had much pleasure with his falcons and his

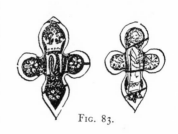

FIG. 83.

harriers, one of which had the nice name of " Sturdy." The second boss has the Despencer arms ; another has four lions' heads, and the minor intersections have roses—the lions and roses of England.

I call attention to the " topical interest " of the details as leading up to the identification of several carved heads of label terminations of the doorways. Two (Figs. 85 and 86) are a king and queen. These should be Edward III. and Philippa, as the Cloister entry was built in 1362–64. Two other heads are of younger royalties, doubtless, the Black Prince and Joan, to whom he was married in 1361 ; the prince's head is well preserved, and one might think interesting (Fig. 87). A third

FIG. 84.

* The lights were doubtless of quarry-work, possibly with foliage like Fig. 163.

L

pair of heads is of an abbot—obviously Litlyngton (Fig. 88)—and apparently a layman who might be the mason.

FIG. 85.

The custom of carving portrait heads of kings and craftsmen has never been worked out. In the North Transept of the church there is a perfectly preserved marble head of a king, which must be Henry III., while higher up is a head which, I believe, is that of his master mason. Outside the door, from the church to the Cloister, are two crowned heads, and there are several other portraits. At St. Albans are a king (Edward III. ?) and queen, an abbot, and a master mason.

In the Angel Choir at Lincoln is a series of fine portrait heads. At Exeter Cathedral, there is an important mason's head, and there are several more in other places. At Southwark Cathedral are some important heads at the crossing which, if they are authentic, should be recorded ; the king looks like Edward I. In certain Continental churches heads of the craftsman type have long been identified as master masons and crowned heads as definite portraits.

FIG. 86.

Such heads, when found in significant positions, must represent particular persons, and in the latter

146

part of the fourteenth century portraiture was a special interest.*

The Abbot's House at West-minster is the most perfect, indeed the only approximately complete, mediæval house now existing in London, and it has special beauties which must always have been exceptional.† The Cellarers' building, facing Dean's Yard, is also Litlyng-ton's work. It contains a vaulted ground floor and, in one upper room, the heavy oak roof under the leaded roof is preserved. The entrance to this range seems to have been by the vaulted lower story of a tower to the south of the

Fig. 87.

Fig. 88.

* I find that Mr. Page in his *Guide to St. Albans' Cathedral*, says that part of the Nave where the heads are, was begun by Abbot Hugh after 1323, and was completed by Abbot Mentmore (1335-49). " The easternmost is the head of a bishop or abbot (probably Hugh), next is a queen (probably Isabella), thirdly a king (Edward), and the last is probably Master Geoffrey, master mason and surveyor of the works to Abbot Hugh."

† The large central hearth of the hall remained in use as late as 1850. " It was only removed during the improvements of the time of Dean Buckland . . . being probably the last instance of this ancient usage to be continued to this day " (Hudson Turner's *Domestic Architecture*, with illustration). The hall is raised above an undercroft with a floor supported by a big longitudinal beam and oak posts.

147

Cloister entry ; in the north wall of this vaulted story is a blocked doorway. Another range of buildings, which stood opposite to these in Dean's Yard, and was destroyed about a century since, is represented in original drawings by Carter and by Buckler in the British Museum collections.

.   .   .   .   .

Later Building Masters.—Now, I turn back from the building to a fuller account of the building masters. In 1360, Henry Yevele had succeeded Thomas of Gloucester as King's mason. In the Patent Roll for that year is entered the " appointment of Henry de Yevele to be disposer of the King's works pertaining to the art of masonry in the Palace of Westminster and the Tower of London, taking in the office 12*d*. a day." He was also directed to take (press) masons for the works and put them on the King's wages, and to commit to prison all contrariants. In accounts of 1365, when the old clock tower of the Palace (the prototype of the present clock tower) was erected, he is called director of the work at the Palace.*

Again, in 1366, Yevele appears as master mason of the King's works, with William Winchester acting as *apparitor*, or second in command ; Master William Herland being master of carpenter's work and Hugh Herland his *apparitor*. This Hugh, thirty years later, was to be the great architect of that supreme work of carpentry, the roof of Westminster Hall. He was, doubtless, the son of Master William, and born to timber traditions. (For Master Hugh, see Sir F. Baines' *Westminster Hall* Report, 1914, and my *Westminster Abbey and the Kings' Craftsmen*, 1906.)

In 1368, Yevele was one of the Keepers of the Works of London Bridge ; and, in 1383, he was repairing Rochester Bridge. A grant was made, in 1369, " to Henry de Yevele,

* In this year he supplied 7,000 Flanders tiles (bricks) (Britton & Brailey). The name shows that the modern brick came to us from Flanders. They were used for chimneys and paving. He also supplied stone for the repair of Rochester Castle.

that whereas by Patent 34 E. III. the King appointed him disposer of Masonry in the Palace of Westminster and the Tower with 12*d.* a day, he shall take the 12*d.* a day for life as well as a winter robe yearly at the Great Wardrobe, of the suit of esquires of the Household, or the allowance in place of it." In 1370, he and Master William de Wynford were each ordered to press fifty hewers of stone for the King's service. Wynford was to be the architect of the nave of Winchester Cathedral and the College. In 1371, Yevele contracted for beginning to build the London Charterhouse. " Lord de Manny and the Prior made an agreement with Henry Yevele for building the first cell and beginning the great cloister of the fabric for which the said Lord gave 600£ and laid the foundation " (Dr. Gerald Davies' *Charterhouse*).

A mandate was addressed, in 1374, " To the Keepers of the Port of le Pole (Poole) by mainprise of Master Henry Yevele, Masoun, and Jordan de Bartone [a Simon de Bartone was one of the masons at the meeting in 1356], citizens of London, to de-arrest the ship *Margarete*, of Wareham, of 48 tons burden, and two high tombs of marble for the Earl of Arundel and Eleanor, his late wife, one great stone for the Bishop of Winchester, and other things of theirs. To be taken to the port of London and there unloaded " (Patent). These marble tombs in a ship at Poole were, doubtless, from Purbeck, and possibly they still exist. At Arundel, there is a tomb which is said to be of an earl who died in 1406, and his countess.

Master Henry Yevele was himself tenant, in 1376, " of the Manor of Langetone, in Purbike,'' or rather of two parts of it, at first at a rent of £8 6*s.* 8*d.*, and afterwards on still more advantageous terms (Patent). In this same year, the rebuilding of the Nave of Westminster Abbey was begun.

In 1385, an order was issued by Richard II. to pay Henry Yevele 12*d.* a day, and confirming the patent of 43 Edward III. appointing him director (*dispositorem*) of the works of the craft of masonry with 12*d.* a day for life (Patent). This grant was surrendered, in 1390, because he was then granted the Manors of Tremworth and Vannes in the county of Kent (Patent). Our mason was, evidently, become a person of much " consequence." He had now reached old age, and in this year he was granted exemption from juries, etc., in consideration of his being King's mason and surveyor of works at Westminster Palace, the Tower, and Canterbury Castle, and on account of his great age (Patent). We may suppose that he was born about 1320.

Richard II., in 1394, appointed John Godmerstone, clerk, to make provision for the repair of Westminster Hall. The next year Richard Washbourne and John Swalwe (Swallow, so spelt by Chaucer), masons, were engaged to heighten the walls of the old hall 2 ft. with Reigate and *Pierre de Marre* (Marr, Yorks), according to the purport of a *fourme e molde* made by counsel of Master Henry Yevele, and delivered to them by Watkin Waldon, his warden, with twenty-six corbels carved according to a pattern, all the materials being supplied, except the instruments used by the masons in their art.

The accounts for remodelling the hall mention Master Hugh Herland, carpenter to the King, also Robert Grasington, William Canon, and others, carving angels, etc., in wood. Even in 1383 the great carpenter was said to be verging on old age, and in 1394 N. Wilton was made master carpenter and engineer of the King's works for the art of carpentry throughout the realm.* This may have been to relieve Master Hugh. The accounts of work at the great hall are guaranteed " by the sight and testimony of Master Hugh Herland, the King's capital carpenter and controller of the works, who received 12*d.* a day. Thomas Wolvey, whose tomb is at St. Albans, did the masonry work of the south gable with the window.

Richard II. was deposed in the autumn of 1399 and his superb hall was hurriedly prepared for the coronation of Henry IV. on October 13, 1399. William Burgh, glazier,

---

* Carpenters were now the engineers, cf. p. 27.

was employed filling the great window with " flourished glass " ; William Chuddere executed four images, possibly those for the pinnacles ; and a Thomas of Gloucester did the painting, including the making and painting the stage at the south end for the coronation. John Chaundeller supplied candles for the carpenters, who, we may suppose, had to work overtime (*Accounts* 473, 11 and 13). Both Master Hugh Herland and Yevele, the mason, must now have been very old ; it was the end of an era as well as of a century. Chaucer, who had been clerk of works to the King's palaces, would have known them well, and the Carpenter of the *Canterbury Tales* may suggest what the status of a well-to-do carpenter was at this time. I cannot find when Master Hugh died ; but his father's will was proved in 1375. He had lived in the parish of Paul's Wharf, and Hugh probably also lived in the City. Henry Yevele died in 1400. His will was dated May 25 in that year and enrolled on October 28. In it, he called himself " masoun " citizen and freeman of the City of London and parishioner of St. Magnus at London Bridge. He directed that he should be buried in the said church, in St. Mary's Chapel, where his tomb is already prepared. He left considerable property ; Katherine, his wife, was to enjoy a life interest in certain tenements charged with the maintenance of two chantries. Under certain circumstances, the property was to be devoted to the use of London Bridge for two chantry priests in the chapel upon the same. He also left property at Alvythele and elsewhere in Essex. Stowe saw the tomb in St. Magnus', and says it was that of " Henry Yevele, Freemason to Edward III., Richard II., and Henry IV., who deceased in 1400." Apparently, the inscription must have been to that effect. The reference to London Bridge chapel, taken in connection with the fact that he had been keeper of the works of the bridge, suggests that he may have been the architect of the chapel which was destroyed just a century since. On referring to illustrations, I find that it was very like the Cloister at

Westminster, which was being built just at the time the master was keeper at the bridge. The drawings of Cooke, at the Guildhall, may be consulted on this.

Our mason's bequest to the Chapel of St. Mary at St. Magnus, where his tomb was, may be traced further in an account of the endowments of London Bridge, to which this had been transferred. Among " the properties formerly belonging to the fraternity called *Le Salve* in the Church of St. Magnus " was a " tenement held by Henry Yevele, mason, paying 5*s*., situate between the King's road on the east and the Oyster gate on the west." Stowe gives an account of the Guild or Fraternity of *Le Salve Regina* : " The better sort of the Parish to the honour of God and his glorious Mother caused to be made a chantry to sing an anthem of our Lady called *Salve Regina* every evening, and ordained five burning wax lights at the time of the said anthem in reverence for the five principal joys of our Lady and for exciting the people to devotion " (*Chronicles of London Bridge*). The house referred to, which must have been close under St. Magnus, was probably Yevele's own residence, and we may think of our mason stepping into the church to join in the anthem before the altar with its five twinkling candles. (I suggest that the story of Yevele, including his interviews with the King he served, with Chaucer and, possibly, with Wycliffe, and, in its setting, of plague, war, adventure, and art, might make a good subject for a little pageant-drama.)

Another point that arises in interpreting the will is : Did not Alvythele, Essex (now Aveley, near Purfleet), give Yevele his name ? In the index of the Patent Rolls, it is equated with Yeovil. In the *D.N.B.*, Yeaveley in Derbyshire is suggested, and it is said that there was also a manor of Yevele in Surrey (?) But may not the Essex place, where the master had property, and his own name have both been pronounced Yaveley ? *

* For references see *D.N.B.*, and *The Builder*, xxiii., p. 409. In this account, I have used the recently issued Calendar of Patent Rolls.

At the Abbey, Yevele was followed by William Colchester, who is called chief mason in the account for 1–2 Henry IV. He received 100s. the year, with dress and furs. He is mentioned again in 1413 and 1416. The Guildhall of London, which seems to have been begun within a dozen years of Yevele's death, is so much like his strong, bare manner of building, that it must belong to his school. It may have been designed by Colchester. In or before 1420, John Thirsk took the place of Colchester, and he is mentioned again in 1433, and about 1448 as the mason of Henry V.'s Chapel. John Smith is named in 1452 and John Reading in 1460. He, in turn, was followed by Robert Stowell in 1471, who in 1488–89 vaulted several bays of the Nave.*

Fig. 89.—Henry Redman, King's Mason.

Thomas Redman succeeded in 1505, and he was followed by his brother Henry in 1516.† Then John Molton and

* In 1470 "John Stowall freemason did the masonry craft of a Jesse front" at St. Cuthbert's, Wells.

† Henry VII.'s Chapel was a royal work, and is here omitted, see p. 161.

153

William Taylor were joint masters from 1528 (Rackham). These, I suppose, were responsible for Islip's Chapel.* Henry Redman was also master mason at St. Margaret's, the building of which was begun in 1491 ; the steeple and porch were begun *c.* 1515, and were dedicated in 1523. (Bishop Hensley Henson.) The entrance door remains a pretty and authentic piece of work. Henry Redman was buried in St. Lawrence's Church, Brentford, where he was commemorated by a brass on the west wall. In the Lysons' collection at the British Museum is a drawing of this, from which I am able to give the portrait of one of the King's master masons.† He appeared praying on the left (Fig. 89) ; on the right were his wife and two daughters, and between them was a small plate, probably of the Virgin and Child. The inscription was : " *Pӯ for the Soule of Henry Redman sutyme chefe M Mason of ye Kyngs works and Joha his wyf sp'all benefactors of this churche.*" It goes on to speak of lands and tenements, half stipend of a curate, and sufficient for a perpetual obit, and ends : " *deceased July 10, 1528. O' whos' soulle Jhu have M'cy.*" According to Lysons, he bequeathed the " George " Inn and £3 6s. 8d. yearly for the curate ; his will and that of his wife were still in the parish chest.

* See Note 3 at end.

† Other tomb portraits of masons are those of Crowland and Lincoln. To these I would add the carved heads before mentioned, especially those of Westminster, St. Albans, Ely, and Exeter. See Note 12 at end.

CHAPTER VIII

HENRY THE SEVENTH'S CHAPEL

" 1502.—*This year in the month of January was the Chapel of Our Lady, standing at the east end of the high altar of Westminster, pulled down ; and the tavern of the Sun there also standing with other housing ; and the foundation begun of another chapel at the costs of the King* " (*Kingsford, " Chronicles of London," p.* 258 : *the date is* 1503 *in modern reckoning*).

My purpose is less to describe what still exists than to discuss what Henry VII.'s chapel was like when first completed. This chapel, one of the latest of our mediæval works, is also one of the most perfect buildings ever erected in England. It is profusely decorated, because it was customary, at the time it was built, to panel and fret all surfaces, but, beneath this system of surface patterning, the structure is amazingly frank and energetic. It was clearly seen as building, although it was finished as a sort of cabinet-work of stone cutting. The work has always been acclaimed as a masterpiece, even during the dangerous reactions of the generations directly following that in which it was erected. This is well shown in Norden's description (MS. Harl., 570), which, I believe, has never been fully printed, and, as it is the longest piece of early building description known to me, I give it here from the manuscript. Original spellings are in italic :

" *The new Chappel by whome it was buylded and of the admirable bewtye thereof.*—There is adjoining unto this famous temple, in the east end thereof a chapel erected by H. 7, the beauty and curious contrived work whereof passeth my skill at large to set down so curious and full of

155

exquisite art it is both within and without. And which is not least to be considered the foundation is most artificially proportioned and it showeth most exquisite invention and skill in the builder, for the foundation is the guide to extract a formal and artificial work. Out of this curious foundation groweth, as Leland saith, *miraculum orbis*, the wonder of the world. In regard of the most curious and artificial workmanship thereof, whereof I dare not wade too far in, describing the beauty and form thereof, lest my skill failing me I be forced to retire without performing what I began. Only this much I dare to adventure to report that whoso beholdeth the exterior parts with due consideration of every matter of singular art, will consider it to be a work whereof (be he never so wise or eloquent) he cannot sufficiently demonstrate every particular point of beauty that therein may be noted. But beholding with judgment the body and internal glory he shall find it so admirable both in the *vautinge on the roofe* in regard of the curiosity of work as also in the proportion. And the walls, windows and the rest so exquisitely performed that he will deem them to be the only rare work in the world and as Leland says *the wounder of the worldes*. This mirror of *art and architect* is not only in itself beautiful, but it is also beautified with many rare and glorious monuments and curious sepulchres of kings and queens, among whom the founder lyeth, Henry 7, under a most royal tomb framed and most artificially formed wholly of brass richly laid over with gold which now seemeth something to have lost the beauty."

The uncertain use of the new and grand word architect may be noted, but what interests this contemporary of Shakespeare is invention, contrivance, skill, curious and artificial workmanship.

According to Stow, the Chapel was built of stone brought from Huddlestone, Yorkshire, but Wren says " it was performed of tender Caen stone." Neale is probably right in saying that the springers of the flying buttresses were from

Huddlestone and the superstructure of Caen stone. Original work, fortunately, remains in the " Well " between the west window and the great church. This west window is an exceptional work fifteen lights wide and delicately wrought ; even on the outside the cusps have terminations of roses, etc. (Fig. 9c). Within, the side compartments have a crocketed label added to the tracery, and the transomes (as throughout) have little battlements. Neale states that " all the windows except those at the west end were rebuilt and reglazed during the late repairs." A few stones of the original exterior have been found re-used with the wrought face inside, and these show the sharpest and most minute cutting.

There is something wrong with the upper parapet and its row of tall, lean pinnacles. Neale says : " The design for the present parapet was furnished by Mr. T. Wyatt ; yet there is strong reason to believe that it bears very little resemblance to the original battlement, which had been

FIG. 90.

entirely destroyed long before the commencement of the late repairs. . . . The whole is terminated by elevated pinnacles, the crockets and finials of which were partly designed from some remnants of ancient ones found among the rubbish ; but, as they now stand without any merlons between them, they are decidedly too high. In some old prints the battlement appears as though perforated by a twofold range of openings. . . . Above the coping was a sort of pierced merlon with an angular termination in the centre."

Carter had collected authorities on this question, in the *Gentleman's Magazine* for 1811. The tomb of Prince Arthur at Worcester has such jutting gabled forms in its parapet, and the whole tomb has so much in common with Henry VII.'s Chapel that it may have been designed by the same master. Mr. Sydney Lee had a drawing of Wren's time which showed a bay of the Chapel with the statues and parapet. The parapet of the eastern Chapel at Windsor follows the same tradition (Fig. 91). Those which crown the western towers at Westminster (*c.* 1740) are like that at Windsor and may have been inspired by the parapet of Henry VII.'s Chapel, where, however, there seems to have been only one gabled form to a bay.*

Again, from the old prints, it is evident that the turrets at Westminster were surmounted by vanes. In the finishing of old buildings, there were imaginations and a gay play element, which are almost impossible for us to think back. A large number of gilt vanes seem to have been one of the ideals of the Tudor time. We know that the King's beasts on the pinnacles of St. George's Chapel supported a similar series of vanes. Some illu-

minations in books suggest that buildings were stages to carry vanes! Flashing as they turned, they gave a building a sort of life.

FIG. 91.

The large octagonal turrets, which surround the aisles, housed a large number of statues : three in each of the side turrets and four in those around the apsidal end. They were removed about 1720 (?), but there are names, carved on labels, attached to the pedestals that once supported them which, so far as they are authentic, show whom the images were intended to represent.

Mr. Micklethwaite, who collected the names (*Archæol.* xlvii.), remarked : " The selection has a very modern look and there seems to be no system of arrangement. Apostles, prophets, and kings are all mixed up in the most complete confusion ; but the apostles and evangelists are all there, as are the greater and lesser prophets. For the rest, the sole qualification seems to be that they should be mentioned in

* Compare also the parapet of Cirencester Church, which has much in common with the Westminster work.

the Old Testament." On the other hand, they are all of " holy men of old." The kings were, I think, ancestors of the Virgin, appropriate to a Lady Chapel, and care was taken to spread the various classes so that apostles, prophets, and kings should not come together. Even the three Hebrews of the fiery furnace did not appear as a group in the three niches of one turret, but all were separated. The appearance of these three, with their names as in the *Benedicite*, suggests, indeed, that the thought behind the sculptures was : " O ye holy and humble men of heart, bless ye the Lord. O Ananias, Azarias, and Misael, bless ye the Lord : praise him and magnify him for ever."

The creatures, which project at the corners of the turrets and run down the slopes of the buttresses, are not mere " grotesques," they are the King's beasts.

The structure, in its essence, is a mausoleum chapel. According to the original arrangement, Henry VII. was to have had his tomb and brazen chantry, with its special altar, in the middle between the stalls ; and Henry VI., made a saint, was to occupy the eastern radiating chapel (see *Gleanings*). Margaret, the King's mother, lies in the southern aisle-chapel, which, as the imagery shows, was intended for her, and it was probably expected that the King's successor (Henry VIII.) would lie in the northern aisle-chapel, where Queen Elizabeth's tomb now is.

Before the original arrangement of the stalls was altered by continuing them eastwards, the eastward bays of the aisles or side chapels opened to the central area by curved screens similar to those in the next bays eastward—like them, doubtless, having doors. What we now think of as the " nave " was thus to be occupied by the bronze tomb of the founder. The south chapel contained the bronze tomb of his mother, and the northern chapel was to contain a corresponding royal tomb. This, the original arrangement, made the " aisles " count for more in the internal space, and opened diagonal lines of sight of great value (Fig. 92 is from a plan *c.* 1600).

Even the " nave arches " of the bays, which opened into the aisles, are different from the others and like those of the eastern chapels. Traces of the screens in these bays may yet be seen on the piers. The four originally unappropriated radiating chapels were almost certainly intended for so many more royal tombs and chantries. There were, thus, to have been eight such chantries surrounding the central altar of the Virgin.

The other main points in the conception must have been : the miraculous vault, constructed wholly of thin wrought

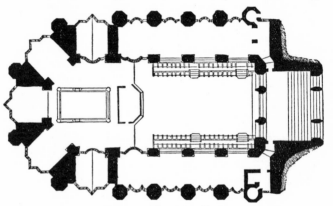

FIG. 92.—Plan from *Gleanings*.

stone, a triumph of geometry and of stone cutting (notice the way in which the springings are pierced to allow of sight of the windows) ; the system of support by a series of octagonal turrets ; the bowed windows between these turrets ; the brazen chantry in the centre of the choir of singers ; the great congregation of stone saints ; the ornamentation with the King's beasts, Lion, Dragon, Greyhound, and with Tudor badges, Rose, Fleur-de-lys, Portcullis, etc. ; the profusion of undercut carving ; brattishings to the window transomes ; and the flood of light through stained windows.

THE KING'S MASONS

The central object of the whole structure, the chantry chapel of the King, in gilt bronze about 20 ft. long, was an amazingly daring thought and a triumphant piece of skilled craftsmanship. Several details, which have now disappeared, are shown in Hollar's delicate etching given in Sandford's *History*. We should realise that, when new, it must have been dazzlingly bright, as also would have been the beautiful gilt bronze entrance gates of the " nave."

Beneath the clerestory of the " nave " and on the walls of the chapels is a great congregation of images of saints, and under these a band of angels guarding the King's resting-place. That this was one of the root ideas in planning the work is suggested by a passage in the King's will:

" I trust also to the singular mediations and prayers of all the holy company of heaven ; that is to say, Angels, Archangels, Patriarchs, Prophets, Apostles, Evangelists, Martyrs, Confessors, and Virgins, and especially to mine accustomed Avouries I call and cry, St. Michael, St. John Baptist, St. John Evangelist, St. George, St. Anthony, St. Edward, St. Vincent, St. Anne, St. Mary Magdalen, and St. Barbara. . . ."

The King's Masons.—The structure, begun in 1503, was completed in ten or twelve years. In 1506–07, " the King's iii Mr. Masons " reported as to the cost of the proposed tomb : they were Robert Vertue, Robert Jenyns and John Lebons, and the first-named was probably the chief master in charge of the work. Mr. Westlake has recently objected that there is no actual proof, and he points out that in the King's will (1509) Prior Bolton of St. Bartholomew's is mentioned as master of the works. A master of the works, however, was the general controller of accounts : Abbot Mylling was " master of the works " of the Nave (Rackham). In the accounts for the tomb of the Lady Margaret the Prior of St. Bartholomew's is mentioned " for his counsel in devising the said tomb and for costs in surveying and controlling the workmen at sundry times and for sending

for workmen beyond the sea for making of the said tomb."
This was in the fourth year of Henry VIII., and the Prior
was probably appointed by Henry VII. in the time of his
approaching death. The workmen from beyond the seas
were none other than Torrigiani and his companions, and
the " Florentine " is mentioned in another passage. All
the devising the Prior can have done was in the sense of
laying down conditions and approving proposals. Of
course, every intelligent employer is in part the designer of
the work he is interested in, but great technical works in
masonry can only be designed in the stricter sense by a
mason. In Neale's day " the credit of designing this
chapel " was generally given to Sir Reginald Bray, who
seems also to have been a master of the King's works, and
he was one of those who laid the foundation-stone of the
Chapel.

Correspondences between Henry VII.'s Chapel and
other works of known craftsmen at Windsor, Eton, Oxford,
etc., afford practical proof that one of the three master
masons of the King, who were consulted on the tomb, was
the chief " architect " of the Chapel, as, naturally, would be
the case. The vault is a developed copy of the vaults of
the Divinity School, Oxford, and of St. George's Chapel,
Windsor. By approaching the Westminster work through
these, we shall be better prepared to consider who was its
designer. The Divinity School was erected during the last
three years of Edward IV. (1480–83). On the vault
is found the monogram of William Orchard, the master
mason (Miss Edith Legge, 1924).* All that is known of
St. George's Chapel is contained in Sir W. Hope's quite
perfect account of Windsor Castle. The works at Windsor
appear to have been begun as early as 1477, under the
direction of Henry Jenyns, king's mason, who may have
been a son of the Robert Jenyns who, about 1450, was the

* William Orchard appears to have been the master mason of Waynflete's
building at Magdalen College, Oxford—" a noted architect and master
builder."

master mason of the tower of Merton College, Oxford. Parker remarks, in *Gleanings* : " It is on record that the work of the Divinity School in Oxford was suspended for several years in consequence of the skilled workmen being sent for to Windsor by royal writ " (p. 70). Of the relation between Windsor and Westminster, Sir W. Hope wrote as follows :

" The Lady Chapel built for Henry VII. at Westminster, apparently by the same master masons who carried out the work at St. George's Chapel, has, towards the east, a polygonal apse, which is strongly reminiscent of the transepts at Windsor. . . . Another feature of the Westminster Chapel is the curious series of lofty bay windows that light the side chapels. The prototypes of these are clearly the oriels in Henry VII.'s tower at Windsor. The masons named in connection with the Windsor work are Richard Nymes and Robert Jenyns. The latter was probably a son or brother of Henry Jenyns, the master mason of the earlier works of St. George's Chapel, and his connection with Westminster is suggested by the fact that he was one of the three master masons who gave estimates for the making of King Henry VII.'s tomb in 1506–07. Another of these was Robert Vertue, evidently a kinsman of William Vertue who, with John Hylmer, contracted to vault the choir of St. George's, and the Lady Chapel beyond, and by himself apparently set up the fan-vault above the crossing." (This vault, it is added, is dated 1528—p. 586.)

" Robert Jenyns was working upon the King's Lady Chapel at Westminster, and was probably the son of Henry Jenyns, master mason of the work of St. George's Chapel from 1477 to 1484, and perhaps later. The master mason of the Windsor work was undoubtedly the same man who designed the Westminster Chapel and who, after the King's death, began in 1511 the noble mansion-house at Thornbury, in Gloucestershire. He apparently also rebuilt the King's palace at Shene after its destruction by fire in 1497 " (p. 247).

HENRY THE SEVENTH'S CHAPEL

Hope had no doubt whatever that the masonry of Henry VII.'s Chapel was designed by a mason, or of the close relation between it and St. George's Chapel, Windsor. He agreed, also, that the master of Westminster would have been one of the three King's masons consulted as to the cost of the tomb in 1506–07. Without giving any reasons, however, he substituted the name of Robert Jenyns for that of Robert Vertue. In speaking of the three masons as giving " estimates " for the King's tomb, Hope may suggest a mistaken view. I should rather understand that they concurred in *one* estimate as to how much a certain project (prepared by a foreigner) would cost. Robert Jenyns, the King's mason at Windsor, might join in a conference as to the cost of a tomb without being engaged at Westminster.

The fact that Robert Vertue is the first named of three King's masons who give their opinion on a Westminster question, while the main work was going forward, is evidence that he was the master actually in charge.

Robert Vertue is mentioned in the copy of Henry VII.'s accounts at the British Museum as receiving, in 1501, £40 in part payment of £100 for building of a tower in the Tower of London. (Was this the " Brick Tower " on the north side ?) Robert Vertue was, thus, working in London at the very time Henry VII.'s Chapel was being prepared for. Only the year before this, I find Robert Jenyns mentioned in the same accounts as " mason of Windsor." Again, in 1503, £10 was advanced " to Vertue in part payment for a new ' platt ' at Greenwich." Later, work was done at Windsor itself by William Vertue, who was probably a son of Robert. In 1 Henry VIII., William was paid £50 " in full content " for vaulting the chancel of Windsor College. I do not know on what evidence Hope assigned Thornbury Castle (1511) to Robert Jenyns except its obvious resemblance to Windsor. In 1516, William Vertue, master mason, was granted 12*d.* a day for life by Henry VIII. ; this must have been for specially distinguished services.

THE KING'S MASONS

In the British Museum manuscript room is preserved a drawing on vellum of a tomb in a style very similar to the King's Chapel (Cott. Aug. II., 1). It is lettered in a somewhat later hand, *The Monument intended for Kinge Henry the Sixte*. Skilfully drawn in a two-sided view that can hardly be called perspective, it clearly must date about 1500, and be by one of the royal masons of the time.

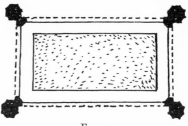

Fig. 93.

Slender octagonal turrets rise from the angles of the tomb proper. These run up the full height, and are terminated above with " ogee " curved cappings cut into scales and similar to the turrets of the chapel. Fig. 93 shows the scheme; arches following the dotted lines spring from " turret " to " turret," and above the arches is a tier of rich niches for about twenty statues. It has been said that this stage must have surrounded an upper chantry chapel, but the scale does not allow of this. This range of imagery is again in the manner of the Chapel, and the images were supported on pedestal pillars, as were the figures of the Chapel. Smaller details, like running foliage in the hollow mouldings and rose terminations to the cusps, also resemble details in the Chapel, and, I think, it is most probable that the tomb drawing was by the master mason at Westminster.

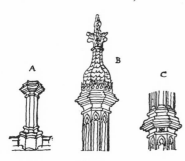

Fig. 94.

The supporting " turret " element was a new thing at the Chapel, but it became a great vogue ; even the brass chantry has open-work octagonal turrets at the angles. In Fig. 94, *A* shows the image pedestals ; *B* the tops of the turrets (compare the brattishing to the cornice with that at Westminster) ; *C* is a band on the turrets (compare those on the brass turrets at Westminster). Altogether, I venture to assign this " platt " to the master of Henry VII.'s Chapel, that is, as I suppose, Robert Vertue.

CHAPTER IX

HENRY THE SEVENTH'S CHAPEL (*continued*)

Decorations and Fittings

" *King Henry the Seventh for the burial of himself and his children adjoined thereto, in the east-end a chapel of admirable artificial elegancy ; for a man would say that all the curious and exquisite work that can be devised is there compacted ; wherein is to be seen, his own most stately magnifical monument, all of solid and massie copper.*"—(HOWEL's " *Londinopolis*," 1657.)

" *In* 1803 *they first began their innovating career and professional blows were dealt against the devoted walls.*"— (JOHN CARTER, 1812.)

The King provided by his will that 10,000 Masses should be said for the " weal of his soul," in honour of the Trinity, the Five Wounds of Christ and the Five Joys of the Virgin ; the nine orders of Angels, the Patriarchs, the twelve Apostles, and All Saints. This indicates what was in the mind of the founder. The sculptured saints, of the interior, nearly a hundred, have been most fully described and identified by Micklethwaite, in *Archæologia*, xlvii. They were to have had their names painted on labels, carved for the purpose, on their supports and similar to the labels under the external images. Since this time, I have had the opportunity of examining some of them from a scaffolding. The central figure at the east end is Christ, Who holds a book open *outwards* in the left hand, while the right is raised. His foot is on the globe of the earth. This would seem to be the Christ of the Second Coming, and it would give a key to the whole assemblage of Saints, if they are assessors of the final Judgment.

To the right of Christ (south) is the Virgin, and to the left is an Angel. This pair has been interpreted as the Annunciation. The angel carried a *sceptre* in the right hand, and this suggests that the meaning may have been the recognition as Queen of Heaven which follows on the Doom. Only the head of the sceptre now remains; the Angel's left hand grasps the end of a long, marvellously undercut scroll, the inscription on which would have made the meaning clear.

Beyond, again, are St. Peter and St. Paul, the former with

FIG. 95.—*a* and *b*.

book and great key, and the latter with book and sword. The rest of the apostles follow. Most of their emblems are described by Micklethwaite; he calls that of Jude a boat, but it is rather the hull of a ship with a raised forecastle and interesting as a model of a mediæval ship (Fig. 95 *b*). The large hat worn by St. James has the plaiting of the straw indicated. Still further on, and now on the lateral walls, we find St. Anne on the north and Mary Magdalen with an aged woman on the south (St. Elizabeth ?). St. Anne is teaching the Virgin to read, but the child's figure is an " emblem " only. Her intent reading face is very true and pretty, also her action in turning over the leaves of the book; it is a delicate and beautiful work.

Saints of the Church fill up the rest of the north and south walls, except in the western bays, where there are ten figures who appear to be ancient philosophers. These last are somewhat unusual, but they occur in some late stained glass in the Cambridge Library. (See also Didron's

SCULPTURE

Iconography, vol. ii.) It may be noticed that the royal saints of England—Oswald, Edmund, etc.—find a natural place in the assembly.

The scheme at the east end may be suggested thus :

5 4 3 2 1	PETER ANGEL CHRIST VIRGIN PAUL	1 2 3 4 5
APOSTLES		APOSTLES

Several careful drawings were made of the images by Mr. S. Weatherley " when they were taken down to be cast " ; this must have been about 1870, and a set of these casts exists at the Victoria and Albert Museum. The whole series should be photographed to a large scale, for the details, which are minutely rendered, are full of beauty and invention. There is fresh observation, realism, and humour in these remarkable works of art which furnish a valuable image of the Tudor mind (*see* Prior and Gardner's *English Sculpture*). Fig. 95 *a* is a sketch of one of the crowns, which is very like that of the Virgin in the Eton wall paintings.* The figures are all in niches above a linked band of angels.

The sculptured angels are not fully distinguished into the nine orders, but there are warrior angels (St. Michael, etc.), and others clothed in feathers (Seraphim), as well as those in ordinary angelic vesture. They are occupied in no less an office than holding up the King's badges : Rose, Fleur-de-lys, and Portcullis.

Amongst a few figures which Micklethwaite left un-identified are two at the east end of the north chapel or aisle. The first of these, an aged warrior who leads a dragon, has since been shown, by Dr. James and the late Henry Bradshaw, to have been St. Armil (Armagilus) of Brittany. This saint was venerated by the Welsh and by Henry VII. Micklethwaite later suggested that St. Ermine's (now an hotel) carries on the name of this saint.

* These paintings resemble Westminster works in other respects, and were probably by a London painter.

Next to the image of St. Armil, in the same north chapel, which, I suppose, may have been planned as a chantry for Prince Henry, later Henry VIII., is the figure of a king, beardless and with a book. Of this image Mr. Mickle-thwaite said: "This has been called Henry VI., but we have reason for putting him elsewhere "—that is, in an empty niche in the eastern chapel. The support, under this empty niche, has the letters H.R. on it, and it is not improbable that the figure once in it was Henry VI.

Several images, however, are repeated in the chapel, and there happen to be two of each of the companion figures of this king. I would suggest that, if the north chapel was intended for the heir of Henry VII., then it would have been specially appropriate to have his name saint here, just as St. Margaret was put in the south aisle where Margaret, the King's mother, was to be buried. It might explain why this image has no emblem, if it could be none other than Henry VI. (See the just published account of the " miracles " of King Henry VI. I may remark here that, in the transcript of accounts of Henry VII. at the British Museum, there are entries for writing and painting a book ; can it be the MS. of the Miracles ?)

The statues and the rest of the works, in a suitable degree, were, or were to have been, coloured and gilded. In the King's will, it was provided that "the walls, doors, windows, arches and vaults, and images, within and without, be painted, garnished and adorned with our arms, badges, cognisants and other convenient painting in as goodly and rich a manner as such a work requireth, and to a King's work appertaineth."

Gay and glittering in bright colour and gilding the long rank of figures ranged along the main walls, and appearing company after company in the several chapels, would have had an extraordinary appeal to the mind by its hypnotising iteration. Such were the thoughts of employers and craftsmen at the end of the period of workmanship and on the eve of a time when imaginative thought and act were

to be washed away in a flood of talk about " architecture "
by professional " art " middlemen.

An important authority for the works of Henry VII.,
at a time just before the new chapel at Westminster was
begun, is the Egerton MS. 2358, at the British Museum,
recording payments of Thomas Warley, clerk of the King's
works to Henry VII. It is concerned with certain works at
St. Paul's connected with the marriage of Prince Arthur,
also with the Tower, Westminster Palace, Greenwich, and
Eltham. It is in Latin, ill-written and abbreviated, so
that I can make little of the details. Only minor masons
seem to be named, Walter Martyn, John Carter and others,
but none is given the title of King's mason.

The most arresting entry is for the wages of " Sculptors "
for sculpturing the dragon, lion, and leopards for the
cipher [?] in the Great Hall at the Tower. They were
John Moore, Richard Codeman, Robert Bellamy, Nicholas
Delphyn, and John Hudde. Robert Duke was employed
painting and gilding the same. John Hudde also sculptured
two lions and a great rose with an imperial crown above
it in Westminster Hall, over the north door. John Hudde
and most of the other sculptors thus named were, doubtless,
the authors of the great array of images at the King's Chapel
—more than a " gross " of statues was a big order which
required many artists. The bronze enclosure of the
King's tomb is described in *Craftsmen*. Six small figures
remain which, Dr. M. R. James says, were the work of
Thomas Ducheman.

.   .   .   .

Stalls and Pavement.—Of the woodwork of the Chapel,
Neale writes : " Neither the stalls nor seats are all of the
same period as may be readily distinguished from the
workmanship ; those which are coeval with the completion
of this edifice extend to the third arch on each side ; the
others were constructed on the revival of the Order of the
Bath by George the First. . . . At the last installation
two of the canopies were displaced from their original

positions near the west end and affixed against the great piers eastward over new stalls, where they yet remain, but the stalls themselves have now been removed. It would seem, too, from the style of workmanship and other circumstances that all the canopies which surmount the stalls added in the reign of George the First originally formed the back fronts of those which are known to be coeval with the Chapel" (Micklethwaite says that the addition was made in 1725. Two modern canopies are now in the triforium). The backs of the canopies most easily seen are several against the south aisle, which have plain backs. Closer observation of others, partly hidden, and of many against the north aisle show that, originally, all were complete at the back as in front. In the north aisle, also, a pierced brattishing over the level lower part is preserved, and thus the complete original form may be understood.

A plan of the sixteenth century in the Thorpe collection at the Soane Museum, which shows the original arrangement of the stalls, published by Burges in Scott's *Gleanings*, was reproduced in Fig. 92 Burges, however, raised some difficulties in his comment, which must be noticed. " Thorpe's plan is not only valuable as showing us the positions of the altars, but exhibits the position of the stalls prior to their being altered in the reign of George I. It is generally asserted that a new bay of stalls was then added on either side ; by a comparison, however, of Thorpe's plan with the actual building we shall find that the number of the stalls remains the same, the only addition being two rows of canopies, which, however, were supplied by cutting off the hinder part of the original ones." This is not so clear as Burges usually was. The fact is, that Thorpe's plan shows the stalls much narrower than they are, and, moreover, as carried right up to the west end where the two " return stalls " are. On this plan the stalls were evidently only roughly sketched ; that the number agrees, or nearly agrees, with the present number must be accidental.

The important return stalls just mentioned were, doubt-

less, on occasion for royal use. There were quite charming kneeling figures of kings in carved oak on the fronts. That on the north side only sur-
vives. From the king's beast, lying behind him, I suppose this one was in-tended for Henry VI. The king saint is represented on the screen at Whimple with an antelope, gorged with a crown, at his feet. Re-member that two bays on either hand, beyond the east end of the stalls, had high

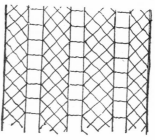

FIG. 96.

stone screens, curved on plan, like the bow windows of the aisles. A good eighteenth-century engraved view of the interior of the chapel shows this arrangement.

A   B

FIG. 97.

The original pavement of the Chapel remains in the aisles, the eastern chapel, and in the tomb chantry. It is of small slabs of grey marble, laid in alternating strips diagonally and square. This is the most general type of mediæval pavement at least in London (Fig. 96). Notice on the west wall below the window three large painted consecration crosses. The original wooden roof above the vault has disappeared; doubt-less, it was very much like that of King's College Chapel, Cambridge. The leaden down pipes of the exterior appear to be original.

I spoke before of the vanes of the exterior. The pre-vailing love for vanes was evident also within. The bronze boy-angels at the ends of the founder's tomb carried banners; and the angle standards of the tombs of the Lady Margaret, Queen Elizabeth, and Mary Queen of Scots all had vanes, some memory of which is preserved in the prints and drawings.

Fig. 97a is from a sketch by Carter, from the vanes once on the " grate " which surrounded Margaret's tomb. The railing without the vanes has recently been given back to the chapel. It was the work of Cornelius Symondson. Fig. 97b is from a small sketch in the Powell collection of the vanes once on the tomb of Mary Queen of Scots. This railing has also been brought back to the Abbey. It

FIG. 98.

was probably by the same smith who made the beautiful " grate " of Elizabeth's tomb, which is shown in Neale's plate 57. " It was surmounted by fleurs de lys and roses, on the frieze were the letters E.R., mixed with lions and falcons ; there had been standards at the angles and in the middle; the whole had been gilt. Patrick the blacksmith received £95 for the work (Fig. 98)." It is marvellous that the learned and powerful of a century ago could decree the destruction of the roses of Elizabeth's tomb. The vanes of the exterior were very similar to those of Margaret's tomb. Carter observed two standards remaining, and one of the vanes is shown on the old sketch which he engraved.

Glazing.—A few fragments of painted glass which remain here and there are sufficient to show what the original scheme was like, even if it is next to impossible to imagine its beauty when complete.

This glazing was, in part, as we shall see, destroyed in the Cromwellian period. It was largely renewed in Wren's time, and again it was subject to injury and loss in the eighteenth century. Of this later time, John Carter wrote : " The whole of the basement part of this chapel is in a damaged state. The windows are broken, their lower divisions stopped up and their mullions hacked. Viewing the windows of the upper story I noticed that their mullions were kept from falling by boards. . . . Wish for an instant to see the place as at first, unsullied by dust and cobwebs ; see the whole in perfect repair ; the stopped up broken windows shining resplendent with their full assemblage of painted glass ; its aisles and chapels unencumbered by intrusive modern objects ; a monument of royal mortality. Our sight becomes distracted, our comprehension loses itself in this labyrinth ; our senses forsake the clue of reason, and we sink entranced into a state of unutterable delight. Six of the windows on the south and one on the north side in the upper tier have been boarded. Several of the eastern stalls are modern and are tolerable imitations. The first small chapel on the north side had its screen destroyed in part. The centre chapel, in which one statue is gone, has no determinations to give a situation for an altar. The fifth chapel : one of the statues is gone, and the screen nearly destroyed. . . . Some small portions of the painted arms and devices in the windows are yet visible ; and in particular in the high east window a good figure. It is rather surprising as these paintings continue to be a general mark for stone-throwers, that a particle of them is in being. . . . The collection of statues represents saints and a small one on the stall on the left of the entrance is pointed out as the portrait of Henry himself " (*Gentleman's Magazine*, 1799).

The story of the destruction of the glazing under the Commonwealth may be gathered from the Fourteenth Report of the Historical MSS. Commission (Appendix, Part II, Welbeck MSS., 1894).

Among payments for " cleansing out pictures " at the Abbey in 1644–45, the following items appear : " 1644, April 19.—Receipt for 6*s*. by Thomas Gastaway from Sir

Robert Harley for taking down the high altar of Henry the Seventh's Chapel. Sep. 30—. . . . taking down the pictures in Queen Elizabeth's Chapel and carrying them to Sir Robert Harley's House.

1645, June 9.—Receipt by John Rutland from Sir Robert Harley of £10 towards glazing Henry the Seventh's Chapel with white glass.

July 15, £10. Aug. 8.—Receipt by John Rutland of £15 from Sir Robt. Harley towards glazing work done in Henry the Seventh's Chapel. (The account includes 498 ft. of glass in the west window, and 360 ft. of glass in the three east windows.) Sept. 11.—Do. for glazing work in the same.

This sad record to some extent confirms *Mercurius Rusticus* (1685) : " Sir Robert Harlow breaking into Henry VII.'s Chapel, pulled down the Altar Stone which stood before the goodly Monument of that King ; it was a curious Touchstone, a Rarity not to be matched ; there it stood for many Years, yet it did not escape the frenzy of this Man's ignorant zeal, for he broke it all to Shivers."

Such was the purging celebrated in the pamphlet *God's Ark over-topping the World's Waves* (1646) : " For the gaudy guilded Crucifixes . . . and Pictures placed and painted thereabout where the sinful Singing was used . . . now a thick throng of pious people . . . what a rich and rare alteration." (Dean Robinson's paper *W. Abb. in the XVIIth Cent.*).

From the fragments of old glass still in the windows at Westminster and from the glazing of King's College Chapel, Cambridge, which is known to have followed the West-minster scheme, we are able to understand the original arrangement at Henry VII.'s Chapel. The Westminster windows were undertaken about 1510, and the Cambridge windows about 1516. Of the latter, we are told : " In this year an agreement was made between the executors of Henry VII. and the provost of the College regarding the windows which were to be glazed with images, stories, arms, badges and other devices. In a contract for completing the Cambridge glazing, dated 1526, it was agreed that the windows are to be set up with good, clean, sure and perfect glass and orient colours, and *imagery of the Story of the Old and New Law after the form, manner and curiosity and cleanness in every part of the King's New Chapel at Westminster.*

From a second contract of the same year, we learn that Barnard Flower had originally contracted for the Cambridge windows, and had been several years engaged on the work. Since he alone was at first employed on so large an undertaking it seems likely that he was the popular man of his day, and possibly had been the painter of the Westminster windows" (*Archæol. Jour.,* vol. xii.). According to Mr. J. D. Le Couteur, "Barnard Flower the Kinge's Glasyer of England," died between July 25 and Aug. 14, 1517. "He was not an Englishman, but a native of Almaine, who had been granted letters

Fig. 99.

of denization on May 6, 1514, by King Henry VIII., and who had held the office of 'King's Glazier' for several years previous to that date. The post was of some importance, the recipient holding it for life, unless a change took place in the succession. John Prudde held the office from his appointment in 1440 till the death of Henry VI. in 1461, when he was superseded by Thos. Bye, citizen and glazier of London, and received such fees and wages as Roger Gloucester held, and all other profits and a ' shedde,' called the ' Glasier's logge ' within Westminster Palace, and a gown of the King's livery, of the suit of the sergeant of the works yearly. He also received the sum of 12*d.* a day. The primary duties of the King's glazier were the windows in the Royal palaces. There was, thus, every reason why Flower and his men should be employed upon Henry VII's Chapel, and, when ready, upon King's College also. His death brought the work of glazing the College chapel to a standstill, for it was not until 1526 that Galyon Hone, a Fleming, who had succeeded as King's glazier was set to work on the task " (*The Builder*, May 9, 1924).

Dr. James thought that Flower had completed four of the Cambridge windows.

In his will, Henry VII. directed that the Westminster windows should be glazed with " stories, images, arms, badges and cognisants."

Now, the King's College windows contain *stories* (subjects) from the Old and New Testaments, arranged as types and anti-types, *images* of prophets, etc., some called " Messengers," and *arms, badges*, etc., in the tracery. The windows both at Westminster and King's College are of five lights in three and two tiers. At the latter, the Gospel series occupies the lower row, and the Old Law the upper row, except for the central light in each case which contains a " Messenger."

The ancient glazing of the tracery at Westminster corresponded entirely with the King's College scheme and the remaining figure at Westminster is very like those at King's College. About sixty years ago, it was pointed out that, when this figure was examined through a glass, it was seen to be " the prophet Jeremiah under a canopy holding a scroll and altogether " a match " for the Messengers in the Chapel at Cambridge. This is a curious instance of a reflex light being thrown upon glass, once a standard in the country, but now lost " (*Archæol. Jour.*, xii.). In 1911, I was able to see this light from a ladder and to make a rough sketch of the head (Fig. 99). The figure, or rather three-quarter figure, rises from a panel or predella of white glass with yellow stain, in which is a little figure of an angel, under an arch, holding a scroll inscribed *Jeremias pph*. The prophet is in a ruby robe and is set under a white canopy on an emerald ground. On the scroll is written *Patre[m ?] laudate nomen domin[i]*.

We may now say that the upper windows at Westminster contained the Gospel story with parallels from the Old Testament, together with messengers of bigger scale in each window, except that the east window would have had the Crucifixion only. At Fairford, again, the scheme is very similar. The fine Crucifixion window now in St. Margaret's Church close to the Abbey repeats the same type of composition. Of this window, indeed, there is a story that it was made at Dort in Holland and sent to Henry VII. as a present for his chapel (see Westlake's *Stained Glass*, where the story is doubted). The exact evidence, however, is against such a theory, and the window appears to have been made for the chapel of New Place, Essex, as rebuilt by Henry VIII., and to be the work of the successors of Barnard Flower.* There cannot be a doubt that Barnard Flower was the glazier of Henry VII.'s chapel. In the Egerton MS. and other accounts, he appears working for the King long before the chapel was ready for glazing. There can be little doubt that the clerestory windows of the chapel contained stories from the Old and New Testaments and a series of " messengers " leading up to a Crucifixion, filling the east window directly above the Majesty in sculpture. Glass and sculpture represented the whole teaching of the Church. All had meaning : it was an encyclopædia.

At King's College Chapel, according to Dr. James, the two north-western windows are those usually attributed

---

* In regard to foreign influence on glass work at this time, see the excellent, recently issued *English Industries of the Middle Ages*, L. E. Salzman : a book full of freshly gathered facts on English craftsmanship and a recent paper by Mr. Knowles in the *Antiquaries' Journal*, 1925.

to Barnard Flower : " they contain the best and most delicate drawing in the chapel." In Westlake's work on stained glass, it is shown by comparing the little figure in the predella with one of the bottom panels in the earliest window, supposed to be by Barnard Flower in King's College Chapel, that both are by the same artist. (A similar treatment is found at Fairford.)

Mr. Le Couteur points out that the " messengers " at Cambridge held scrolls with inscriptions, which explained the Bible scenes with which they were associated. They were not prophets, and if the figure now in Henry VII's Chapel is Jeremiah, he might have been one of a series occupying the west window. The inscription is not suitable for Jeremiah (with the exception of the word *Patrem*), but rather (with the same exception) for *O Angeli laudate nomen domini*.

I may suggest that the little predella angel with the name Jeremias was, probably, not associated originally with the figure above, and so, I think, it is possible that the figure was a " messenger " and not a Prophet. The longer inscription is a mystery ; it seems to fit too well to have been adopted from another light. Probably, this figure was put in place by Wren, in whose time much glazing was done in the chapel. As we shall see, he gathered the stained-glass fragments in the church into the east and west windows. The figure was already in the east window of the chapel when Malcolm wrote about 1800.

In the *Inventory*, it is said that the building was completed about 1519, but the glass must have been earlier than this, if it was by Barnard Flower. The chapel must, I think, have been practically completed about 1512, which is the date of Skelton's eulogy of Henry VII., that was suspended on the bronze enclosure and his chantry.

At King's College, the badges in the tracery include the Lancaster Rose, the Hawthorn Tree, Portcullis, Fleur-de-lys, York Rose, and Initials H.R. and H.E.

At Westminster, the original glazing of the quite small openings in the traceried heads of the clerestory windows yet remains in large part. In the four central piercings of each window are the four *quarters* of the Royal coat of arms, while the still smaller piercings round about are filled with bright coloured glass unpainted; small quatrefoil forms have a disc of ruby at the centre of four pieces of smoky blue—very simple and very effective.

The great west window, which is no less than fifteen lights wide, had tiers of figures under canopies on red and blue grounds (Prophets ?). In the tracery are angels, heraldic badges, and initials. The badges, portcullises, roses, fleurs-de-lys, prince's feathers were on ruby and blue grounds; the initials are H.R. and H.E. for Henry and Elizabeth (see illustration in *Inventory*) The large lower windows in the five radiating chapels must all have had badges in coloured panels set in diamond glazing, such as are now only found in the eastern window. The badges themselves are authenticated by sketches in the Powell collection at the British Museum, with the note : " Taken before the recent repairs." In Fig.

Fig. 100.

100 I give a rough restoration of these badge-panels in relation to the diamond glazing. It will be seen how easily the pretty form was obtained from the conditions.*

* Mr. Le Couteur points out that there are similar badges in the Chapel of the Tower " like them set up by Barnard Flower at the King's command."

The tiny little tracery piercings along the top lights are set with morsels of blue and ruby glass, as described before. Badges are now only to be found in the central chapel; but, as the windows of the other radiating chapels have the red and blue along the upper lights, while they are otherwise the barest in the whole building, it may not be doubted that they also had these extremely effective badges. A few similar badges are now in Jericho parlour and on one of those is scratched the date 1512.

Keepe (1683), after speaking of "the fine wrought wainscot" of the stalls, adds : " nor are the windows, where with this chapel is further embellished to be neglected, every light being composed of diapered and well-painted glass, each pane containing either a red rose, the badge or cognizance of the house of Lancaster, or a text

FIG. 101.

h, the initial letter of this King's name, each crowned with a royal diadem."

Hatton (1708) wrote : " The windows in the N. and S. aisles are painted with the Flower de lis, Rose, Portcullis crowned, and another [window] at the W. end of each aisle."

Malcolm, describing the chapel in 1803, before its restoration, says of the *northern* apsidal chapel " the windows contain painted glass of the arms of Edward the Confessor, Henry VII. his initials, a crown on a tree, with the red rose and *fleur-de-lys*. In the *aisles* the large west windows had many panes of painted glass ; and those on the sides have

182

scraps still remaining. They are representations of the red rose, *fleur de lys*, a rose half red and half white, portcullis, and the initials H. R."

Neale states : " At the present time but few panes are thus ornamented, much of the glass having been broken or ruined while the chapel was in a state of dilapidation. What remains has been distributed in the different windows." " Formerly," he continues, " several of the panes had daisy-plants and others an initial H surmounted by a crown with a branch going through it."

Painted quarries (distinct from the badges) are now only to be found forming a row at the top of the plain diamond glazing in the aisle windows ; these have the crowned letters H. and R. alternately. Fig. 101 is from some quarries in the South Kensington Museum, which look as if they must have been " collected " from Henry VII.'s Chapel when it was being " restored." In the present glazing of the lower east window, there are also some fragments of the old quarries ; one is a nearly complete daisy-plant design (see Fig. 100), a second is part of a thorn tree and crown device (Fig. 101). Another is a crown which looks as if it might be part of the portcullis quarry (Fig. 101). Doubtless, Keepe was literally true, and every pane had its device. Compare the lower windows at King's College Chapel. These badges, devices, and initials are delightful elements for repetition. The glazing was as fresh and interesting as the other parts of the chapel and worthy of the brazen chantry in its midst. Altogether, as William Morris said, the chapel was " the most romantic work of the late Middle Ages."

CHAPTER X

SCULPTURE AND SCULPTORS

Master John of St. Albans, Sculptor.—Any full story of the sculptures of the great church and tombs would fill a book. I can here only discuss a few selected points. Two tall figures, representing the Annunciation above the inner door of the Chapter House, have already been described. They are certainly to be numbered among the most impressive statues in England; casts at South Kensington can most easily be studied. The Chapter House was being completed in 1253, and in the accounts for that year two images, costing 53*s.* 4*d.* (four marks), are mentioned. As Professor Prior suggested, these images may have been the Annunciation group, and this is made the more likely by the evidence that the big figure of the Majesty, now between them, did not exist originally (Fig. 102). Four marks seems a small price for the two figures, but it would be for labour only. The images of the Queen on the Waltham Cross cost five marks each nearly fifty years later.

In 1257–58, John of St. Albans, " sculptor of the King's images," received a robe of office while working at Westminster along with Peter of Hispania, the King's painter, and Alexander, the King's carpenter, who, as we know from other records, were engaged on the Abbey works. John of St. Albans, the King's sculptor, was thus employed at the Abbey at the very time when the first work of the King was being completed. The Angel spandrels, high up in the transept ends, can have been carved only a very short time before, if, indeed, they were completed. As the most important sculptures now in the church, they may with confidence be attributed to Master John and his school of

assistants, but, of course, the chief task of " the sculptor
of the King's images " would be the wonderful northern
portals, the work on which must have continued for many
years. A measured drawing of the angels in the South
Transept, made by my old friend J. A. Slater, in 1883, is
reproduced in Figs. 103 and 104.

Fig. 102.—Chapter House Doorway.

I have examined the angels from a scaffolding, and there
are casts of two of them at South Kensington; they are
certainly of great beauty, serious and yet gay, the very
embodiment of rapture. Fig. 117 is a distant impression of
one of the heads.

The style of the sculptor of the Chapter House Annunciation may, I think, be detected in these censing angels.
Notice especially the hand of the more eastward of the two

Fig. 103.—South Transept.

in the South Transept, which is sharply turned at the wrist; the little lion under the foot of the same angel resembles the lions of the Chapter House capital; compare also the clumsy feet and the drapery of the figures. The chief sculptor could not have done all the figure work in the church, but he would have guided the whole, and, as chief of a school, it would have been his in the sense that the sculptures of the Parthenon are by Pheidias. One master seems to have worked on the Annunciation and the Censing Angels.

Between the two angels in the North Transept were two

FIG. 104.—South Transept.

figures which are lost. Opposite, in the South Transept, two still remain, which seem to have reference to the story of the Confessor's ring. Possibly, the first pair showed the gift of the ring, and the second its return ; both incidents appeared on the tapestry of Abbot Barking.

With these angels of the transepts must be associated some in the smaller spandrels of the wall arcades. One of these in a south-east chapel has an angel carrying two crowns ; another, now in the Museum, probably from the same chapel, plays a harp (Fig. 105) ; yet another, in the west aisle of the North Transept, swings a censer (Fig. 106).

187

These, taken together with the bigger angels, so closely resemble the angels in the spandrels of the wall arcade of the Ste. Chapelle (see Viollet-le-Duc's " Ange," Figs. 4 and 8), that it seems that one series must have been suggested by the other.

These noble figures of angels have a marked affinity with another chief work of thirteenth-century English sculpture — a series of angels at Lincoln Cathedral, which was carved some fifteen or twenty years later than the Westminster figures. They are in the Choir, which is often, in consequence, called the Angel Choir, but the sculptures themselves represent " a choir of angels." Some play musical instruments, others guide the sun and moon and do all the things that angels should. These Lincoln angels, with the wonderful sculptures of the Judgment Door, which is

FIG. 105.

contemporary with the Angel Choir, are so like the Westminster angels and the old north portal that it seems likely that the Westminster sculptors must have gone on to Lincoln.

At the Abbey, there still exists a Choir of Angels, but it is in a position where it can hardly ever be seen, on the soffits of the six window lights above the interior of the great north door.

MASTER JOHN OF ST. ALBANS

In July 1911, I examined these medallions from the high Coronation stand erected in the North Transept. They are on the soffits of the lower range of windows, and there are twenty-four, two on each side of every arch. Most of the medallions are circular, but some are lobed squares (Fig. 107); the frames touch one another, and in some cases throw off foliage in the spandrel spaces. The figures, or rather busts, represent a Choir of Angels, playing music, worshipping, carrying chalice, censer, incense-boat, crown, palm, scroll, book, etc. One bears discs (sun and moon ?) and another a dial. The musical instruments are harp, dulcimer, pipes,

FIG. 106.

and bells. They are in fair condition and of great beauty; the casts that were obtained by Cottingham about a century since seem to have been excessively touched up.* When opportunity offers, they and all the sculpture should be photographed. These sculptures in medallions,

FIG. 107.

* These are now at South Kensington.

touching one another, confirm the view that the medallions in the north porches contained sculpture. The lobed squares (Fig. 107) are of the form assigned to the central panel of the great porch. Below the Choir of

Fig. 108.—Henry III.

Angels, on the extreme window jambs, are two standing figures of kings, one of which stands on a small prostrate figure. This is probably the Confessor and the other Henry III. (see Neale and also Walpole's *Anecdotes of Painting*, illustrated edition).

PORTRAIT HEADS

Another interesting group of sculpture at the Abbey is formed by the portrait heads, to which special study should be devoted. It is curious that we possess no standard set of Royal portraits, and I should like to suggest the subject to any student who wants an interesting task. Directly inside the Royal door at Westminster is an altogether remarkable head (Fig. 108). In rather a dark place, it is hardly ever observed, but it is carved in marble and has escaped injury, so that it is practically perfect. It is of a beardless man crowned, and it must, from its special character and place, represent Henry III. himself. It is recognised in

Fig. 109.

Fig. 110.

France that portrait heads of Henry's contemporary, St. Louis, exist, and the earlier representations of Henry show him as beardless. Higher up, above this head, is another portrait head; this time, I think, of the master mason, Henry de Reyns. Outside another doorway, going into the Cloister, are two crowned heads; these may be of the King and Queen, but they are badly decayed. In the Gallery Chamber, now the Muniment Room, which was probably the Royal Pew, there are other crowned heads, and there were three—now hopelessly decayed—at the Chapter House door. (Portrait heads of later date in the Cloister have been mentioned in another section, p. 145.)

191

SCULPTURE AND SCULPTORS

In the Triforium are many large sculptured corbels under its roof beams. Some have fine smiling heads, others are hideous, grinning creatures ; the former are on the south side and the latter are on the north. It has never, I believe, been noticed that a pair of busts among these corbels, on the south side of the Choir, represents the Annunciation. The angel holds a book and the heads have some resemblance to those of the Chapter House group (Figs. 109 and 110). A corbel head in the British Museum came from the Abbey. In St. Faith's Chapel are a dozen fine heads forming corbels, and, again, there is a difference of character between those on the north and the south, following the idea that these were evil and good quarters. One of the heads on the north side is a negro type. Figs. 111 and 112 are from minor heads.

Fig. 111.

Fig. 112.

The spandrels of the wall arcade are filled either with figure sculpture, foliage (naturalistic and ornamental), or with diaper work. The arcades of St. Paul's, or the north-east, chapel, had subject sculptures of which a pretty group remains behind a tomb, which looks like the education of the Virgin. One of the chapels on the south side, as we saw, seems to have had a choir of angels ; the alternate chapels on this side have diaper spandrels. Of the spandrels carved with a foliage, a delightful one with birds amongst it is illustrated in *Gleanings*. The remnant of a spandrel in one of the south-east chapels, which has just been cleaned, shows that it was filled with a naturalistic vine—a very early example. At the Abbey is a drawing made nearly a century ago of the branching rose spandrel in the Chapter House (Fig. 113). The idea of systematic variation is carried out in the triforium arches of the Presbytery which are decorated thus :

	D		
	C	C	
	M	M	
Diagram of apse	———	———	D=Diapers.
and the Presbytery	D	D	
indicating decora-	C	C	C=Carved.
tion of triforium	———	———	
arches.	M	M	M=Moulded.
	D	D	

With the spandrel sculpture must be mentioned the magnificent set of heraldic shields in the aisle arcades of the Choir. Amongst these are the arms of England, France, and Germany. Of the last it has been questioned whether the eagle was double-headed, but examining it in a good light, I found enough to show that the head

Fig. 113.

was single; there is a turn of the neck which brought the head in profile (Fig. 114). This suggests a comment ; a practice is springing up, following some old examples, of making heraldic charges face to the east in every case, but it was not so here, as may be seen also by the ramping lion of Simon de Montfort near

o

by. The eagle of the German Empire in the early stained glass was single-headed, and so it seems to have been on Crouchback's tomb. Matthew of Paris gives the eagle of the empire either with one or two heads. A shield on the south side, which has long been attributed to Rothsay, has recently been shown to be that of De Ros.

The vaulting bosses of the west aisles of the transepts are big, bold sculptures, about 2½ ft. in diameter, and in high relief. The one nearest the north front is David playing his harp ; the next has two men, who have been

FIG. 114.

called Aaron and Moses, and a cast of this at South Kensington shows that Moses was horned ; another has the Virgin and Child, with angels on either hand, and others seem to be the Assumption of the Virgin and " Abraham's bosom." These are fine work, as may be seen by casts of four of them at South Kensington. Fig. 115 is from a delightful little seated Virgin at the top of the sculptured jamb of the Chapter House door ; there is a companion figure of Christ.

Royal Portrait Statues.—Passing from the structure to the tombs we find a series of figures of great beauty, some of which are of bronze. First must be mentioned the noble bronze effigy of Henry III., the work of William Torel, goldsmith, of London. It formerly had a canopy, lions at the feet, and sceptres in the hands, which are now lost, but the figure is practically perfect. The effigy of Queen Eleanor, by the same artist, is of unsurpassable freshness and grace ; her hand holds the neck-band of her mantle, and the body bends in a slight curve from head to feet. A figure of the Queen on her seal, which was doubtless made several

194

years before her death, resembles the effigy in many respects
and was probably by the same goldsmith. Were it not for
this, we might suppose that the effigy had been modelled
by the sculptor of the stone statues of the crosses. Rather,
we must think that the seal was referred to by the sculptor
as well as by the goldsmith maker of the effigy.

I cannot think why this most lovely portrait of such a
romantic person as Eleanor
of Castile has not attracted
somebody to write her life.
If it were well done, it
might suggest the spirit of
the Middle Ages in Eng-
land almost more than anything else.*

The question how far the
Royal and other notable
effigies are likenesses, will
be important whenever an
attempt is made to form a
series of early national
portraits. In such a critical
book as Sir J. H. Ramsay's
Dawn of the Constitution
(1907), it is again asserted
that tomb statues are not
portraits. He says : " It
would seem that the bronze
effigy of Henry III., executed about 1291, was not
intended for a likeness,
but only as an ideal of the stately and the beautiful.
So J. H. Middleton, *Academy*, March 5, 1881." In this
case the King had been dead nearly twenty years, and

Fig. 115.

---

* In the Wardrobe Accounts of Edward I. are many delightful details
of jewels, plate, and furnishings, which would adorn such a story. Begin
with the *Dict. Nat. Biog.* and Agnes Strickland.

so there would have been special difficulties, but to say that a likeness was not intended, seems against both reason and record. In the account for the making of the bronze figure by William Torel, it is said to be *ad similitudinem Regis*. The orders of Henry III., for images representing himself while alive, are worded in what may seem to us a vague manner, but that must have been a custom. Thus, a picture was ordered which was to have St. Edward presenting a certain King to the (Divine) Majesty. There may very well have been folklore reasons against too close identification while the person represented was living, but these could not hold when he was dead.

Certainly, tomb effigies for country churches were often done under conditions which would not allow of strict portraiture, but with Royal persons the circumstances were different. Their dead bodies were embalmed and were carried open at their funerals. At a later time the actual body was represented by an effigy made up like a waxwork, and it lay long " in state." The tomb statue was a more permanent representation of the body or of the funeral effigy, and was fully coloured even to the eyes, cheeks, and lips. It was a " double " of the dead person. The custom persisted fully till the time of Elizabeth. Stow writes : " The city of Westminster was surcharged with all sorts of people who came to see the obsequies, and when they beheld her statue or effigy lying on the coffin, set forth in royal robes, having a crown upon the head and a ball and sceptre in either hand there was such a sighing, groaning, and weeping as the like hath not been known." Miss Agnes Strickland adds that the effigy was the faded waxwork, which still exists. For embalming from the time of the Conquest, see Sandford.

It is recorded that Queen Eleanor was embalmed, and that Henry III. was also is shown by the fact that his heart was given to Fontevrault. " The King of France died and was embalmed, and buried as befitted so great a prince " (*Jehan de Paris*, French Romance). Such a custom made

196

continuity of record easy. The statues of Queen Eleanor at Waltham and Northampton are very similar to the effigy; all agree in having freely flowing hair, and the same is found on her seal. This must certainly be an individual trait.

.   .   .   .   .

Master Alexander of Abingdon, the Imager.—We have found that Robert of Beverley was occupying the office of King's mason in 1284. Master Richard of Crundale, " cementarius," was in charge of the Royal works at Westminster Palace in 1288, and he, doubtless, directly succeeded Master Robert. He may have had his name from Crundal, in Hampshire. Queen Eleanor died in 1290, and Edward at once set about building the series of memorials, now known as Eleanor Crosses, and tombs in the Abbey, at the Blackfriars, and in Lincoln Cathedral. The Abbey tomb and Charing Cross were the work of Richard Crundale, the King's mason, who, however, died about 1292, before Charing Cross was completed. The full original accounts for these works still exist, and it thus appears that the statues of this cross, as well as those which, most fortunately, still exist about the Waltham Cross, were sculptured by Master Alexander of Abingdon, " *le Imaginator.*" (These most beautiful works of such historical importance are all the time decaying in our acid atmosphere, and, little as I like meddling, I think it might be wise to remove the best preserved figure from this and the Northampton Cross to a museum, and substitute a copy. I should like to ask the S.P.A.B. to consider this.)

Edmund Crouchback, the King's brother, died in 1296, just as the crosses were completed, and there can be little doubt that his superb effigy in the Abbey must be Alexander's work. Alexander is mentioned several times in the *Letter Books* of the City of London. In 1305, Alexander " *le Imagour* " acknowledged a debt of £6 to a merchant of " Besaz." This is repeated two other times (Letter Book, B). In 1312, Master Adam the painter, and others, were sureties for Master Alexander " *le Imagour* " that he would complete his contract with the parson of Stanwell before All Saints' Day (Letter Book, D). Adam the painter is mentioned again in 1313 (Letter Book, E). We thus have a period of over twenty years of Alexander's working life marked out— 1290–1312. The persistent calling of him " *le Imagour* " (" *Imagour* " was a not infrequent craft title), seems to point to some office or special reputation, and his work on the most important of the Queen's crosses, conjointly with the King's mason, indicates that he was the King's sculptor. He was certainly the most important sculptor of his time. The entries in the Letter Books show that he was a citizen of London—and they suggest that he had, what is sometimes called, the artistic temperament; even his name was romantic.

The effigy is that of a very perfect knight. Crouchback was not taken to the Abbey until 1299–1300, but his tomb was probably erected, together with that of his wife Aveline (who died as early as 1273), about 1290. The graceful tomb statue of Aveline is in style remarkably like the figures of Eleanor on the crosses, and there is every probability that it was by the same master.

Another effigy of a lady, at Chichester, is so akin to the Aveline statue that both should be by the same artist. Professor Prior says of this : " The effigy of Lady FitzAlan, who died *c*. 1280, shows a handling some way towards that of the Westminster lady." He observes also a resemblance between the weepers of both tombs, which " do not turn sideways as in the St. Denis model." While writing this, I have re-examined the figure at Chichester, and noted the following points : The axis of the body bends in a slight curve from head to feet ; the drapery falls in long lines from the shoulders and covers well the feet, which rest against two dogs ; the mantle is caught up under each elbow ; hands are palm to palm on the breast ; linen around the head and chin leaves only a triangular opening for face ; she has also a veil over the head, which falls on the shoulders; the head rests on two square pillows, the upper smaller one being placed diagonally; two angels at the head are rather big and have their hands on the upper pillow; in profile the figure forms a long low curve terminated by head and feet. The two figures are so much alike that one is practically a repetition—that at Westminster seems a little more developed, elegant, and later; I do not doubt that both are by the same sculptor.

Professor Prior compares another lady's effigy in Aldworth Church, Berkshire, with the Waltham queens and Aveline. " These ladies would seem executed *c.* 1280–1300, and are sufficiently alike to suggest their source from a special *atelier*. Is it possible that they show the style of a single artist ? " Mr. Shearman points out to me that the effigy of a lady in Romsey Abbey is very like Aveline.

The weepers of the tombs of Aveline and Crouchback are also of one style with the queens of the Waltham Cross. Among these weepers are queens and princesses, which are practically reduced copies of the Queen's statues. (See for these Fig. 395 in Prior and Gardner's *Sculpture.*) There is the same swaying attitude, the drapery caught up by the arm, the hands on the mantle strap ; above all, there is the same expression of sweetness and dignity. The weepers of Aveline's tomb are much injured, and those of Crouchback's tomb have been defaced (literally), so that at first sight the little figures have a rather blunt look. Recently, however, they have been cleaned, and this, revealing the sharpness and delicacy of the modelling and the perfect measured grace of the poses and proportions, as well as the colouring, even to the flushed cheeks, shows that they were master works. I should like to see coloured casts set up in a museum.

The tombs of Aymer de Valence and John of Eltham also have weepers—there must be more than sixty of these figures altogether. The weepers about the tomb of Aymer are still more elegant, so that, at first sight, one is inclined to prefer them to those of Crouchback's tomb. The weepers of John of Eltham's tomb are even affectedly jaunty, but

very gay and amusing ; fortunately, twelve of them still
keep their heads—as they never did when alive ! A little
study of the series shows that there must have been a decline
of manners between 1290 and 1330—the high time of
Edward I. and after the reign of Edward II. The weepers
of the tomb of Aymer, like the whole work, follow the
tradition of the Crouchback tomb, but they can hardly be
by the same master—rather by a pupil. The tomb of
John of Eltham must, I think, be by the same master who
wrought the monument of Edward II. in Gloucester
Cathedral.

Later Sculptures.—The tomb of Queen Philippa is a new
departure in portraiture. It has suffered much violence ;
even the head has been at some time broken off, but it is a
remarkable work of art. The figure is realised through
the drapery ; even the pillow is not formal ; it is the portrait
of a pillow. The queen's left hand held her mantle strap,
which was " under-cut " ; the right hand fell lower and
held a sceptre ; an iron rod which projects from the head
must have supported its higher end. Her hair was arranged
in an elaborate net studded with little pins, to which
precious stones or gold beads must have been attached.
Sandford shows a crown still existing. The canopy is
astonishingly delicate ; the small tracery forms were set
with deep blue glass, which remains in places. Traceried
margins on each side of the figure contained little figures,
now lost. From an account of the tomb in the Liber Niger,
it appears that these were kings—probably the Saint Kings
of England. Two of the weepers remain (hidden by
Henry V.'s Chantry), and these still show remnants of
" picking out in gold and colour." This tomb was by
Hawkin of Liège.

The sculpture of the Reredos of the Chantry of Henry V.
(the Chapel of the Annunciation) has recently been cleaned,
and this has brought out, in a remarkable way, their exceptional quality. In the middle is an empty niche, once,

I suppose, occupied by a crowned figure of the Virgin. On either hand is the Virgin and the announcing angel. Beyond are Edward the Confessor and Edmund, King and Martyr, while at the extreme left and right are the patrons of England and France, St. George and St. Denis. These life-size figures are framed up in tabernacle work, containing a multitude of small figures of prophets. The large heads are full of expression, human and pathetic; the head of St. Denis, carried in his hands, is placid and beautiful, yet so true that it might have been studied from a corpse. The head of the Virgin is that of a frank English girl, with her hair thrown back in a natural, modern way (Fig. 116). These heads show close observation of ordinary living types; they are not traditional conventions. The tomb effigies of Abbot Colchester and Philippa, Duchess of York, have something of the same character, which was clearly typical of early fifteenth-century sculpture.

FIG. 116.

When I described these sculptures before, I thought that the central niche would have been occupied by Christ in Majesty, but from the prophets in the tabernacle work the glorified Virgin is more probable. I suggested also that (a) two important figures on the staircase are the Confessor and the pilgrim; (b) that two kings above, in the middle, who hold churches, are Sebert and Henry III., or the latter and

Henry V. himself as builder of the nave ; (c) two bishops or abbots, SS. Wulsin and Dunstan. The identification (a) is certain, for, seen from above, it is clear that the king's head is cut to receive a metal crown, and the other figure has a pilgrim's hat. The pairs (b) and (c) are, doubtless, like the Confessor, *founders*. A group of " founders " appeared on some thirteenth-century tapestry which once hung in the Choir, and the paintings on the sedilia comprised the Confessor and the pilgrim, two other kings, and two ecclesiastics. We are justified, therefore, in speaking of the statues on the front of the Chantry as a group of Founders of the Church. Some old casts of these sculptures are preserved at South Kensington.

On the big hollow of a table moulding, below the main sculptures, are three pretty little reliefs in trefoils, formed by a ribbon (compare the reliefs on the screen of the High Altar). The two lateral reliefs are similar. Each contains a figure of the Virgin with the infant Christ ; she is seated on the moon and is surrounded by a glory of rays ; beneath is a woman seated holding an animal ; this is a unicorn, which might only be caught by a Virgin. The central relief is half destroyed, but apparently it figured the Annunciation. In the right lobe of the trefoil the Virgin is seated holding a book, and again surrounded by a glory of rays ; in the left-hand lobe was doubtless the announcing angel ; above, in the upper lobe, appears a heart-shaped body, in which is struck a sword, the hilt of which is towards the Virgin. This upper object is also surrounded by rays ; on the ribbon border was an inscription, the last word of which seems to have been *diem*. Between these reliefs were painted shields which are so obliterated that they probably had reference to the cult of the Virgin.

The Altar Screen with its frieze of sculptures from the life of the Confessor was probably by the same mason as he who built Henry V.'s Chantry. It is fully described by Neale, and Dr. M. R. James has shown that the subjects were copied from a manuscript now at Cambridge.

LATER SCULPTURES

The tomb portraits of Henry VII. and his Queen, with a third figure of the King's mother near by, all of gilt bronze, are really great works of the Italian Renaissance by Torregiani, the contemporary of Michelangelo. They follow the tradition of Donatello and, if they were in Italy, they would be noted among the most wonderful things that could be seen on tour. The King's face was probably modelled from the remarkable effigy, in the Abbey Museum, which was carried at the funeral of the King. The face of this effigy seems to be an actual death mask taken in the Italian manner. It has been slightly injured, but a cast could easily be completed. (See Notes 6 and 7 at end.)

Fig. 117.

CHAPTER XI

ILLUMINATION

Whitening, gold, and colour.—The purpose of these chapters is to understand and " see," as far as possible, how the church was built and what it looked like in its first freshness ; sharp, unencumbered, light and undirtied. We must try to gain some idea of the fairness of the exterior— mostly as white as flour, but here and there touched with colour and gilding. From the wide spaces of the interior, we must banish the terrific modern monuments, many screens, and the seating which hides the columns as they rise from the once shining floor. We must hold in mind the fact that the church was flooded with light, passing through glass which was not only transparent but glittered.

Besides these main conditions, the internal effect depended on the large use of polished marble in varying tones of grey ; on the whitening and red lining of the whole of the masonry where not otherwise decorated ; on a lavish use of gilding ; and on the assembling of specially splendid objects, such as the gold shrine, the exquisite retable, and the polished porphyry floor—like glass mingled with fire.

At Westminster the remnants of the original decoration are so few and small that it would hardly seem possible to find sufficient evidence for the original scheme, but comparison with St. Albans, Salisbury, and other great churches, prepares us in such a way that the merest hints allow of large conclusions. The schemes of decoration of a dozen great churches might now be worked out in quite a trustworthy way. Some who are not well acquainted with these results, when they hear of the tale of white and vermilion, azure and gold, hasten to say that they would not " like it." But the people who did it loved bright things, and students who have come to see just a corner of this field of gleaming beauty, are likely to tell us, " We like it very much indeed, thank you."

Parts of marble columns, which have been protected here and there, yet retain some of the original polish. A window recess, now blocked at the end of the wall passage around the southern apsidal chapels, had still, when I saw it some dozen years ago, the stonework covered with the original whitening, red lining, and roses, a precious remnant of the general decoration of the wall surfaces (Figs. 118 and 119). From many orders of Henry III. we know that it was the common fashion of the time to whiten walls and divide them up with red lines into spaces of the shape of large bricks with sometimes a simple flower in each. This was called pointing, quarrying, or illuminating. To the roses we have more than one allusion. In 1240, the King ordered that the Queen's chamber in the

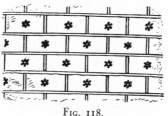

Fig. 118.

Tower should be " thoroughly whitened internally and painted with roses." The wall whitening at the Abbey was being done in the year 1253 by Adam the *dealbator* and his mate. Scott knew of the wall decoration. His son, G. G. Scott, says: " The interior was whitened and stoned in red lines. The diaper work of the triforium was gilt on a red ground ; the sculptured bosses were gilt and coloured."

I have not found any direct proof that the diaper of the triforium was coloured and gilt, except that the diaper in the eastern arcade of the Chapter House still shows traces of gold and red. There is little doubt, however, that the diaper of the apse and Presbytery was, at least, intended to be gilt. Gilding of the interior was one of the ideas taken from the Ste. Chapelle, where the whole interior recalled a goldsmith's shrine.

There are traces here and there that the wall arcade was painted; in a protected part behind a big tomb in St Benedict's Chapel the capitals are copper-green and the roll mouldings red. In the bay over the mosaic tomb in the south ambulatory the capitals are gilt, but the painting here seems to be later work. In several places red remains in the space under the arches. Since this was written it has been found in cleaning the wall arcade of one of the south-east chapels that the vine carved in a spandrel was gilt, while the background was bright red; touches of similar red on a capital showed that it also had a red ground and therefore gilt foliage. This speci-men shows what would have been treatment in all the Chapels.

Fig. 119 (half-size).

The shields of arms in the wall arcade of the Choir must have been painted from the first, as they are at present.

The ribs and bosses of the high vaults of the Presbytery and Choir are gilt, and this has certainly been so from ancient time. Keepe (1683) writes : " The vault whose arches dividing themselves into several squares compose a most stately roof, wrought with divers figured stones [bosses], and in some places curiously gilt with gold." Hatton (1708) says : " The next thing remarkable in the ornament is the gilding of the arches over the chancel, done in gold, which has been of many years' continuance." Wren, in his report on the church, says : " The vaulting of the Quire, though it be more adorned and gilded, is the worst performed." Crull (1713) writes : " You may still perceive that the arches of the roof of this Quire have been richly gilt and are at this time adorning with new gilding as well as the cross aisle [transept] on the south side."

The new gilding was done during Wren's great work of restoration, begun in 1698. In 1700, Samuel Clothier and David Legge, painters, were engaged " painting upon stone in imitation of Sussex marble in the ribs of the two bays and face of the great arch over the choir . . . being first thoroughly soaked in oil." Other items are " Raffled leaves round the 5 roses " ; " for laying 5,550 of double gold upon capitals, ribs and roses." The roses are the bosses, the raffled leaves are borders round them on the field of the vault. The latter and bands up the sides of the ribs may be over old painted work. The account for gilding is followed by " The gold beater's bill." Large surfaces of the interior seem to have been covered with drab paint and this may be what was meant by " painting in imitation of Sussex marble."

The sculptures of censing angels high up in the South Transept were fully painted, and this is evidence for all these spandrel carvings. In 1910, I examined the angel on the left, from a ladder, and found red in the creases of the drapery. On the upper garment was a pattern of three spots distributed at intervals (∴ ∴). The right-hand angel had stars on the drapery, which are plainly recorded in the drawing of Fig. 104. I also have a note of traces of gold. Patterning of draperies in this way was common in paintings of this time (see recently issued *Life of St. Alban*). There was red, also, on the little lion below the angel on the left.

ILLUMINATION

Photographs of the angel spandrels at Lincoln, given in Prior and Gardner's *Sculpture*, show that they, too, were coloured and had painted square-diaper backgrounds that appear to have been adapted from the carved square diapers at Westminster.

The tombs of the interior, lately cleaned, show what the painted sculpture was like. The knights and ladies had bright eyes, flushed cheeks, and coloured garments. The effigy of the Lady Aveline was painted all over; she had a red robe and green mantle lined with blue. The pillow was diapered with coats of arms, which were painted in transparent varnish colours over gold. Crouchback's effigy had a red surcoat diapered with a pattern imitated from the retable; on the front of it was a big coat of arms. The flesh was painted, the cheeks flushed, and his eyes had blue circles. The little angels at his head were fully coloured and their hair was gilt. On the edge of the slab could be read, " Ici gist Emon Fiz [Henri jadis Roi d'Angleter ?]re."*

The weepers had red cheeks and painted garments—in some cases, at least, these seem to have been in varnish colour over gold. The ornamental painting of these two tombs was so elaborate that no description would serve without full illustration. Little panels were inlaid with glass over pattern-work on gold, other parts were in raised gesso gilt, even the little knight in the gable of Crouchback's tomb had red cheeks, and he rode a dappled horse.

The wooden sedilia opposite were decorated in the same way; the carved heads on the canopies were like " waxworks." The tomb of Aymer de Valence also followed the same general scheme, but it was simpler. There was still much gilding on the prominent mouldings and the carvings, so that the general aspect was that of a gilded work. Panels, hollows of mouldings, and other plain spaces, were coloured red and green with smaller quantities of black and white to clear and harmonise the whole. The effigy with little angels and the weepers were fully coloured. The weepers

* Compare the inscription on the tomb of Henry III.

stood against backgrounds alternately scarlet and green, spotted with gold ; the small pillars between were patterned alternately gold and black and gold and red with hollows at the side alternately green and red (Fig. 120). The chamfers of the panels and the delicate tracery above were a fair ivory white with gilt fillets. The bases of the little shafts and the plinth mouldings were " marbled "—an innocent little spotted colouring, but still marbling.*

The tomb of Queen Eleanor was of polished Purbeck marble, with gilt carving harmonising with the gilt bronze figure. Recent cleaning showed traces of the brightest red on the iron railings, which appeared to be original, and it is recorded that there was painted pattern-work on the railings of Henry V.'s Chantry.

FIG. 120.

The Cloister, so far as built by Henry III., was painted like the church. The sculptured entrance to the Chapter House was brilliant in gold and colour. In Allen's *History of London* (1828) is this description : " One range of the mouldings [of the arch] contain circular scrolls [of foliage], which have been gilt, and the depths coloured black and another scarlet ; a third is divided into small niches by waved scrolls, and within these are twenty [little] statues— the Blessed Virgin and infant Jesus, and David, much broken. Fragments of the paint and gilding yet adhere on various parts of them, enough to show their former

---

* Many years ago Mr. Philip Webb told me that he had observed alternate lengths of dark and light colouring on some of the great arches in the transept, spotted like marble. Such decoration of arches has recently been found in the south transept at Rochester Cathedral. Painting like marble is mentioned in the Liberate Rolls of Henry III. Some marbling of the slab of the Crouch-back tomb seems to imitate the green porphyry of the pavement.

P

splendour. Before this doorway, the vaulted roof [which is later than the doorway] has a greater number of ribs than the rest, and some of the keystones [or bosses] are rich in carving and gilding. The remainder of the divisions on the east wall [of the cloister] have a string of gold once about 3 in. broad, horizontally about 3 yds. from the pavement. The wall was painted a dark colour, on which are a number of white trefoils " (Compare Ackermann). One of Neale's plates shows this band in the Cloister, which had a scroll pattern. Traces of the gilt bosses outside the Chapter House and bright red on the vaulting ribs were found in May, 1925.

The general original ground wash would have been white with red lines struck on it. Many traces of such a treatment exist in the cloister of Salisbury Cathedral.

Comparison with the façades of Wells and Crowland, and the great porch at Lincoln shows that the sculptured portals at the Abbey would have been painted and gilt. Masonry within and without was not properly completed until it was washed over and " illuminated." This traditional treatment, as Burges remarked, was really a necessary protection to stone work. In our climate, we must paint or it will rot. What was founded in necessity, however, flowered, under the magic hands of mediæval craftsmen, into fairy beauty.

Later work shows the same liking for gay colour. The small chapel, usually called after St. Erasmus but properly Little St. Mary's, opposite the tomb of Aymer de Valence, and founded by his widow, Mary de St. Pol, preserves much colouring, which has recently been better revealed by cleaning (March 1923). In a shallow niche fronting the door is the general form left by the removal of a carved image ; from the head of this long rays spread over the background. The vaulting is starred in red on a white ground, ribs have barber's pole bands and rosettes ; the boss is a pretty little Assumption of the Virgin. The walls are spotted over with pine-shaped units, on each of which is a fleur-de-lys. This pine-shaped element was very popular in the latter half of the fourteenth century; it appeared in St. Stephen's Chapel and is found on existing Norwich paintings (Fig. 121). The pattern also appears on costumes in the illuminated Life of Richard II at the British Museum; it was taken from textiles. The wood door was also gaily painted. In the

Fig. 121.

Muniment room is a wooden partition (*temp.* Richard II.), painted bright red and powdered with white stars (Fig. 122).

Fig. 122.

The fifteenth - century altar-screen was fully decorated in colour, and some traces still remain on the east side. The backgrounds were bright red and blue. The soffits of the canopies are carved into a delicate network of tracery, the interstices of which are red and blue. Above the canopies, the space in the centre is red, while the rest was blue. According to Neale, there was much gilding on raised patterns, which would have been in gesso.

There are still traces of Catherine wheels of gesso on the elaborate tomb of Lord Bourchier, which forms a screen to St. Paul's Chapel; as Neale says, they were " thickly powdered " over the monument and gilt. His engraving shows them and also the band of angels above, each holding a pair of painted shields and having gilt wings. This tomb, also, has lately been cleaned. The cornice and battlement were blue picked out in gold, as apparently was the whole work. In the hollow of the cornice, between the arms and badges, was an inscription in big gold letters : " Non nobis dñe non nobis sed nñi tuo da gloriam," some of which can

still be read. Below, on two deep bands, several of the shields can be distinguished with traces of the angels' wings. The bands were edged at the bottom with a fringe like the valance of a funeral hearse. There was further lettering over the shields, in white on black, which is given in Keepe's MS. as " + L'onnour a Dieu a nous Merci + " and " + Learne to Dye to live ever

Fig. 123.

+ ." These were several times repeated. According to Keepe's drawing, the big flags, and the lion and eagle which support them on either side of the monument, were fully coloured, and traces of this can still be seen. The sides of the tomb proper have quatrefoil panels, with red and green fields alternately, the colours counterchanged on the chamfering. Keepe gives twenty-two shields of arms, which, he says, were of " the nobility both of England and of Henault, viz. Robsert, Bourchier, Swinford, Chaucer, &c." (Fig. 123).

WHITENING, GOLD, AND COLOUR

The chapels on the east side of the North Transept were dedicated to St. John Evangelist on the south, St. Michael in the middle, and to St. Andrew on the north. The Chapel of St. John had a screen which, Keepe states, was " adorned with several carvings and coats of arms, by John Estney Abbot, painted and gilt with gold, who lies on the south side with his effigies engraven on brass ; he died 1438." Dart says the screen was wood finely carved and gilt. The middle chapel still has the ruin of a fine late Reredos. A sculptured figure of the Virgin and Child, painted and gilt, a fragment of which now rests in the St. Erasmus

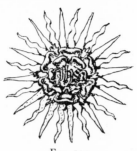

Fig. 124.

panel in the north ambulatory, may have belonged to this Reredos. According to Keepe, " the screen of St. Andrew's Chapel was adorned with imagery work of birds, flowers, cherubim, devices, mottoes, and coats of arms." A drawing (dated 1722) of this screen, which Dart says had been destroyed, has lately been presented to the Abbey from the Gardner collection.

It was of stone tracery, with a central door in the spandrels

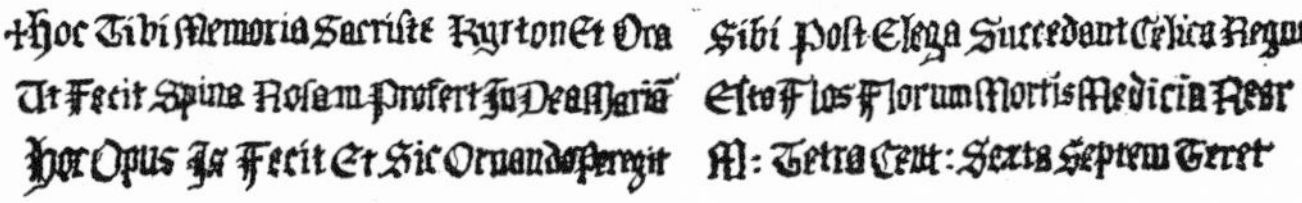

Hoc Tibi Memoria Sacriste Ryrton Et Ora   Sibi Post Elega Succedant Celica Regna
Ut Fecit Spina Rosam Profert Ju Dei Maria   E To Flos Florum Mortis Medicia Pear
Hoc Opus Ja Fecit Et Sic Ornanda Pergit   M: Tetra Cent: Sexta Septem Terct

Fig. 125.—(Rose Fig. 124 was in centre).

of which were two big crowned eagles holding inscribed labels ; above was a blazing sun or rose (Fig. 124), and a long inscription on either side of it. On a handsome carved cornice were arms, with trees and inscription ribbons between. Rising from the cornice were two pinnacles. In Keepe's MS. collection in my possession are further

213

details and a copy of the inscription. The sun surrounded a red rose, on the heart of which was inscribed I H S it was a symbol of the Virgin—*flos florum*. The inscription (Fig. 125) ended with the date 1467. Thirty shields of arms are given ; the one in the centre bore the device of the Trinity, two others were the ordinary Abbey arms and the keys of St. Peter impaled with the Confessor's Cross. The birds in the cornice were gilt eagles and black raven holding labels inscribed *Kyrie Eleson*. (In giving a sketch of this in 1906, I understood the carving to be a wooden cresting, but, as now said, it was part of a stone cornice.) The painting of the tomb of Sir Bernard Brocas is described by Crull. Malcolm says that, while he was examining the Chantry of Henry V., " a large portion of two canopies fell by their own weight which had scarcely more solidity than lumps of sand dried in the sun. They have been covered with whitewash that remains perfect till the stones powder into dust beneath it." Slight traces of painting have recently been found on the front of the Chantry.

There was much painting of later date in the Cloister. Keepe states that at the entrance towards the west was a crucifix with the Virgin and St. John " curiously painted and very pitiful to behold." Round the Cloisters were other paintings " with variety of verses alluding to the history of the foundation and the figures." Opposite the walls were " windows of tinctured glass " [in the tracery only]. The description by Allen, quoted above, goes on to say that the north-west bay of the Cloister " has been painted with orange-coloured sprigs on a dark ground." In the south-west bay above the entrance are " fragments of black-letter inscriptions on serpentine labels."

A fragment of this lasted on until Micklethwaite's time, who says that, above the door, " on the wall just below the vault are a few mouldering elements of a picture " [the Crucifixion ?]. All that can now be made out is part of a ribbon with an inscription in letters, of about 1500, which

214

Mr. J. T. Fowler has read, with some hesitation, " *in s'cla s'clorum. Amen.*"

As lately as October 1923, colour was found on the ribs of the Cloister vault in the south-east bay —red on the rolls, fair blue in hollows, and a morsel of gold on the boss. It is clear that the whole Cloister was as clean and bright as paint and gilding could make it.

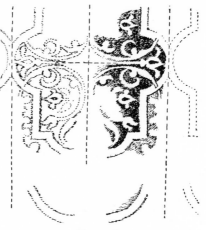

FIG. 126.

Feckenham, the restored Abbot, accomplished a considerable work in refitting and redecorating the church. In 1557, the Confessor's coffin was put back in, rather than on, the marble basis. A quite pretty shrine-like structure of wood—recalling in its form the old shrine proper—was set above the basis, where it yet remains. The marble work received an additional cornice, and large spaces, where the mosaics had been picked out, were filled with

FIG. 127.

plaster, and had the patterns completed by painting. A new inscription was painted around the frieze, signed by the Abbot's monogram. Remnants of plaster filling are found on the mosaic tombs of Henry III. and of Katherine. Several of the Royal tombs around the Confessor's shrine received new painted inscriptions, which have recently been more clearly revealed by cleaning. The often-quoted words " PACTUM SERVA " on the tomb of Edward I. belong to this work. These inscriptions are in a good form of Roman letter (Fig. 127). The old sculptured coats of arms in the Choir aisles were now repainted and inscriptions written over them in " Lombardic " characters. The continuation of the heraldry to the west end seems now to have been done for the first time, and the recess where the tomb of Katherine is also appears to have been painted. Recently a fragment of wall painting of Holbeinesque style, and very pretty, has been discovered in one of the Canons' houses Fig. 126).

CHAPTER XII

THE ITALIAN MOSAICS

AT Westminster, there are six remarkable examples of Roman mosaic works of the thirteenth century, a group unequalled outside Rome itself : (1) The Pavement of the Presbytery, dated 1268 ; (2) The Pavement of the Confessor's Chapel ; (3) Tomb of the Young Princes, John and Alphonso, and of Katherine, daughter of Henry III. ; (4) Tomb Slabs of John and Margaret de Valence ; (5) Basis of the Confessor's Shrine, 1279; (6) Tomb of Henry III. We may begin our examination of the Presbytery floor with the description of Keepe, 1683 : " Ascending by two or three Steps until you come to the Rails that compass in the High Altar, you there behold that noble and most glorious inlaid Floor still remaining intire that was done by the command of Richard de Ware, Abbot of Westminster ; where in most artificial Work and delightful Figures you have the *Jasper*, the *Porphyry*, the *Lydian*, the *Touch*, the *Alabaster*, and the *Serpentine* stones, so laid and wrought to the Spectator's satisfaction that you are unwillingly drawn from the sight thereof ; round the Squares and Great Circles, in Letters of Brass, are some of the verses still remaining, which when entire were thus to be read, concerning the duration of the World. *Si lector*," etc.

The floor was, in fact, of red and green porphyry and glass mosaic, inlaid in Purbeck marble. On it were Latin inscriptions : (*a*) a single verse around the central circle to the effect that it was an image of the archetypal sphere ;* (*b*) a curious prophetic calculation as to how long the

* " The Universe, the macrocosm (as opposed to man the microcosm) was symbolised by a central circle " (Dr. M. R. James).

world would last ; (*c*) words dating the work to this effect,
+ the year of Christ, 1268, King Henry the Third, the City
(Rome), Odoricus (mosaic-worker), and the Abbot (Richard
Ware) assembled these porphyry stones together.

The minute details, given in the accurate woodcut in

Fig. 128.—Plan of Mosaic floor, 1810.

Gleanings, can still, for the most part, be verified, although
some letters and indents of the inscriptions have disappeared
in the sixty years since the drawing was made. Around
the central disc six letters now remain of the words,
MoNsTrAt aRchEtypum. Of the straight band on the
north side there only exists a letter of lapidEs ; and O and

218

THE PAVEMENT OF THE PRESBYTERY

E remain on the east side. Most of the straight band on the east can be read from the indents beginning + Xri, and the important line containing the names is still certain on the west—*Tercius Henricus Rex, Urbs, Odoricus et Abbas.*

The curious prophetic inscription was on the strip round about the four circles next to the big central circle (see Neale and *Gleanings*). Here I have found two brass points (:) in a continuous sunk groove. The lettering

FIG. 129 (one line).

on Abbot Ware's grave-slab seems to have been of the same kind. Both of these have entirely disappeared. The dots on Fig. 128 show the positions of the inscriptions. Fig. 129 is a restoration of what remains of the name of Henry III., and Fig. 130 is the name of the artist; this is usually given as Odericus, but the second vowel was certainly O. Both names are in a single line.

Many parallels to the prophetic inscription are known.* In the evening *Westminster Gazette*, October 26, 1906, a correspondent quoted an old Gaelic saying, " *Tri aois coin aios eich,*" etc. :

FIG. 130 (one line).

" Thrice dog's age, age of horse ;
Thrice horse's age, age of man ;
Thrice man's age, age of deer ;
Thrice deer's age, age of eagle ;
Thrice eagle's age, age of oak."

A complete record of this wonderful and romantic pavement, fully illustrated by a

---

* There was an old Irish form going back to the eleventh century : stag, boar, hawk, salmon : Welsh ; stag, owl, eagle : German thirteenth century : Indian, Venetian, and Portuguese. See *The Academy*, Oct. 13, 1888. Dr. M. R. James says in *Inventory* that " the gist was proverbial in the middle ages."

minute survey, should be made at once—there is some necessary loss by age, and probably the last trace of a letter disappears every year.

The plan of the floor given by Ackermann, together with Malcolm's detailed description, when compared with the minutely accurate plan in *Gleanings*—made before the repairs of 1866—make it possible to decide that in 1800 the details of the pavement were much as they are to-day. Talman is recorded to have made a careful plan in the eighteenth century, but I cannot discover if it now exists. The plan (Fig. 128) is from an outline print of Ackermann's tinted engraving, and on this I have dotted the position of the inscriptions.

The floor, as we have it now, has been much repaired; often it appears with plain marble in place of intricate mosaic patterns. Burges observed that the big central circle " has a very modern look," also that the fillings of the four smaller circles round about it were not satisfactory. Most of the fillings of the small circles in the wide margin look equally doubtful. Neale speaks of injury " by wear and the removal of thousands of tesseræ." Ackermann (1811) cites the " lamenting enthusiam " of Malcolm. Malcolm himself (1803), beginning his description of the Presbytery with the then existing altar, continues: " Descending two steps which cover parts of the mosaic, we tread on the wreck of the most glorious work in England; venerable through age, costly in its materials, and invaluable for its workmanship. What must have been the glories of this holy place soon after the completion of the church ! An admirer of the arts must view it with deepest regret. . . . since it has been the custom to show the Choir for money, it is trodden, worn and dirtied daily by hundreds. Is it not a national treasure ? When it is quite destroyed can we show such another ? " He then gives a detailed description, from which it appears that the number of brass letters which remained were much as at present, and that the band of stars around the central circle was " much depredated." It is clear that the floor, as we have it now, must, to a considerable extent, be the result of successive repairs.

It is said that the larger circle near the north-west angle was renewed about sixty years since. This would be in 1866, when Scott refaced the Reredos and " restored " the destroyed half of the eastern margin of the floor. The pattern of the circle and, doubtless, the other repairs of the time carried on the old design. The plainer strips filling out the spaces on the north and south sides were added.

An abbot's coffin, thought to be Crokesley's, now in St. Paul's Chapel, was found at this time in front of the Reredos, and another coffin—probably Ware's—was seen on the north side. The foundations of the Confessor's church were also then discovered.

I consulted the late Mr. W. Brindley about the large central circle, and he said : " It certainly

Fig. 131.

would have been more worn if it had been there from the first ; circles like this for table-tops have long come into the country." The original centre may have been of porphyry or have had some device relating to the surrounding inscription. As was observed by Miss Mary Hervey and myself independently, Holbein's portrait of the Ambassadors in the National Gallery represents this floor, and the central circle here contains two interlocking triangles. Fig. 131 gives, as a complete plan, the indications of the perspective in the picture. The same pattern of interlaced triangles also occurs in the stained glass of the apse windows made in Wren's time. It occurs too in the original mosaic pavement of the Confessor's Chapel (Fig. 136). From these facts we might certainly infer that the central circle had these interlacing triangles were it not that it is possible that the Confessor's pavement was the source from which the pattern was taken by both Holbein and Wren. This symbolic device is sometimes called the Shield of David. The short inscription round about would seem to have had reference to some special design or representation here. The late mediæval writer, Sporley, says that the meaning of the short inscription was that the round stone had the colours of the four elements—fire, air, water, and earth. This brings to mind a plan of the universe given by Matthew Paris, in a British Museum MS., which shows four concentric circles inscribed fire, air, water, and earth.[*] Either by the mixed tints of porphyry or by some definite arrangement of colours the universe was s y m b o l i s e d. This central circle is surrounded by a band of glass mosaic forming a star pattern (Fig. 132). Glass mosaic is also found in the graveslabs on the north and south sides. Burges seems to have thought that the use of glass tesseræ was confined to these places, but it appears originally to have been distributed all over the floor.

Fig. 132.

The intricate and altogether remarkable filling of circle E on the plan Fig. 128 is largely of glass. It is now, so far, obliterated that, without the help of sketches and a rubbing

[*] This scheme he obtained from Elyas of Dereham, who has sometimes been called an architect.

222

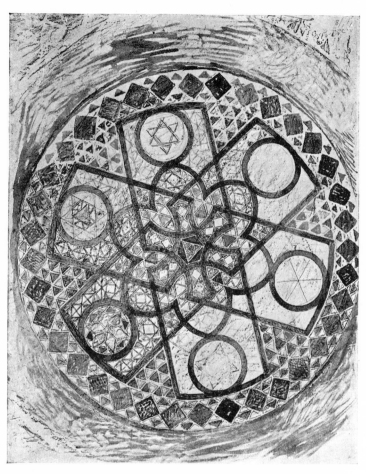

Fig. 133.

done many years ago, it is doubtful if it now could be made out. It is certainly entirely original (Fig. 133). Medallion A, Fig. 128, looks modern in workmanship and material, but the design may be old. B almost certainly had the spandrels of mosaic like a similar circle in the Confessor's Chapel, but all is now of marble; C seems largely ancient; D, of marble, is probably an old renewal; E is discussed above; F is, doubtless, semi-modern; G still retains mosaic about

a small square slab, and this may be, or represent, ancient work (Fig. 136). H to M were cut off by semi-modern steps; the circles were restored by Scott in 1866. K, perhaps in part, follows the old pattern. The rest, N—T, seem to be all semi-modern.

The history of the floor is fully documented. The lettering, formerly around the grave on the north side, told how Abbot Richard Ware brought the stones from "the City." In the Patent Roll for 1269 is this interesting entry, which I have never seen quoted: "Acknowledgment of £50 to the Abbot for the pavement which he brought with him from the Court of Rome to the King's use to be put in the Church at Westminster before the King's great altar there, and for the service which he did the King at the Castle of Kenilworth." This reference to the Vatican suggests that the materials may have been a gift from the Pope. In the Pipe Roll for 1267–68 appears an entry for the stipend of certain *cementariorum pavatorum* working before

Fig. 134.—Detail of Circle G.

the Feretory of Saint Edward. These craftsmen must have been Odoricus and his assistants. In the Roll for 1271–72 occurs a similar entry " for making the pavements before the various altars." This may refer to the Confessor's Altar and an Altar of Relics in the same chapel.

The Confessor's Chapel.—When I studied this floor before, I thought that the mosaic could not have been laid until Henry III.'s tomb was in place, for the pattern stops short of the tomb, and that it might be as late as 1285. On the other hand, provision for this tomb and its execution, or at least commencement, is probable during the life of the King. The grave-slab of John de Valence (died 1277) seems to form a considered part of this floor, and I would now suggest that it was begun on the completion of the Presbytery pavement. Burges thought that this floor was an English work made in imitation of the Presbytery

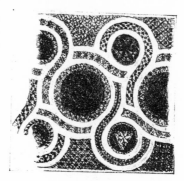

Fig. 135.

pavement, but a mosaic in Sta. Prassede in Rome may be put in as evidence on this point. This example is only a panel, but the pattern and details are very similar, and it is cut in on a slab in the same way as ours. See the illustration in Mr. A. Christie's delightful book on *Pattern Design* (Fig. 135). The Roman panel, he tells me, forms the front of an altar, and it bears an inscription with the date 1238. It might be by one of the masters who later worked at Westminster.

One idea of these mosaic workers was constant variation of the minor patterns. Some sketches, hurriedly done when the floor was uncovered, are here added to those I gave

Q

FIG. 136.

before (Figs. 136 and 137) (see an excellent general plan given in the *Inventory*). Fig. 138 is an enlarged detail. Some others with a general plan are contained in the first volume of the Architectural Association Sketch Book (see also Scott's *Gleanings*, Malcolm, and some rubbings in the Print Room, South Kensington, from one of the floors).

. . . . . .
The Confessor's Shrine.—
The high marble and mosaic basis which supported the golden coffin or shrine was of minute workmanship. As some existing portions still show this was largely of gilt-glass tesseræ, the glow and glitter of gold must have been the most marked characteristic. An inscription in large letters of blue glass on a gold ground recorded that it was the work of *Petrus Romanus Civis*, 1279.

About 1910, an American student, Miss Cecilia Waern, sent me a small photograph of the monument of Pope Clement IV. at Viterbo with the note, " This is said to be by your Westminster Pietro

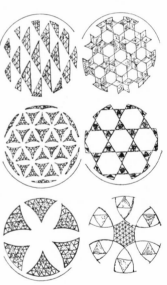

FIG. 137.

226

d'Oderisio. It looks *new*, for it has been moved about and set up again and, finally, decently restored about fifty years ago, and again in 1885 ; but the simple elegance is still very charming after first shock *of scrape* " (Fig. 139). This tomb of Clement IV. (died 1268) was signed by Petrus Oderisi, and in a guide book to

Fig. 138.

Viterbo, published as early as 1894, it had been noted that it must have been made by the artist who worked at Westminster. This identification was adopted by Professor Frothingham in *Monuments of Christian Rome* (1908), and by Mr. Gerald Davies (1910). Frothingham thought that Petrus and Odoricus of the Westminster inscriptions were probably one, for " it was sometimes the habit to call a man by his patronymic." Mr. Gerald Davies writes :

"The father wrought the pavement of the Presbytery, while the son Pietro Oderisi completed and signed the tomb of the Confessor. . . . Another son of Oderisi, Stephane, is known." The best reading of the facts would, I think, be that Odoric and his sons were the most famous mosaic

workers in Rome in the period 1260–70, that Henry III., advised by the Pope, through Abbot Ware, attracted the father to Westminster. The Pope died in 1268 while Odoric was away from Rome, and Peter, his son, made the Papal tomb. When this was done, Peter came to Westminster to execute the basement of the Confessor's shrine. He may have been here before with Odoric. Frothingham wrote of him thus : " A leader of the Roman School, Peter, son of Oderisius, made the first attempt to introduce both sculpture and mosaic decoration in sepulchral art in

FIG. 139.

his tomb of Clement IV. at Viterbo in 1268. . . .

He also *for the first time* substituted for the antique architrave and classical orders the Gothic trefoil arch and foliated capitals ; it was quite a revolution." Our shrine base has trefoil arches, and we may ask, Was the revolution in the Roman marble-workers' style a consequence of their contact

228

THE CONFESSOR'S SHRINE

with Westminster ? A comparison between the works at Westminster and Viterbo shows such resemblances as confirm the view that they are both by the same master. The main arch of the Viterbo tomb has cusps in the Westminster style. One of the arched compartments at Westminster is filled in a singular way by circles at top and bottom connected by vertical strips, and the same awkward arch-filling is found at Viterbo ; there, one of the columns is inlaid with an inverted chevron pattern, and the same occurs on one of the niche heads of the shrine base. Again, on the tomb of Henry III., which was certainly by the same master who made the shrine base, there are similar patterns and large crosses in the two recesses ; crosses of the same kind occur on the Pope's tomb.

The shrine basis was surmounted by a flat cornice band which bore the inscription giving the name of Peter. A fragment of this cornice exists, which must have been part of the west end ; this is wrought on three sides, and a rebated joint shows that it projected as a " break " about 9 in. beyond the angle.

On comparing the record of the whole of the inscription with a part which is now apparent on the east front, it will be found that extra space was required at the west end for several letters more than those at the east end. This extra space was provided by the projections just described. These projections of the cornice of the west front of the basis were probably supported by the larger spiral mosaic columns, which are now half buried.

Scott says that these pillars at the west end were found to agree in height with those at the east ; that is, they would rise to the bed of the inscribed cornice. The best-preserved portion of mosaic is on one of these columns, and the part formerly buried may have been placed uppermost by Scott. In the Print Room at S. Kensington is a careful drawing, inscribed, " Done in 1850 by uncovering the base of the columns of the tomb of the Confessor. I made this drawing, and we then covered it up again.—A. MacCallum."

THE ITALIAN MOSAICS

Among the fragments in the triforium, I recognised. some years ago, two of small spiral marble columns with lines of gilding following the twist. The shrine at St. Albans had detached spiral columns around the shrine, which are almost exactly like these, and fragments of similar pillars exist at Winchester (for these, see *Antiquaries' Journal*, October 1924). In all these cases, the pillars probably supported candlesticks. There is a Westminster record that, in 1290, 46s. 8d. was paid for making three marble columns around the shrine, and our fragments are probably of those (Fig. 140, without base).

The original cornice of the Basis was the inscribed course consisting of a " face " with a few mouldings above. When the existing wooden shrine was set on the marble basement by Abbot Feckenham (1556–58), the sides of the marble work were heightened by the addition of a new projecting cornice. At the same time, what now appears as a narrow frieze under this new moulded cornice was made longer and wider. It had been the margin of the slab on which the shrine proper rested, and it was originally narrower and shorter than the inscribed band or cornice, forming a " step " above it. This

FIG. 140.

step course was enlarged in an irregular way, as may be seen by the spacing of the pattern, and a few years ago Mr. Westlake found that, on the south side, there was hidden a complete angle piece and return, near, but not at, the west end. (Compare Fig. 171.)

The Presbytery pavement, the shrine basis, and the tomb of the Pope at Viterbo were all signed prominently by the artists who made them. Examination of similar works in Italy shows that this school of Roman mosaic workers made a practice of putting their names on monuments, frequently adding (as in the case of our shrine) the words, " *Civis Romanus.*" This points to the existence of some guild of workers who prided themselves on seeking the inspiration of ancient Rome and turning away from the art of the Tedeschi of the Lombard schools. Such a thought was the germ of the whole Renaissance, which, in essence, was the rebirth of national culture and the repudiation of Germanism. The Westminster inscriptions are thus specially interesting, and they resemble other inscriptions in Italy so closely that it is probable that they were suggested by the craftsmen themselves.

If all the artists who signed themselves Oderisio were of one family they must have been an artistic clan comparable to the Cosmati. The fine bronze doors of Troja Cathedral in South Italy, made in 1119–27, bear the name of Oderisus of Benevento. At Eboli, near Naples, a fine picture of the Crucifixion is signed Robertus de Oderisio, a follower of Giotto (W o l t m a n n and Woermann, *History of Painting*).

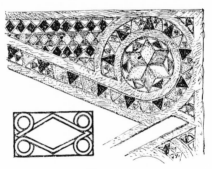

Fig. 141.

Dante tells of Oderisi of Gubbio, " the honour of that art which, in Paris, is called illuminating." According to Vasari, he was working in Rome about 1295.

The shrine basis is, in many ways, a work of extraordinary interest. The recent cleaning of it has revealed many details of the mosaic patterns. By the evidence of small portions remaining here and there, together with imprints left in the matrix where the mosaic has been picked out, the designs could almost fully be made out and a restored drawing made by any student. Fig. 141 is a restoration of one of the frieze panels. A patient study of this one monument, and more still of the series of mosaic works, would be instructive to do and valuable in result. The point has been reached when special work on details is required.

. . . . .

Tombs.—Recent cleaning has also revealed the glittering splendour of Henry III.'s tomb. It was a surprise to find that much pure white was used to set off the gold and colour. In the borders, where one pattern is continuous, the background colour is varied in lengths of a few inches. At the east end, where it is sheltered, the panels are largely complete.

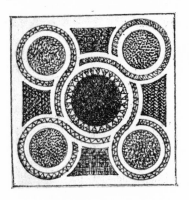

FIG. 142.—Minor details conjectural.

The small tomb of the royal children, Katherine, John, Alphonso, etc., now in the south ambulatory, has also been cleaned and the general disposition of the mosaic work can be traced. At the east end the now mostly hidden panel was like the restored sketch, Fig. 142; the central disc remains and the two on the left may also exist. The side of the tomb, which was placed against the wall here, about 1395, may still be in good condition.

Two grave-slabs close in front of Henry V.'s tomb form a part, as has been mentioned, of the floor of the Confessor's Chapel and must be contemporary with it. They were memorials of John and Margaret, son and daughter of William de Valence. Both had brass crosses and one of them had the field set with mosaic; this was probably the tomb of John; it occupied a position on the central axis of the pavement and thus seems to have been the first to be put in place. With the mosaic a few letters were found, . . . LAME : on one side, with traces from which

232

the name Willame could be safely inferred, and on the other side RLEA. About twelve years ago, a portion of the plain paving by Henry V.'s tomb, which overlies the slabs, having been lifted, the end of the second slab was exposed and this retained several letters and imprints giving VALENCE : KI : PUR : LA . . . The name Valence began under the foot of the cross and the rest continued up the south side of the slab.

Putting the remnants of the two inscriptions together, it is evident that they must have been in French, and of the well-known form : + Here lies John son of William de Valence for whose soul God have mercy.

The systematic cleaning of the structure and monuments, which has been referred to several times, has given me more pleasure during my little term than almost anything else— the one greater pleasure is new work I have *not* done in the ancient church.

CHAPTER XIII

THE STAINED GLASS

From many precise orders recorded in the " Liberate Rolls," it appears that Henry III. had a special love for stained glass. In 1237, for instance, a command was issued " to make a chamber with beautiful glass."

There is evidence to show that the King must have glazed his church at once with stained glass. Much of it was ornamental, for figure work, as usual, would have been reserved for special positions. Most of it, too, was very fair, either " grisaille " just touched with points of colour or white quarry work. The glass was attached to wooden frames in the lights. Several window irons in the foiled circles still retain " lugs " to which the leaded glazing was attached by wedges, some of which have actually been found. In two of the traceried compartments of the north walk of the Cloister, such irons with lugs may easily be seen. The early glass at Canterbury was fixed in the same way. The window lights are of large scale varying in width from about 3½ ft. in the apse to 5½ ft. in the north bay of the aisle of the North Transept.

Grisaille.—Some precious fragments of the original stained glass, which used to lie in the triforium, were, in 1908, carefully framed and put up in a window in the west aisle of the North Transept. There are about 20 ft., being portions of three different patterns. They were taken out of one of the south-east apsidal chapels in Scott's time and show what the glazing of those chapels was. Set up as they now are, it is easy to see how the patterns were arranged to fill the lights (Fig. 143).

234

GRISAILLE

When I gave some sketches of the details before, I did not allow for the exceptional width of the window lights ; the patterns would have been arranged as in Figs. 143 and 144. This doubling of the units agrees with windows at Salisbury and elsewhere. Fig. 145 is a diagram of the third variety. Full-sized drawings of this beautiful grisaille glazing, made

FIG. 143.

many years ago, may be found in the Print Room of South Kensington Museum.

FIG. 144.

Shields.—The glass now in the windows of the apse, besides containing some late mediæval figures, have backgrounds made up, in part, of fragments dating from the thirteenth to the seventeenth century. When these windows were taken out in 1916, I was able to draw many ancient quarry patterns and three beautiful shields. (This glass may now be studied in photographs sold at the Victoria and Albert Museum.) The three early shields of arms which now exist are those of Henry III., of his wife Eleanor of Provence, and of Richard of Cornwall (his brother). They are about 16 in. high and are

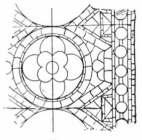

FIG. 145.

precious examples of the earliest heraldic glass which we

have; they are probably twenty years earlier than the
similar Salisbury shields. The King's shield is, fortunately,

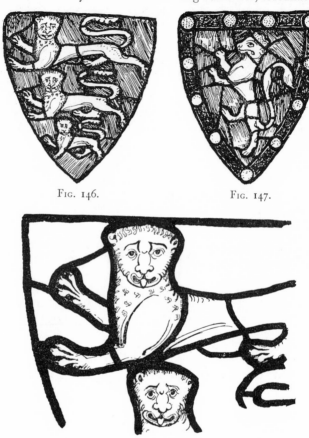

FIG. 146.   FIG. 147.

FIG. 148.

very complete, and so is that of Cornwall. Figs. 146 and 147
show these, and Figs. 148 and 149 are enlarged details. The
Queen's shield is in worse condition, but enough remains to

allow of a drawn restoration being made. There were four red pallets on a gold ground. Three pieces of deep yellow glass, which are still associated with the red stripes, are patterned a good deal like borders, and examination shows

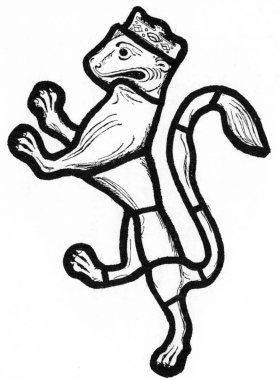

Fig. 149.

that they are parts of the diapered golden field on which the ruby pallets in fact were charged. In Fig. 150 the three upper pieces of diaper pattern are original. From records, we know that such shields were set in the ground-storey windows, which we have seen were of grisaille glass;

237

at Salisbury, some of the windows were practically copies of those at Westminster, and these had two shields to a light.

Sandford records that there remained many royal shields in the windows of the Westminster Church and Chapter

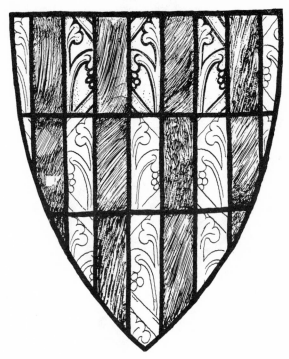

Fig. 150.

House, and mentions particularly that one of Eleanor of Castile was in the aisle of the North Transept. The ground-floor windows, we may suppose, were mostly of this lovely kind of " jewelled grisaille," with pairs of shields set on the lights. In the British Museum (MS. Lansdowne, 874) are sketches of about a dozen of these shields on a sheet signed William Camden. Here, besides the three now existing, are England with a label (for Prince Edward); the castles and lions of Castile and Leon and the three bends of Ponthieu (both for his wife Eleanor); the

Fig. 151.

black eagle of Germany (for the emperor Richard of Cornwall); the cross and birds of the Confessor; then the three

Fig. 152.

chevrons of Clare and the quarterly coat of De Lacy. Some were twice repeated. Fig. 151 shows the varieties other

239

than the three existing ones. The selection of arms must mark a date earlier than the death of Henry III., and the three now existing in the apse windows were, doubtless, made

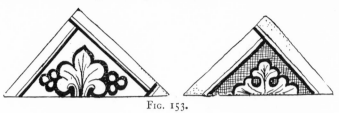

FIG. 153.

before the consecration of the church in 1269. In the orders of Henry III., shields of arms in glass are frequently specified.

Quarries.—Following a usual custom the clerestory windows were probably simpler than those below, as at

FIG. 154.

Salisbury and York. In the much " made up " later glazing of the high apsidal windows are a large number of early fragments, including several varieties of thirteenth-century quarries. These, according to the early custom, are squares which were set diagonally. This is shown by analogy with examples at Lincoln, etc., and also by the fact that some of the pieces seem to have been half-quarries. One of these early quarries was found in my time at the clerestory level on or in the masonry (for similar quarries, see Winston, plate 31, Fig. 15). " The quarry is generally bordered on all or only two of its sides." These windows

240

of diapered glass also, probably, had one or two bright heraldic shields set in each light (see Figs. 152, 153, and 154). Fig. 155 may be from a border, and Fig. 156 shows two fragments of grisaille work.

Kings.—Among the fragments in the east windows are also some pieces of large crowns, on deep golden glass, which are certainly of mid-thirteenth-century style. Fig. 157 is a restoration of one of the crowns; three or four of the central knops and two or three of the low intermediate ones exist, but I have not found any part of the end knops. These crowns must have been 12 or 13 in. wide, and the figures which bore them can hardly have been less than 8 ft. high. Exactly similar jewel patterns to those on the circular bands are found on the early glass in Jerusalem Chamber. A further most interesting point is the form of the knops, which are roses. As we have seen before, rose decoration was a special characteristic of the work

Fig. 155.

of Henry III.; roses appear on his coins, and the Chapter House inscription shows that he was a rose admirer. The large figures which wore these crowns can hardly have been anywhere else than in the apsidal windows, and we reach the conclusion that there was a king in each of the lights. Possibly they were the saint-kings of England, among whom Edward and Edmund would appear; or the founders, Edgar, Edward, and Henry III. himself may have been included. These figures would have been named by inscriptions, and there is, at least, one fragment existing in the present windows of an early letter (R ?) which must have been full 6 in. high (Fig. 158). There are also other fragments of later naming inscriptions in black letter as big or bigger. Such large standing figures are well known in France; those around the apse of Notre Dame, Paris, were some 16 ft. high. A set of kings, if I remember aright, were (I had written " are," forgetting the war) in the clerestory windows at Reims. One of the figures at Westminster would assuredly have been the Confessor, and taking a large, contemporary, painted head of the white-haired King in the Cloister at Windsor as a guide, I can " see " him in his place appearing above his golden coffin.

Fig. 156.

Medallions.—In Jerusalem Chamber are preserved, set in its big northern window, seven pieces of the finest thirteenth-century medallion work with small figures. These precious panels were first described in *Archæologia*, 1834, but they must have been here long before. They appear in an engraved view of the Chamber while it was in the Strawberry Hill style, and on one of the panels (St. Nicholas) is scratched " Wm. Miles, glazier, May 12, 1794." Now on one of the apsidal windows in the church is scratched " Wm. Miles, No. 20 Tufton Street, Westr., Repaired this, 1797." On the same panel in the Chamber other glaziers have put their names and the dates 1762 and 1746,

FIG. 157.

while on another (Murder of the Innocents) is written " Thomas Manning [?] glasd. this win. 1680." Winston dated these medallions *c*. 1250–70, and we may be confident that they were part of the original glazing, in place, when the church was consecrated in 1269. They are from windows of big scale and could only have come from a church of the first rank. The subjects show that they were parts of special " theological windows " in such a church. Two of the panels form a pair which would require a light from 4 to 4½ ft. wide, and the other medallions associated in pairs (compare Fig. 143) would be suitable for such lights.

FIG. 158.

The two panels, which make a pair, are of the form shown in Fig. 159, and they contain, as subjects, the Ascension, and Descent of the Holy Spirit. In the centre of the former stands the Virgin with Apostles on either hand, and the feet of the ascending Christ appear above. The second panel has eleven Apostles with the head and wings of the descending Dove, from which fall red streams—the tongues of fire. The pair were joined together by a quatrefoil containing coloured foliage, and the filling between the medallions would, doubtless, have been of the same kind. A third piece is a circular medallion (1 ft. 9 in. diameter) of the Resurrection. Christ rises from the Tomb holding a long cross and having a ruby nimbus crossed with white. At

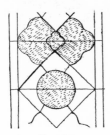

the head and foot of the tomb is an angel, a very pretty pair, and the whole is as good as may be. From the subject, we may suppose that this medallion was associated with the two just described; they may have been arranged as in Fig. 159. This type of arrangement is found in France and at Canterbury, Beverley, and Salisbury (Fig. 160). There are drawings of two or three of these panels in the Winston collection at the British Museum, made in

FIG. 159.

1839–43, and these are valuable as evidence of condition before restoration.

The fourth and fifth panels are pointed quatrefoils about 2 ft. by 1½ ft. These contain St. Stephen's stoning and the execution of St. Paul, and they, doubtless, belonged to one light devoted to St. Paul or SS. Peter and Paul.

The sixth panel is a pointed oval, and contains the Murder of the Innocents. This belongs to the Infancy group of subjects, and probably occupied a different light. A persecutor in one of the panels has a monk's head. Was this leaded up by mistake, as Winston supposed, or is it a craftsman's malicious joke?

FIG. 160.

The seventh panel is of similar form, but different size; the subject is St. Nicholas and a drowning man, and it must be from yet another light. The sea is formed of wavy bands of blue and white.

These medallions all have blue backgrounds and ruby outer borders, with an inner strip of white pearling;

nimbuses are red, green, yellow, and white. Hems of the garments of Christ and Apostles have jewel patterns. Fig. 161 is a figure of the Virgin from the Ascension group. In the later windows many small pieces are leaded in which may have come from "mosaic" grounds of medallion windows.

Some medallions at Lincoln have borders which are similar to ours. One of these is illustrated by Winston with part of the surrounding ornamental foliage; such foliage would have formed the filling between our medallions. This glass must have been in some place of honour, possibly in the Lady Chapel or in the windows of the South Transept directly opposite the gallery which, I suppose, was the King's pew. By comparison with Lincoln and Salisbury, we may form some imaginative thought of the fair interior full, flooded with light through windows mostly of pearly white, heightened here and there to dazzling splendour of colour.

We probably learn who was the glazier of the church

Fig. 161.

at the time of its consecration from a charter witnessed by Robert de Beverley (the mason), Edmund, goldsmith, and William le Verrer, in 1272.

.   .   .   .   .

Later Glazing.—In the east and west windows are several

fragments of fourteenth-century glazing, quarries (Fig. 162), and oak-leaf borders. Fig. 163 is from a piece of fourteenth-

century grisaille found in 1907 over the vault of the south walk of the Cloister. It may very well represent the glazing of the refectory as transformed about 1350–60.

The new work of building the Nave was begun in 1376, but went forward very slowly, and it is doubtful if any glazing was done for nearly a century. In 1462, an entirely new rose window in the South Transept was glazed by Thomas Pedeler for $1\frac{1}{2}d$. a foot, except for the arms of England at the centre in colour, which was 4s. In 1469, two glaziers worked ninety-two days glazing two windows of the Nave (probably the aisle). Glass of " Rene " and English glass are mentioned ; also a plate of *auricalco* (brass) for grinding

Fig. 162.

colours, an " anelyng herth " and " papiro " bought for the glaziers. The next year Thomas, the glazier, worked forty-two days, and in 1489 a glazier employed in the church is still called Thomas.

From 1506 to 1510 the windows in the western part of the church were glazed. In 1505–06, 3s. 4d. was paid to a glazier coming from Malvern to see the windows. In 1507–08 Richard Twyge, glazier,

Fig. 163.

received £37 6s. 8d. for the glazing of fourteen windows in the upper story of the church. In 1509–10, Richard Twyge filled the great west window with glass, for which he received £44, and also one window in the upper story for £3 (Rackham).

In April 1643, Parliament appointed a committee to demolish monuments of superstition in the church. In May the copes were burnt. It was then used as a " preaching house," and bills for " cleansing out pictures " suggest much destruction of glass, although the only specific notice I find of this, apart from Henry VII.'s Chapel, is for 40 ft. of new glass, in 1646, for a window next the " Redd-Door."

The Nave at least retained many windows with figures up to the beginning of the eighteenth century, but any within reach seem to have been of the nature of royal portraitures. Hatton (1708) says that the windows of the Nave were " finely painted but now ruined. The windows were adorned with various portraits, of which there yet remain such at the east and west ends, and many on the south side in the upper range westward from the cross roof ; and in the south-west window

below is the portrait of Edward the Confessor."* Hatton's text may have been written just before the transfer of the figures of the Confessor and the Pilgrim to the apsidal end, or he may have followed Caxton's *Chronicle*, from which it also appears that there was a representation of the Confessor, giving his ring, on the south side. Dart (1723) states that the story of the Confessor had been in the glass of the south aisle, but implies that it was no longer there. Another of these windows, according to Sandford, contained a portraiture of Richard II. with his badge of the White Hart.

Gathering together the large stained-glass figures into the east and west windows appears to have been done by

* According to Crull the Confessor's shield of arms was also in this window.

Wren, when most of the church was largely reglazed, from 1700 to 1722.

Edward Drew was the glazier, and in 1700 he repaired 34½ ft. of painted glass " in the Spiritual Court." In this year ironwork was put to " the eight windows over the altar." A board was provided " to draw out the glass," and also a model of one of the windows. In 1701, " the lights of old glass in several places " were " fitted up." Much glazing now and later was done in Henry VII's Chapel. In 1703, Edward Drew was paid for 1,650 ft. of new glass " in seven windows over the altar or shrine : which finishes the east end entirely above, at 9*d*." These

Fig. 165.

must be the seven clerestory windows of the Confessor's Chapel, as it appears that the stained glass was not yet there. In 1704, nine new windows on the north side required 2,202 ft. of glass. In this year an item appears for " new leading the figure of Edward the Black Prince in the west window and putting a border and the College arms under the same." This was the west window of the south aisle. In 1705, new glass, worth £42, was used " for the great west window with twelve figures of old painted glass." According to Dart, the glass in the big west window was fragmentary in 1723.

In 1706, £70 was paid " for 566 ft. painted glass amended at the east end of the church." This must refer to the three stained-glass windows in the apse. The lights are here narrower than the average, and 188 ft. for each window seems a full allowance. Names and the dates, 1709–11–13–35 are scratched on these windows, which are here easily reached from the leads. That they were there from the earliest date is confirmed by entries in 1716 : " For mending painted glass east end that the boys broke." " Six frames for the wires for the three painted glass windows at the east end over the altar." It is interesting to find windows protected at so early a time ; the Westminster boys were already at it ! In this same year other entries occur as follows :—" Taking down the old glass next the Cloister garden." " Figure work done over mason's shed next to the east door " [of Nave ? this is under the heading Spiritual Court]. " Work done in the belfry [lantern ?] for a painted window taken down from top of the church and fitted up."

The three eastern apsidal windows have six large single figures in as many lights. They are surrounded by work which even from below is seen to be semi-modern, but the whole is of pleasant colour for the glass, of which the added work is made up, is mostly ancient. Even the figures in the first window seem to be of the semi-modern kind.

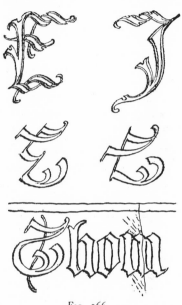

FIG. 166.

The figures in the two central lights are ancient (sixteenth century) and of fine quality and colour. They represent the Confessor giving his ring to St. John, disguised as a pilgrim. The King stands before a green curtain in a blue robe and crimson mantle. St. John, with blue mantle, is in front of a crimson curtain. The colours of the curtains seem to have been counter-changed in the backgrounds above them. The figures were about 7 ft. high and their

249

nimbuses 1½ ft. in diameter. They stood on castellated pedestals. On the garments, the distinctive letters E and J are scattered.

These two figures are very fine of their kind, the King being developed portraiture, the faces and hair highly wrought, and the eyes in three-quarter aspect with high lights. There is an approach to perspective in the pedestals and the curtain bent back behind the figures. These lights have a German look, and the initial letters, which powder the garments, seem to be of Renaissance character (Fig. 166). These letters and a coarse damask pattern on a robe are ground through flashed ruby into the white glass beneath. The other two figures are also late, but they are in a more conventional glass painting manner. One looks like an apostle; he is without headdress, carries a long staff, and seems to have had bare feet (a fragment is leaded in, out of place). The sixth figure is a bishop or mitred abbot, on his robes are letters E (possibly out of place) and C (?) ground into the flashed ruby glass (Fig. 166). These two lights must be nearly of the same date as the other pair. However, the second pair of figures does not seem to have been done to range with the middle pair; there are no curtains behind them and no pedestals for their feet.

In the work around the panels of ancient glass is a collection of fragments from the thirteenth to the seventeenth century. There are several broken inscriptions. One is " Sanctus Greg . . . . . . ecclesia. . . ." Two fragments, which may have belonged together, are the tantalising words:

Regina M . . .	. . . me fecit R . .
. . . therefo	. . . anno re . . . . .

Can these be Margaret, wife of Henry VII., and Richard Twyge, the glazier ?

One fragment of inscription, Thom[as] (Fig. 166), appears from the initial to be by the same hand which ground out the bigger letters.

LATER GLAZING

The making up of the glass to fit these lights is quite interesting, bold and workmanlike, yet with an effort to harmonise new work with the place and the old figures. Mr. Drew should find a place in the history of glazing. We have his signature scratched on a quarry preserved at the church.*

A further record of the Nave windows was given to me, about 1910, by Dean Armitage Robinson. This is a photograph of a drawing, by Ashmole in the Gough collection at the Bodleian, of two armed figures. It is inscribed: "A draught of the pictures of St. George and the Black Prince taken from a glass window in the South Isle at the west end of the Choir in Westminster Abbey." There is no doubt as to the identification of the former, for his name appeared in big black letter beneath. The second figure still exists in a badly repaired state with a new face in the S.W. tower, but it is good to have it authenticated. Neale quoted Walpole (1762) for the identification, but objected that the armorial surcoat had no label. The label, however, was there when the drawing was made, and the figure seems to have been in perfect condition. It stands on a hexagonal base, which, doubtless, was the top of a pedestal somewhat similar to those under the central pair of figures in the apse, which probably ranged with it and its companion.

These two figures—St. George and the Black Prince—certainly filled the lights of one window; they match exactly; indeed, they seem to have been drawn by the "trace and turn over" method. The St. George has gone where all glass goes, but the data are so full for these two figures, that it might be worth while to make a reconstructed drawing of them.

It seems, from the evidence, that the Nave aisles were glazed at a late time with a series of portraitures of English kings and patron saints. Above, in the clerestory, may have been ecclesiastics, and the third pair of figures in

* A panel of some signatures has lately been leaded up, also others of such early fragments as have been found.

the apse could have come from this range. In this case, they are probably the work of Richard Twyge (1506–10), as may also be the figures of the Confessor and St. John. The west window in the N.W. tower is made-up as a companion to the Black Prince, but the figure here is like the semi-modern pair in the apse and was, doubtless, by Drew. Below it is a big portcullis with side chains and a handsome arched crown—a fine panel of Tudor work. From its scale, this badge may very well have been in this

Fig. 167.

light, which is probably part of the work of Richard Twyge (1506–10). There are other big badges in the east windows, which were probably transferred from the west end.

Islip's Chapel, finished about 1530, had stained window-panes. In Keepe's MS. volume, which I have, he says: "In the windows of the Chapell above, where several of the Kings and Quenes of England are placed in

Fig. 168.

Fig. 169.

Effegie in divers presses [the waxworks] you shall find sometimes an Eye with the slip of a tree; then a great I with the aforesaid slip, and sometimes one slipping from a tree with the wordes in a label coming out of his mouth (I slip)." One of these panes has recently been restored to the Abbey and is now in the window of the lower Chapel. (See also an illustration given by Malcolm and *Gent. Mag.*, 1802, sup., p. 1185.) Figs. 167 and

169 are from late quarries, and Fig. 168 is a fragment of background.*

In connection with glazing, there are references to the Palace workshops. Thomas, of Gloucester, did some work in Westminster Hall, including " flourished glass," in 1398–99. John Prudde was appointed to " the office of glazier of our works " by Henry VI. in 1433, to hold it as Roger Gloucester had held it with a shed called the " glazier's lodge " standing " upon the west side within our Palace of Westminster." Under Richard III., in 1484, " a house which John Prudde late had " within the Palace of Westminster is again mentioned (Brayley's *Palace*, p. 337). For Prudde also see *Burlington Magazine* about 1912. A palace in the Middle Ages was a school of art and university of crafts.

* See Note 8 at end.

CHAPTER XIII

ALTAR, SHRINE, AND CHOIR

The Altar.—The high altar was the altar of St. Peter, in the special sense that he was said to have dedicated the church itself.

In the great retable, now preserved in the ambulatory, we have a precious part of the high altar, which was, doubtless, in place when the church was consecrated in 1269. It consists of delicate paintings on gilt backgrounds. The frames around these and other surfaces are encrusted with glass, and the whole resembles a splendid piece of goldsmith's work. More particular description must be reserved for a study of the paintings.

The size of this retable represents the size of the frontal also. The frontal was a superb work of gold embroidery of the kind called *Opus Anglicanum*, enriched with pearls, garnets, and enamels. It may be imagined as a flexible piece of goldsmith's work, and the King's goldsmith seems to have been in charge of its execution. It echoed, in general style, the retable and the shrine—they were all golden. This piece of embroidery was probably the most splendid and costly thing of the kind ever worked, not excepting the cloth at Canterbury, called the " glory," which was burnt for its gold about 1645.

The frontal occupied three women for nearly four years. The foundation was 12 ells of canvas, which was waxed, and on this the artist would have painted the design ; 54 marks of gold (say £800) was made up into gold thread for the embroidery ; white pearls cost £71 and great pearls £13 13*s*. 4*d*. (say, £1,500) ; 786 enamels, weighing 53 shillings, were in the border, and 76 large enamels, weighing

65 shillings, were also used, these cost £81 16s. ; 550 garnets placed in the border cost £3 6s., and their golden settings £5 12s. 6d. with £1 2s. more for making.

As we know from analogous, if inferior, work, it would have been treated as a flat panel divided into compartments, and the description shows that it had a border set with precious stones and enamels. In the *Archæological Journal*, vol. xiii., Burges illustrated a fragment of the border of a royal robe of twelfth-century Sicilian work, which was covered with little plates of gold and ornamental enamels, not more than a quarter of an inch in size, the interstices being entirely filled with pearls. This type of encrusted work is best known in mitres, but jewelled borders frequently appear on garments in thirteenth-century MSS. and stained glass. The enamels seem to have been of silver, some of them were over figure subjects (*pictura argenti*) and these may have been translucent ; " clear enamels " are mentioned in the wardrobe accounts of Edward I. They may have been brooch-like plates, linking the compartments of the central portion of the frontal. The cost of the work was something like £4,000 of our money.

As the name *Opus Anglicanum* suggests, we were specially famous for these splendid embroideries.* It is interesting to get a record that the actual needlework was a woman's craft. This is confirmed by the fact that when Isabel, sister of Henry III., married the German Emperor in 1235, she retained, in her new land, two English attendants, Margaret Bisset, her governess, and Katherine, a skilful needle-woman—*aurifrigiaria*—orphrey worker (Ramsay, *Dawn of the Constitution*, 1907, p. 75, from Matthew Paris).

Hudson Turner observed of these elaborate embroideries that King Henry III. " chiefly employed Mabel of Bury

---

* English embroidery and goldsmith's work are mentioned as famous by William of Poitiers. Lappenburg cites a writer who says that *Opus Anglicanum* was famous in Italy. In the thirteenth century, some English goldsmiths were working in Paris.

St. Edmunds, whose skill seems to have been remarkable, and many interesting records of her curious performances might be collected." In his index, he calls Mabel " a celebrated embroidress."

I have found Mabelia of Bury St. Edmunds doing work for Westminster. In 1242, she was paid for an embroidered chasuble, orphreys, cloth of gold, etc., offered to the Abbey church. It would be interesting to know whether she lived long enough to take charge of working the glorious frontal, but, in any case, the women who wrought it must, practically, have been pupils of hers. Drawings for the figure work of these embroideries would have been supplied by the best painters of the day. It may be noticed that the gold patterns on the coronation chair, decorated by Master Walter of Durham, King's painter, are exactly in the style of the golden backgrounds of the embroideries. There is in the British Museum (show-cases of books) a binding, embroidered with the Annunciation, so much in the style of Walter the painter, that, I think, it may actually have been designed by him—as drawing and colour, it is one of the most lovely pieces of painter's work we possess. A wonderful cope (now preserved abroad), embroidered with the Days of Creation and the Sabbath Rest, resembles in style very closely the pictures in a fine MS. at Holkham. The *Artist's Sketch Book*, recently examined at Cambridge, might well have been used by an embroidery designer.

In the Golden Legend account of the Confessor's miracles is the story of a London embroidress—" a noble woman right cunning in silk work," who discussed with " a young demoiselle that was fellow with her in the same work," whether they might disregard St. Edward's day. From Saxon days onward embroidery was an art practised by women. In the French life of the Confessor, Queen Edith is said to have been skilled *d'or e argent brodure*. In the will of Matilda, wife of the Conqueror, she bequeathed certain church embroideries, worked by the wife of one Alderet. This carries us back to Saxon days, and the accounts of royal ladies working embroideries under the direction of St. Dunstan. In the thirteenth century, it had probably become a trade craft, and, I think, it was practised in this way mainly in London.*

The name for this gold embroidery, *aurifrigia*, seems to be the source for the word orphrey.† In 1231, Henry III. ordered a cope of red samite, great and well ornamented with good *aurifragiis*. John of Hertford gave to St. Albans a choir cope of red samite *bene aurifrigiatam*. Henry III. gave two copes, one called *Vinea*, the other *Paradisus*, in which the ejection of Adam was nobly figured in *opere plumaro* : these two were, I suppose, without gold. Orphrey, it has been said, means Phrygian gold work, and this is made the more probable by the fact that, in a map of the western part of the world by Matthew Paris in a MS. at the British Museum, the name Frigia appears on a part of what we now call Asia Minor.

The frontal and the retable would have been very similar in general appearance. It was the tradition of the time to have pairs of painted " tablets " made to go in front of, and over, altars. Frontals, wholly plated with gold or silver or with enamels, are known to have existed, and ours was in this general tradition.

The Lady Chapel had a new altar provided before the consecration of the church in 1269. In the account of 1272, for the frontal of the high altar and other works is an item which shows that Master Peter of Spain, the King's painter, provided two well-painted tables (panels) for the Altar of St. Mary. They were valued at the great price of £80 (say, £1,600), and must have been exceptional works (*Gleanings*, p. 113). These must have been frontal and retable. In the records of St. Albans Abbey are several examples of the provision of these together. For example, Brother Richard's nephew with the latter's son painted the

---

* See the " Broderers of London and *Opus Anglicanum* " in the *Burlington Magazine* some years ago.

† See *Aurifrigium*, Camden's *Remains* " Apparel."

tables of St. Thomas's altar, lower and upper. We have what is practically a retable still in place at Westminster in the low panel-like painting on the wall behind St. Faith's altar, and this, it is interesting to note, echoes the great retable in its design.

A beautiful foliated cross appears on a picture of the altar in the Cambridge *Life of the Confessor*, and silver altar crosses are mentioned in the records. Around the altar were probably four bronze curtain standards, as in French Cathedrals of the time—Amiens, Notre Dame, St. Denis, Bourges, etc.

Altar rails are mentioned in the accounts for the coronation of Edward III.: " For fitting up and ornamenting the rails of the Great Altar and the pavement with cloth of gold and silk diapered . . . 4 cloths of purple velvet for the same. Cloth of silk for the same."

Mercurius Rusticus, writing of the ills of 1643, says that " some soldiers quartered in the church broke down the rail about the Altar, and burnt it on the place where it stood ; they pulled down the Organ and pawned the pipes at several alehouses."

The Coronation Chair, made in 1300, was wholly gilt and painted and set with glass ' enamels,' entirely in the same style of workmanship as the retable. The original account for making the chair tells that it was made to contain the stone upon which the kings of the Scots had been crowned, which had been found at Scone in 24 Edward I. (1296). It was placed " near the altar before the feretory of St. Edward," and was made by Master Walter, the King's painter. Later, the same artist made a platform (*gradum*) for it to stand upon. Burges thought that the chair was for the priest at the altar of St. Edward, but the younger Gilbert Scott supposed that it was the Abbot's seat placed behind the high altar, and facing west. It is difficult to interpret the evidence with certainty, possibly it, at first, occupied the position suggested by Scott, but was shifted when the sedilia were made. That it required a platform to raise it above the floor is in favour of Scott's view.

The stone of Scone, inserted under the seat of the chair, is a roughly squared mass, at the ends of which are inserted two staples to which iron rings are attached. In the recently published *Inventory*, it is suggested that the rings might have allowed of the stone being carried on a pole. I am inclined to doubt if the stone would have balanced on such support, and it is possible that they were for some ceremonial rite, like swearing fealty, while grasping the ring. As the " stone of Bethel," it had the sanctity of a relic, and swearing on relics was customary.

The existing sedilia on the south side of the altar were not made until several years later than the chair. They, too, were in the style of the retable, and the tombs on the north side of the altar were also largely gilt. The whole region of the high altar glittered with gold.

The arrangement about the altar was modified when the high screen was built between it and the shrine. Even then, it is possible that an abbot's chair was placed in front of the screen on the south side of the altar. Kings, at their coronation, occupied a chair in this position, and the abbot's chair at Peterborough seems to have been in a similar situation.*

The wide cornice of the new screen served as a loft on which stood a sort of triptych and great figures of Peter and Paul. Above this stage was a large tester, with the Tabernacle of the Sacrament suspended from it. This tester was attached to the underside of a rood beam, above which was a large crucifix with SS. Mary and John and Seraphim on wheels to the right and left. These facts are made known in a remarkably accurate drawing on the Islip Roll. (Compare a modernised version by H. W. Brewer in *The Builder*, July 2, 1892.) In 1644, £1 8s. was paid to Thomas Stevens and others " for taking down the angels in the Abbey and cleansing out pictures."

* See Gunton's account of Peterborough.

The angels, here mentioned, may be the Seraphs shown on the beam over the high altar in the Islip drawing. Another crucifix " at the north end " may have been in the transept ; at St. Paul's there was a rood at the north door.

The tester under the rood beam may have been the thirteenth-century arrangement. Above the high altar at Bourges Cathedral was a *ciel* or tester with the Choir rood and images over ; from it hung the Tabernacle of the Sacrament. The *celatura* above the altar at St. Albans was probably a similar tester.

Liberal provision for the suspension of lamps may be noticed in the vault of the apse and presbytery. Not only are the five bosses pierced, but there are nine holes in the cells of the vault as well. A large silver crown for candles was given to the old church by Henry III. In 1243, the King ordered that the church should be illuminated at his coming by lighting all the candles of the great lampadarium.

The deep cove of the cornice of the high-altar screen has sculptures of the Life of the Confessor on the side towards the shrine ; the other side towards the great altar had similar sculptured subjects. Keepe, describing this screen (it is true, from the east side), says the carvings represented " much of the Life of St. Edward and the ancient History of the Church." Already in Abbot Barking's choir tapestries, described below, the Confessor's Life is followed by subjects from the history of the church, including its Consecration by St. Peter. Probably this subject appeared over the altar. This story is long drawn out by the Westminster Chroniclers and itself would have furnished incidents enough to fill the space. At the end of the series representing the Life of the Confessor is a scene with a church, and it has been suggested that this may be St. Peter's dedication. It is more likely to be the Confessor's church which is represented in this position.

Shrine.—Beyond and above the retable rose the golden

shrine, the shining beacon of the whole church. As Mackenzie Walcott, speaking generally of church arrangement, said: "The chest enclosing the saint's body, plated with precious metals, was visible above the reredos to all entering the church, and in some cases the west end of the shrine was the reredos of the high altar, as at York, St. Paul's, and Lincoln."

"The King, grieved that the relics of Saint Edward were so poorly shrined and lowly, resolved that so great a luminary should be placed on high, as in a candlestick, to enlighten the church. And on the day of St. Edward's first translation the King summoned the nobility and the burgesses to Westminster. And the chest being taken out of the old shrine, the King and his brother Richard carried it upon their shoulders: his sons Edward and Edmund with the Earl of Warren, Lord Philip Basset and other nobles supported it with their hands to the exalted new shrine of gold and precious stones" (Wyke's *Chronicle*). This was in 1269. As early as 1241, the shrine had been commenced, and, doubtless, the rebuilding of the church was already at that time being discussed.

Under this year Matthew Paris wrote: "The King employed chosen goldsmiths of London to construct the shrine of purest gold and precious stones, and the workmanship surpassed the materials." In 1244, an image of the Virgin with an emerald and ruby was given by the Queen. In 1248, Edward, keeper of the shrine, was ordered to go to Woodstock to show the King the image of the Confessor. In 1253, the King, by will, left 500 marks towards it, and the *opus* of St. Edward. It was hardly complete, however, when the church was dedicated in 1269; probably, as with the church, there was an interruption in the work from about 1253 until 1258. At the time when it was begun, the King's favourite man of business was Odo the goldsmith, who is mentioned from about 1226. His son Edward, mentioned from about 1239, continued in his craft and place, and became "keeper of the shrine" and the Abbey works generally.* These must be the designers of the shrine.

Two documents at the Abbey show that Odo, in 1241, received a grant of a free chantry in his private chapel, and that he was at one time provost of Westminster.

In 1272, just after King Henry's death, an audit was ordered of the accounts of William of Gloucester, goldsmith, "who received great sums of money" to make divers jewels, a frontal for the greater altar, an image over the tomb of Katherine and the shrine of St. Edward; whereof William did not render an account (Patent Roll).

The account itself is printed in *Gleanings* (p. 114). It goes back to the year 1256–57, but only small details " *ad operaciones feretri beati Edwardi* " appear. Items are for the stipend of Master Edward, goldsmith; Master Walter, goldsmith, and Robert and Thomas, goldsmiths. The last two worked on bases and columns about the shrine— probably little shafts dividing the sides into compartments.

The shrine was a large gable-ended coffin, entirely cased with sheet-gold, jewelled and enamelled. A competent Italian observer in England, who visited the shrine about 1500, says that the shrine of St. Martin at Tours could not be put into comparison with it. He then describes more fully the shrine at Canterbury, which was similar, but, at this time, still more extravagant. " The tomb of St. Thomas surpasses all belief. This, notwithstanding its great size, is entirely covered over with plates of pure gold, but the gold is scarcely visible for the variety of precious stones with which it is studded, such as sapphires, diamonds, rubies, balas-rubies, and emeralds. These beauties are enhanced by human skill, for the gold is carved and engraved, and agates, jaspers, and cornelians are in relievo, some of the cameos being of unbelievable size; but everything is

* In 1244, the King granted Edward of Westminster water from the conduit which the King had caused to come to the Great Hall at Westminster.

left behind by a ruby the size of a man's thumb nail "
(*Relation of England*, Camden Socy., condensed).

The most precise details known of the Westminster shrine
are contained in two documents published in *Gleanings*
(cf. Rock's *Church of Our Fathers*).

One is a drawing of a shrine of the Confessor in the MS.
Life of the Saint now at Cambridge, the other is a list of the
golden figures, which had been made up to the year 1267,
for the new shrine. The drawing has recently been published in *fac simile* in Dr. M. R. James's edition of the Cambridge MS., which was, he thinks, with the drawings the
work of Matthew Paris (died, 1259). It does not profess to
show the new shrine, but an older one; however, the style
is so advanced, that it must resemble the new shrine, the
design for which would have been known to Matthew
Paris, who quite possibly was consulted about it.

The golden images described in the schedule were ten,
with five smaller ones of angels; their crowns, sceptres, and
the borders of their garments were set with rubies, sapphires,
garnets, and pearls, while specially large precious stones
were on their breasts (as brooches ?). They were valued as
follows, and these sums should be multiplied at least twenty
times.

The Majesty £200 (say, £4,000). The Virgin and Child,
set with rubies, emeralds, sapphires, etc., £200. These
two, we may suppose, were placed at the gable ends; the
drawing, mentioned above, shows the Majesty with two
little angels, occupying one gable. The Virgin's figure
would seem to be that given by the Queen in 1244.

St. Peter trampling on Nero, £100; St. Edmund, £86;
King holding a cameo with two heads, £100; King holding
shrine, £103; four other kings together, one of whom
held a flower, £215; five angels, £30. The King holding
the shrine, was, doubtless, as Burges remarked, Henry III.
himself; it was the most costly of the single figures. Another,
almost as valuable, was the King, who held a cameo. This
may have been the image, shown to Henry in 1248, of the

Confessor himself. His figure would hardly have adorned his own shrine, unless he was one of a series of English saint kings, of whom St. Edmund was another ; the incident of his giving the ring to the Pilgrim, however, is represented in the MS. drawing by a pair of isolated figures standing above pillars right and left of the gable end of the shrine, and this probably was the arrangement.

The resemblances between the MS. drawing and the new shrine of Henry III. are so many, that I think the artist must have intended to represent the new shrine, which would have been well advanced by 1250–55. That the drawings are by Matthew Paris himself seems, as shown by Dr. M. R. James, to be almost certain. I may further point out that a second drawing of a shrine in the same MS.

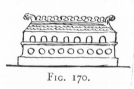

FIG. 170.

(*Gleanings*, p. 138) is closely like a little marginal sketch, representing the new shrine of the Confessor in the MS. of Matthew Paris's *Chronicle* in the British Museum (Fig. 170). The row of circular holes at the bottom followed the fashion of the time in shrine basements, but when, later, this part was executed, an arcade was substituted.

What the details of workmanship of the shrine were may be gathered from a smaller shrine of mid-thirteenth-century work at Evreux, which is well illustrated in the *Architectural Association Sketch Book*, vol. i. At Tournay, I have seen another shrine in the church of St. Pierre, which is said to date from 1247 ; this is also set with short lengths of enamel and with precious stones in a manner remarkably like the existing Westminster altar painting, which, itself, is obviously in the style of goldsmiths' shrine work, and is thus a guide to the general character of the shrine with which it was closely associated. An elaborate triptych of goldsmith's work from the Abbey of Florette in the Louvre is of similar style, so is yet another shrine in the library of Rouen Cathedral.

THE SHRINE

The bones of the Confessor are now contained in a coffin of thick planks, strongly bound with iron. Keepe, otherwise Taylor, professed to have found this coffin broken in 1685, and to have taken from it an enamelled golden cross. At a meeting of the Society of Antiquaries in 1722, it was reported that Mr. Talman, who had viewed the shrine, and coffin " will not allow Taylor's account of the crucifix, etc., to be true, from the appearance of the coffin which appears to have been nowhere broken or new cased as Taylor represented " (S.A. Minutes). Neale cautiously wrote:

" In the year 1688, a singular narrative was put into circulation, under the name of Charles Taylor, Gent., but actually written by Mr. Henry Keepe."

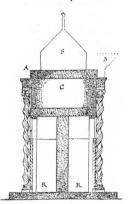

Fig. 171.

Micklethwaite, in an examination of the evidence in *Proceedings of the Society of Antiquaries* (N.S. ix.) proved that a cross was brought to King James and added, " the coffin is now such a one as James is said to have ordered." * On this point it is to be observed that already in 1683, Keepe in his *Monumenta* wrote : " I have seen a large Chest or Coffin, bound about with strong bands of Iron, lying about the midst of the inside of this Shrine [the marble basis] where, I suppose, the body of that pious King may still be conserved." The coffin, as it now exists, agrees perfectly with the description written before the alleged remaking. It is nearly 7½ feet long and two feet in width and depth ; this chest is banded around with five iron bands about three inches wide and again lengthwise with similar bands.

Scott and Burges at first thought that, when the feretory

* Crull (1713) says the King ordered the old coffin to be enclosed in a new one 2 in. thick.

was destroyed, the body was taken away and buried some-where in the Abbey, " the shrine [that is the marble basis] was only disturbed so far as necessary to effect that purpose " (*Gleanings*). Later, in his *Recollections*, Scott remarked : " The fact has been ascertained that the whole of the shrine [basis] had been taken down and rebuilt, and that even the steps had been reset and misplaced, the marks worn by Pilgrims' Knees—still very distinguishable—being quite out of their proper places."

Taking down either a part or the whole of the basis would have been quite unnecessary to get at the golden shrine and the body it contained, for it rested free on the top of the marble work. However, this basis was, I believe, taken down when Henry V.'s Chantry was built and set up again a few feet farther west, as shown by the plain space in the mosaic pavement. A second displacement of the upper part of the basis only was caused by forming a recep-tacle for the coffin in Abbot Feckenham's time (Fig. 171). The cavity is nearly 8 ft. long by 3 ft. wide and deep. Above are two strong iron bars across the top of the coffin, built into the sides of the marble work to prevent its being lifted out. The original position of the shrine was S, and A is the " step " below it ; C is the cavity and present position of the coffin, B being the semi-modern cornice, R.R. are the recesses.

A portion of the original mosaic inscription was seen by Geo. Virtue, in 1741 ; it may have been revealed by the falling away of some of Feckenham's plastering. " The old mosaic inscription, almost defaced, was thus written [text given] ; and the calcined glass, yellow like gold cut and set in. No more than what is marked with these turned commas [*Petrus duxit in actum Romanus Civis*] at the east end of the shrine was remaining in April 1741, and in June following they were erased, picked out, and taken away." The imprints of these letters can still be traced, and on the south side there are some traces of the actual inscriptions in gold glass on blue. Virtue's large engraving

THE CROSSING

of the base was from a drawing by Talman, and he may have been engaged on it when he made the examination mentioned above.

The Crossing.—The square area below the lantern was at an intermediate level between the choir and presbytery. Here stood the choir altar and the great Pascal candlestick. I have a note that the candlestick was seven branched, but cannot now find the authority for this. A great branched candlestick was given to Winchester Cathedral by Canute in 1035, and another was given to Canterbury in the twelfth century. At Durham, there was a seven-branched candlestick, the arms of which, it is said, almost extended across the choir, while the tall central candle nearly reached the vault. In a Durham book, which was exhibited at the Burlington Arts Club, is a drawing of a seven-branched candlestick, so like the splendid late-twelfth-century example now at Milan, that I wonder if it is not the same (Fig. 172). Details recorded of the Durham candlestick tell that " The

Fig. 172.

stand was of latten glistening like gold and enriched with figures of the evangelists, flying dragons, curious antique work of archers, bucklermen, spearmen, knights, and beasts." The Milan candlestick is said to have been given to that cathedral in 1560.* We shall see that " idolatrous bronze lecterns and candlesticks " were sold from Westminster in 1549, and probably the Durham candlestick disappeared about the same time. Walcott, who knew Westminster records well, says that the high tapers weighed 300 lbs.

* It is attributed to Nicholas of Verdun (died 1183) by Otto von Falke. (*Prussian Jahrbuch*, vol. xliii., p. 49.)

Great candlesticks from Henry VII.'s chapel are now at Ghent.

The central space was specially used for the coronation stage which was erected at the midpoint of the church. It was raised upon pillars, so high that, it is said, men-at-arms might ride under it ; it also had stairways to the front and back, so that the King ascended by one stair and descended by the other. It appears for long to have been called the pulpitum, a name which it bears in the accounts of the coronation of Queen Eleanor in 1236, and the word is of parallel meaning to ambo (see *Jube* in V.-le-Duc's *Dictionnaire*). In later times it was called the scaffold or high place. This pulpitum, at the centre of the church, is likely to be a remote derivation from the great ambo in Sta. Sophia, Constantinople, where the emperors were crowned. This ambo was a large structure on pillars, having a canopy above and standing out in the centre of the vast church, having staircases giving access to it both at the east and the west, that is, in front and behind. Of the coronation of an emperor, we are told that he was first shown to the people and acclaimed. The ceremony was completed in the church of Sta. Sophia, where they put on him the purple. The patriarch took his place on the ambo, when the prince and his companions, rising from their seats, joined him there. The patriarch then said the prayers appointed for the anointing and anointed the head of the prince, in the form of a cross, with the holy oil, saying, with a loud voice, " Holy." After this the crown was brought from the bema to the ambo, and the emperor was crowned. He then descended, but not on the side by which he ascended, and then the empress was crowned.

Fig. 173.

THE CROSSING

Even as late as the coronations of Queen Mary and Edward VI., the stages at Westminster were of the ancient type. For the former was provided " a mounting scaffold with stair up to the same and down to the altar, and thereupon a throne of seven stairs ; and in the middle a great royal chair." The stage for Edward VI. had a flight of twenty-two steps up to it, and on this was the throne of seven steps and the chair.

In a little book *Westminster Abbey and the Coronation* (1911), further details are given, and I suggested a restoration of the pulpitum with its canopy. At the corners of this canopy silver bells were hung (Fig. 173). For the coronation of Edward I. a mass of silver, weighing 32*s*. 6*d*., was purchased and delivered to Edward of Westminster, goldsmith, to make little bells thereof, which were hung to the canopy that was carried above the King's head. It cost 35*s*. 2*d*. to purify the silver, so that it must have been worth about £50 (Hudson Turner, i., p. 129). The bells seem to have been taken by the Abbey as a " perquisite." In Bentley's *Cartulary* is noted a document (519) being " *Le supplicacion Will. Colcestre abbe de Westom fait a seneschal d'Engleterre, come en droit da sa esglis, pour les iiii hastiles ou bastons qe supporteront le drap en la coronacion, ensemble avec les iiii campanynelles pendantz entour mesme le drap.*" The four shafts of the canopy are mentioned by Matthew Paris in describing the coronation of Eleanor of Provence in 1236.

Here, at the crossing, dead kings lay in effigy under elaborate canopies or " hearses," supporting a multitude of burning candles.* Henry VII. provided by his will that at his funeral a hearse should be set up, with 100 tapers and four great candles in the lantern space, until the King's great chapel was finished. The elaborate candlesticks from Henry VII.'s Chapel, now at Ghent, would be a permanent provision for the great candles mentioned in the will.

---

* Effigies represented the actual corpse. In the obsequies of an abbot of Canterbury, at the close of the fourteenth century, the payment is entered for the image (*Corpus fictum*) and hearse.

We have a picture of a funeral hearse in Islip's mortuary roll, which shows it to have been an elaborate canopy of open-work supporting hundreds (?) of candles. The corpse of John Islip, Abbot of Westminster, who died in 1532, was placed " undre a goodlye Herse wt manye lights . . . which was left standing until monethes mynde." *
The hearse of Edmund Crouchback had no fewer than 559 candles, and this odd number suggests that there was a single one at the apex.† These canopies of lighted candles —*chapelles ardentes*—must have been a remarkable sight not without consolation for rich relations. The effigies now in the Museum were those carried at the funerals.

Choir.—In Flete's account of Abbot Barking, who died in 1246, he tells that the abbot gave to the church " two curtains or dossals of the choir " on which the Life of Christ and the Life of St. Edward were represented in beautiful work. They were in being as lately as 1631, when Weever noted two inscriptions " wrought in the cloth of Arras, which adorns the Quire." Dr. M. R. James found copies of the complete set of inscriptions in a MS. at Cambridge, and these are printed in Dr. Armitage Robinson's edition of Flete. These " hangings about the Quire," as Weever also calls them, contained, according to this transcript, " on ye south syde of ye Quier ye history of Christ in faire arras worke " in twenty-six subjects. The story of St. Edward, opposite, contained twenty-two. Each subject was explained by an inscription in two or four lines. Weever noted of one that it contained " portraitures of the King [St. Edward], Hugolin [his treasurer], and the Theefe ; under which are these verses," and the copyist of the inscriptions puts headings before each inscription, which he evidently noted from the figured subjects themselves, thus—(1) *The Angell Gabriell saluteth our blessed Lady*, (2) *Christ borne betwixt an oxe and*

* Sharpe's *Cal. of Wills*, ii., 662.
† Rock's *Church of Our Fathers.*

an asse. From the length of the inscriptions it appears that each subject must have been of considerable size, and although the words " two curtains or dossals " are likely at first to suggest only a pair of pieces, it may not be doubted that a complete suite of hangings for the choir existed. At Canterbury and elsewhere, we have records of similar choir hangings. The last four subjects on the south side at Westminster showed : the Coronation of the Virgin ; the Abbot praying to her ; She intercedes for him ; Christ answers. In the inscription of the last one, Abbot Richard is mentioned by name. There is thus no doubt that these were the very hangings given by Richard Barking. From some slight indications in the grouping of the subjects, it seems probable that they were arranged in pairs, and this would, doubtless, mean a double band of subjects. They probably disappeared in the cleansing out of superstitious pictures in 1644–45.* Barking's tapestries would have stopped the holes in some barn.

The fine set of tapestries which adorned the choir of Canterbury Cathedral are now at Aix-en-Provence. " They still bear the relics of the donor's inscription recorded by Somner. The date is 1511." They were sold in Paris in 1656. " The set consisted of fourteen panels, representing scenes from the Life of Christ. Nine of them are illustrated in Jubinal's *Tapisseries.*"

Barking's tapestry, described as arras, may really have been woven. In a wardrobe account of Edward II., 1317, is an item : To Thomas de Stebenwith, mercer of London, for a great *dorsorium* of wool wrought with figures of the King and Earls for the King's service in his Hall on festivals, £30. (Brayley's *Palace*, p. 436. See also " cloth of arras," p. 49, and compare the tapestries at Angers.)

Lecterns at Westminster are mentioned in a document

---

* Compare Neale, ii., 273, who seems to confuse them with tapestries in the presbytery, which was often called the choir by older writers. The recently uncovered choir paintings at Eton are in the tradition of such ornaments, and here the subjects are arranged in two tiers.

dated January 13, 1549, printed by Dr. Armitage Robinson. " Also it is likewise determined that the two lecterns of latten and candlesticks of latten with angels of copper and gilt, and all other brass latten, bell-metal, and brass shall be sold by Mr. Heynes, Treasurer, by cause they be monuments of Idolatory and Superstition, and the money thereof coming to be received by the said Treasurer for making the Library and buying of books for the same " (*Westminster Abbey Manuscripts*, p. 13).

Sir John Mason, ambassador to France, reported to our Privy Council in 1550 : " Three or four ships have lately arrived from England, laden with images which have been sold at Paris, Rouen, and other places, and being eagerly purchased, give to the ignorant people occasion to talk according to their notions ; which needed not had their Lordships' command for defacing them been observed." England must have been very rich in works of art before the two great exportations about the years 1550 and 1650.

Two fragments of an original stall elbow (*c.* 1265) have recently been recombined and set in a new stall in St. Faith's chapel. In the Museum is a fragment of a " miserere," which, in form, is like the one I illustrated in *Craftsman*, but different in detail ; we may suppose that this was the case with all of them. The repair of organs in the choir is mentioned in an Abbey document (19635) of 1374–75.* Henry III. gave a hanging to the church, to be placed opposite the organs (Liberate Roll). A payment was made in 1644 " for taking down part of the organ loft." The present choir gate is a beautiful piece of ironwork of Wren's time. The stone wall, against which the tomb of Newton and its companion are placed, is ancient, and so are the enclosing walls of the choir on the north and south sides.

To the west of the choir screen or permanent pulpitum

---

* Another document (19663) refers to the " Repair of small pair of organs : Item the Duke of Exeter's Organs " ; and there are several other organ makers' bills for repairs, one of 1553 (37566).

were the nave altars of the Holy Rood, the Trinity, and the Virgin, and there was a great rood beam above. In the series of sculptures of the Life of the Confessor, on the east side of the screen behind the high altar, is one which contains a representation of the altar of Holy Trinity, where Saint Edward had a vision. This sculpture may indicate what actually existed in the fifteenth century; it is appropriate for an altar in such a situation.

The Sacrist's Rolls of the latter part of the fourteenth century speak of " an image of the crucifixion in the north part of the church " (Westlake). This, doubtless, means a rood in the north transept, for the chief entrance to the church was through the north door. At old St. Paul's there was a rood by the north door. In the accounts for purging out superstitious images, in 1644, occurs a " receipt for £1 8s. by Thomas Stevens for various destructive works including " cutting out a crucifix at the north end of the Abbey."

Fig. 174.

Outside the north portal a later porch was erected which, from Hollar's representation, looks as if it were as late as the reign of Richard II. Mr. Westlake, however, would identify it with a " galilee " mentioned in 1361–62, and again in 1372–73, " so that it was evidently built at an earlier time than that supposed " (ii., 315). In Miss Strickland's *Life of Queen Elizabeth* is a reference to the Abbey, which may be noted here. On opening Parliament in 1565 the Queen went to the Abbey and " alighting at our Lady of Grace's chapel, she entered at the north door " ; then, having heard a sermon, she proceeded " through the south door to the Parliament chamber, then evidently held in the Chapter House." " Offerings at the image of the Blessed Mary outside the door of the church " are noted in the Sacrist's Roll of 1338, and again " St. Mary at the North Door " in 1363–65. An image of St. Peter outside the north door is also mentioned in 1428.

CHAPTER XIV.

RELICS AND TOMBS: WOOD, METAL, TILES.

Relics and Royal Tombs.—We have seen, from the evidence of the mosaic floor and of the work itself, that the position of the shrine was changed in the Confessor's chapel, probably at the time when Henry V. chantry, which encroaches on the space, was built. In what appears to have been the original position about 2 ft. more to the east than at present, the shrine would have been under the central boss of the apse, and, doubtless, the wooden shrine-case was suspended from this point.

The chapel as well as the actual shrine of the Confessor acquired the name of "feretory." Sporley says that Abbot Wenlock was buried before the south door [in the altar screen] of the feretory. At Winchester the shrine chapel is still known as the feretory, so also is that of Durham.

Before the building of the chantry of Henry V., the eastern point of the Confessor's chapel would have been occupied by the great relic aumbry, and possibly an altar. In his will the King directed that a chantry, ascended by steps, should be erected in which place the relics were to be plac-d, and an altar founded. In the existing chantry there are recessed lockers, which were evidently provided for the relics. Some of the doors of these appear in Carter's drawing, dated 1786, now at the Abbey.

The design of this chantry was suggested by the structure for exposing the relics behind the altar at the Ste. Chapelle, which was reached by spiral stairs in turrets of open-work. There was a similar arrangement at Amiens Cathedral, and variations are recorded at Arras and elsewhere. At a later time a relic cupboard stood on the north side of

275

the Confessor's shrine (see *Stanley's Memorials*, first ed. and *Archæologia*, 1907). The relics of Westminster were many and famous. Several belonged to the Abbey from the days of Dunstan (see Dean Armitage Robinson's volume on Dunstan, also his edition of Flete's *History* (1909) and a 1520 list of relics, printed by Mr. Westlake. At this time four great shrines were in the chantry of Henry V. Abbot Barking (died 1246) ordered that the Feast of Relics should be more solemnly celebrated than in the past. It was observed July 16. In 1247, Henry III. obtained a portion of the Holy Blood; the scene, when it was received, is described by Matthew Paris. In Abbot Ware's *Customary*, it was provided that the high altar and the relics should be watched at night, and what is probably a slight record of one of the watchers exists on Crouchback's tomb. When it was cleaned two years since, I made out that a roughly scratched word high under the canopy and hidden in darkness was Ypeswic. Now a sacrist at the end of the fourteenth century was named Ipswich. The name could hardly have been written, except at night, and it is probably an idle signature of a watcher.

The chapel of the Confessor or of the relics was intended for a royal mausoleum from the time when it was planned. In 1246, the King formally provided that he should be buried in the new church by the side of King Edward the Confessor (Charter Rolls at the British Museum). His tomb occupies the bay on the north exactly by the side of the shrine ; in such a position on the north side of an altar a founder's tomb was not infrequently placed.

The bay to the east of the King's tomb was taken for Queen Eleanor on her death in 1290, and the bay to the west was reserved for Edward I. His tomb is a great plain chest of black marble. It was specially decorated from time to time. At the coronation of Edward III., the tomb of the Lord Edward, the illustrious grandsire of the King, "was covered with cloth of gold in silk with diaper work sewed together on account of the breadth of the tomb."

When the embalmed body of the King was examined more than a century since, interesting vestments, a specially made sceptre (very pretty) and a crown were found, sketches of which are at the Society of Antiquaries (Fig. 175).

The robes in which the kings were anointed seem to have been preserved for their burial. The accounts for the funeral of Edward II. show that he was buried in the linen shirt and coif which he wore at his consecration, as well as with the tunic and gloves. Much earlier, in 1183, the younger Henry, son of Henry II., was buried in " the linen vestments, anointed with crism, which he had at his coronation."

The Queen's tomb is about as lovely as any work of man may be; it was wrought at the balanced moment of highest perfection in our national arts.* Although the sides of the tomb are elaborately panelled, they are in large single slabs of Purbeck marble.

These three tombs are on the north side of the chapel, the south side of which is now occupied by the later tombs of Queen Philippa (eastern bay), Edward III. (middle), and Richard II. (western bay). The tombs of Edward III. and Philippa have suffered much injury ; as lately as when Crull wrote the latter had " a crown on her head sup-

FIG. 175.

ported by two angels." The smaller images which surrounded these two tombs are recorded in the Liber Niger at the Abbey. Those in the framework of the Queen's effigy seem to have been the saint-kings of England. In the ambulatory opposite the tomb of Richard II. is the mosaic tomb of the children of Henry III. and Edward I., usually called

* A drawing made in 1641 of the second tomb of Eleanor at Lincoln is in the possession of the Earl of Winchilsea and Nottingham (*Proceedings Socy. Antiq.*, N.S., xiii.

277

the tomb of Katherine. Record and material evidence agree in showing that this tomb was removed from the Confessor's chapel to make room for the tomb of Richard II. To the evidence I gave before, I would add that Sandford, writing of Alphonso (died 1284), the son of Edward I. and Eleanor, says, following the chronicles, " he was buried on the south side of the shrine among his brothers and sisters."

Two other remarkable, early monuments now occupy places in the first apsidal chapel on the south side, both of which, there is good reason to think, have been removed from the Confessor's chapel. These are the tombs of William de Valence, half-brother of Henry III. (died 1296) and of John of Eltham, younger son of Edward II. (died 1337). The enamelled effigy of William de Valence is exceptionally interesting and valuable, as representing a beautiful way of workmanship, of which very few examples now exist.

A similar effigy of Blanche of Castile (died 1283), once at St. Denis, now in the Louvre, is said to be from *les ateliers Limousins*. It has a wooden core covered with thin sheet metal nailed on ; the face is repoussé, hands are joined on the breast, the pillow is enamelled with a lozenge pattern. Resemblance to our effigy is so close as to suggest that both were by the same artist. An account exists for a tomb of Walter de Merton, Bishop of Rochester, made by Master John of Limoges about 1276, for which he was paid £40 5s. 6d. (say £1,000). A messenger was sent to Limoges and he and Master John returned with the work (*Archæol. Jour.*, vol. ii.).

Our effigy has recently been cleaned, and this has brought out some details. It was gilt, and over the gilding the tunic was painted green in varnish colour ; on it were set about a dozen bright little enamelled shields of the De Valence arms. Around the brow is a coronet band, once jewelled ; Sandford describes it as " a circle of the same metal enriched and embellished with stones of several colours." There were plainer bands around the junctions of the plating—at the shoulders, elbows, and wrists—some of which still exist on the more hidden side of the effigy. They appear in a drawing, by Stothard, in the Print-room of the British Museum, also in Neale's minute engraving. Keepe, who made his notes *c.* 1680, wrote : " Around the wooden chest on which the effigy rests were thirty little brazen effigies, some of them now remaining. About the inner ledge of this tomb is most of the epitaph remaining in ancient Saxon [' Lombardic '] letters, and the rest of the chest is covered with brass enamelled."

In another part he gives a long inscription in verse, which contains, what is said to be, the wrong date 1304, and this would seem to be from a later written inscription hanging by the monument on a tablet. In 1680, twelve of the small enamelled roundels beneath the " weepers " remained, and of these there are sketches in my Keepe MS., one being Stutville. About twenty existed when the Lancaster Herald made his notes, *c.* 1610 (B.M. MSS., 874.) The inscription about the inner ledge in ancient letters, we must suppose, was on the outer margin of the enamelled plate on which the effigy rests, for the outer raised ledge was cased with thin metal plating, having a punched pattern, some of which still remains up to the edge. In the Wallace collection are some little enamelled figures, which must be similar to the " weepers " that were around the tomb chest. It is difficult to believe that so costly and splendid a monument was from the first in a secondary chapel. The young children of this William de Valence were buried in the Confessor's chapel, under slabs in the mosaic floor, and Aymer de Valence, his longer surviving son, has one of the best places in the presbytery for a tomb. Now Burges observed that the masonry under the enamelled effigy looked as if it had been disarranged—" at the angles are pieces of diaper so irregularly placed that one is inclined to believe that they at one time have done duty somewhere else. These diapers are of two sizes. The west end of the tomb is quite plain." Examining this question, it may be seen that, at the north side of the tomb, there is, on the left hand, one row of big diaper, while on the right there is a similar row, and on a separate stone two more—three next one angle and one next the other. On the south side there are three rows of small diaper next one angle and two by the other. Further, the stone slab covering the masonry is irregularly jointed in several pieces. There can be little doubt that this masonry has been shifted, and, I think, that it was made shorter and narrower at the same time.

The tomb of John of Eltham, now in the same side chapel as that just described, was as beautiful and costly as any in the Abbey. "The funeral appears to have been celebrated in the most sumptuous manner." This tomb, with its twenty-four weepers and knightly effigy, "was formerly surmounted by an elaborate triple stone canopy, something like that of Edmund Crouchback, but the little buttresses which supported it went down to the ground. They, as well as the canopy, were, doubtless, highly coloured and gilt " (*Gleanings*).

Keepe says " a canopy covering the whole with delicate wrought spires and masons work, everywhere intermixed and adorned with little Images and Angels, was supported by eight pillars of the same curious wrought work. There is no epitaph." The canopy was destroyed about 1760.

Sandford and Dart give engravings of it and from these, together with the evidence of the existing stumps of the buttress-piers, it would be possible to make a fairly accurate paper restoration. It was of three equal bays, delicately vaulted. The side bays were gable-roofed, and had small figures carrying candlesticks on the finials. The middle compartment rose as a spire from its square base, and had a larger figure of an angel on the finial. The sides of the existing tomb with the sculptured weepers are pierced and backed with dark slabs. From Sandford's engraving it looks as if this treatment had been carried into the canopy as well.

This tomb, with its elaborate three-bayed canopy, many weepers, and candle-holding figures aloft, is a variation and development of the tomb of Crouchback by the high altar, and like that it must have been made for some most honourable position. About twenty years ago I remarked: "There is a reference to this tomb which I can hardly explain. In 1351, Edward III. wrote to the abbot that the body of his brother John, Earl of Cornwall, should be moved to some fitting place " entre les roials " agreeable to the devise of the Queen-mother Isabella, places being reserved for the King and his heirs." We may not doubt that this removal was from the position now occupied by Edward III. himself. The small thirteenth-century tomb, now in St. John Baptist's Chapel, was probably also removed from near the shrine, as Burges thought. The state of the Confessor's chapel, when the ring of royal tombs was first completed with the erection of that of John of Eltham, and when the enamelled effigy of William de Valence formed a *pendant* to the figure of Queen Eleanor, must have been amazingly romantic.

The great tomb of Richard II. again filled up all the available space about the shrine, and when Henry V. was buried here, a further displacement had to be made, as mentioned above in regard to the relics. His tomb-effigy was a costly work, in method following the precedent of that of William de Valence, but the casing was of silver—" a royal image of silver gilt, made at the cost of Queen Catherine." The sceptre, orb, and the antelope at the King's feet were already lost when a late mediæval inventory was taken, and it was plundered as early as 1546 (Kingsford's *Chronicles of London* and *Historic Literature*).

In seeking to form some total impression of the Confessor's chapel, we must think of the lamps and candles burning at the shrine and the tombs. In the records there is a recurring entry for renewing the wax about the body of Edward I., according to custom (*de cera renovanda*). This was thought to mean renewal of a cere cloth, but many similar records show that, as Sir W. Hope concluded, it referred to candles lighted about the tomb. Abbot Crokesley, who died in 1258, left an endowment for the celebration of masses and for candles, including iv *cerei* about his tomb (Flete). Lights were also provided for burning at the tomb of Queen Eleanor, and the late chronicler Fabyan, mentioning her burial, adds: " she hath ii wax tapers brenning upon her tomb both day and night, which so hath continued syne the day of her burying to this present day."

At the tomb of Richard II. four wax tapers were " to burn perpetually without extinction," and Henry V. provided in his will for eight wax lights for ever, burning on the tomb during high mass and vespers every day.* A church became a building to burn candles in, and a multitude of little twinkling lights is an impressive mystery suggesting spectacle. The splendour and associations of the place, the royalty, relics and rites, the still effigies of the dead, the polished surfaces of marble shafts and mosaic floor reflecting the lights, must have made a strange hypnotising impression on the minds of those admitted to " experience it."

.   .   .   .   .

Funeral Effigies.—The history of these is fully given in *Crowns and Coronations* by William Jones, 1902, and in *Archæologia* by Dr. Armitage Robinson. Their importance as royal portraits is hardly recognised, but when an effort is made to form a series of likenesses of the kings, these will be among the authorities. The head of the effigy of Henry VII., which is of gesso or plaster, seems to be from a death mask, and thus to be a really authentic portrait.

The latest of the old kind of effigies is that of Queen Elizabeth, and this has been maintained, fully clothed, by

* For much more concerning this cult of candles, see Mr. Westlake's volumes.

restorations. According to the records, an effigy was actually carried at the funeral. It is mentioned as being put in order in 1606, when it was seen by the King of Denmark. It was restored in 1760 by the Chapter; " the original figure carried at her funeral had fallen to pieces a few years before." Probably there was a death-mask record from which this and the tomb effigy were executed.

A drawing, made in 1786 by Carter of eight of the earlier effigies which were then in the chantry above Henry V.'s tomb, has recently been presented to the Abbey; one with a carved-wood head retained some of its cloth drapery.

. . . . .

Tomb Slabs.—The oldest tomb slabs in the Abbey are that with the large incised cross which covers the Roman coffin,* and a slab now in the Museum with two small crosses on a central stem. The latter, which may be Saxon, was found in the cemetery on the east side of the south transept. The stone coffin called Sebert's tomb has a black Tournay marble cover. Works of this marble were imported early in the twelfth century, and this must be the date of this coffin, which has the usual tapering shape.

In the south walk of the cloister are three abbots' tombs with effigies, one of which is also of black Tournay stone, and of the first quarter of the twelfth century. This is the tomb of Gilbert Crispin, of which an illustration is given in Dr. Armitage Robinson's *Life* of the abbot. The book in his left hand, however, is not indicated, but it was shown by Dart and can still be just traced. Compare the graves of two abbots of Peterborough, illustrated by Prior and Gardner (Figs. 649, 650), which are also of Tournay work. The head of our effigy is usually described as having been bare, but there are signs on each side of a cap-like headdress, such as I have seen on some twelfth-century door sculptures in France.† There are traces of delicate cross

---

* In the *Inventory;* this coffin is said to be, probably, of the fourth century; but from the fine style of lettering, it can hardly be later than A.D. 200.

† These are usually worn by prophets, I think. Was it a doctor's cap ?

folds on the sleeves, and this effigy was evidently finished with details more or less incised (Fig. 176).

Another effigy is that of Abbot Laurence (1176). In *Craftsmen*, I pointed out that this figure had no mitre, although Dart gave it one. In the text of his edition of Flete, Dr. Robinson followed Dart, but put a note at the end " I did not know that Sporley adds the words *absque mitra*." The rounded top of the head may, I think, still be distinguished.

Fig. 176.

The third effigy is that of Abbot William de Humez, 1222.

A marble coffin with a cross on the lid, which rested on the tomb of Abbot Fascet in 1713, " in which is yet to be seen the skeleton of an embalmed body, but whose admits of dispute " (Crull), has recently been cleaned and placed on the east side of the same chapel. If the body was really embalmed, it may be doubted whether it was that of a churchman.

Another very similar grave-slab discovered in the east aisle of the north transept, however, had a leaden chalice associated with it. This is now fixed vertically against the wall by the entry to the aisle.

A third slab, of somewhat the same type, is still in the floor of the same aisle against the great tomb at the north end. A fourth is in the Museum.

· · · · · ·

Brasses.—The best old illustrations of these are in Harding and Maule's volume; some are in Dart. Sandford gives the fine brass of Thomas of Woodstock with part of the epitaph, also that of Eleanor de Bohun with the inscription complete. The former was in French to the effect . . . " here lies buried among the [royals]: As you can

284

here see, be it morning, noon, or night : Pray to God for the soul of him that He have mercy on him." Eleanor de Bohun's brass is one of the most beautiful existing. On the bottom ledge were several swans in silver or enamel, with scarves around their necks, which, being of brass, still remain. Neale gives part of the inscription of the once very fine Galofer brass, with the date [13]96 ; " between every verse there appears to have been a stag couchant amidst foliage." The foliage was broom. Except for a part long protected by a heavy bench, this is now entirely worn out ; a fragment is in the Museum. One or two brasses have recently been moved, so as to be more out of the way of trampling feet. These are an inscribed plate in the south ambulatory, another in the north, four shields farther to the west at the angle of the North Transept aisle, and the slab with the indent of Abbot Kirton's brass in this aisle. Kirton's slab was not in its original position, and lay in a north and south direction. From old descriptions it appears that it was formerly the covering-stone of a raised tomb, and had a long inscription around the edge, which had been cut away (see Keepe). From the indents on the slab, one may still see that there was a small figure of the abbot in the central division of tabernacle work and coats of arms in the lateral divisions. The mitre of the figure and cusps and pinnacles of the canopies can still be traced. On the ground were several small scrolls, which bore the words ihū mercy (see Neale).

Inscriptions.—Several lost or imperfect inscriptions have been mentioned incidentally. The important records on the Presbytery and Chapter-House floors, on the shrine and on several of the tombs, have never been properly published ; nor has the painted inscription on the altar piece in St. Faith's Chapel. Scott gives the words, but omits crosses before each of the lines and prints Christum for a contraction which appears to be XPC. It is best given on plate ii. in the *Gentleman's Magazine*, 1821.

Malcolm seems to have been the first to record it. In Camden's *Remains*, epitaphs on Abbots Vitalis and Laurence are given, but these may have been on " tablets " and not on the tombs. The epitaphs of John and Margaret, children of William de Valence, on the slabs in the Confessor's chapel were inlaid in brass letters ; when that of Margaret was uncovered the name VALENCE was perfectly clear.

A portion of the epitaph of Queen Eleanor, which is hidden, is represented in a plaster cast in the Abbey Museum, and the words are given in *Craftsmen*. Near by, in the pavement, is a fragment of a grave-slab, which was re-used as part of the mosaic floor of the Confessor's chapel. On it are the imprints of letters, once of brass, KETINI : followed almost certainly by DE and preceded by N (?). The name Anketin may probably be inferred, as was suggested to me by Mr. Peers.

The tomb of Sir Bernard Brocas has a long inscription on a brass strip. In the *Inventory*, it is said that the tomb was restored in the eighteenth century, and that the effigy is of doubtful antiquity. The tomb is described by Crull (1713) when it retained its ancient painting, and he gives an engraving of the effigy which appears as at present, except that the sword seems to have been detached. Brayley says : " after some repairs about the middle of the last century [1750] it was entirely painted over of a yellowish colour. On the ledge was this inscription in brass with some animal or flower after every word. . . . On his right arm is a restored shield." Crull only gives the first half of this inscription in his text, and speaks of it as broken. Keepe (1683) has only the same part of the inscription, but from the two descriptions it is clear that Crull followed Keepe. The latter says that there was " a deep shield on his left arm almost broken away," the painting was defaced, and " nothing remains but a piece of broken inscription in brass."

Fortunately, Camden's notes of the Heraldry (Lansd. 874) contains a copy of the inscription which agrees with the existing brass and Brayley. It is so pretty and authentic looking that it was confusing to have to doubt it. The same is true of the effigy, which is very fine, however much it may have been repaired. Burges says: " The effigy is a very good illustration of the armour of the period, but serious doubts have been entertained as to whether it is not a restoration. The shield shown in Stothard's engraving, and which has now disappeared, must certainly have been modern." Stothard may be trusted not to have drawn a modern effigy. The tomb was thoroughly cleaned in March 1925, and now there cannot be any doubt as to the authenticity of the effigy. The head rests in the helm, the feet on a lion ; this keeps them up from the slab, and the body makes a graceful curve. The battlemented edge of the tomb proper, within which the figure lies, is appropriate and most effective. " Sir Bernard Brocas served in the French wars and, being afterwards sent against the Moors, overcame the King of Morocco in battle, and was allowed to wear for his crest a Moor's head crowned."

Chaucer was buried under a grave-slab near the existing memorial, which was erected by Nicholas Brigham in 1556. According to Caxton, Chaucer's " body lieth buried tofore the Chapele of seynte Benet, by whose sepulture is wreton on a table honging on a pylere, his epitaphy maade by a poet laureat, where of the copye foloweth." It was thirty-four lines long, and was by Stephen Surigonus of Milan. Keepe supposed that the existing memorial was the actual tomb.

Dart tells of the destruction of the original grave-slab. Dingley (*History in Marble*), after giving the inscription on the memorial, adds : " His grave-stone (before this was erected by Brigham) carried this inscription : GALFRIDVS CHAVCER VATES ET FAMA POESIS MATERNE HANC SACRA SVM TVMVLATVS HOMO

Some notes by R. Commaunder (*c.* 1600) at the British Museum give these two lines as by Surigonus of Milan (Egerton, MS. 2 p. 24, cf. 213), and it may be doubted if they do not come from the tablet. Crull (1713), after giving the inscription on the memorial, goes on : " But if we may credit Mr. Wever, the old verses on his grave were these [two lines as above]. And the verses about the ledge of his tomb were as follows : *Si rogitas*," etc. [three lines]. It must be understood that there was originally a grave-slab with an inscription, a long epitaph was suspended on a tablet close by, then, in 1556, an old tomb, ejected from a city church, was brought and set up to the memory of the poet. The inscription " about the ledge of his tomb " suggests that there may have been a brass figure in the midst ; was this the source of the traditional portrait ?

Several scratched words and signatures occur here and there. On the newel of the north turret of Henry V's Chantry are words which have not been read. The signatures of Jhon Bylson of Hull and Stephen Gy . . de of Hull are on the tomb of Henry III. The name of Ipswich the sacristan on another tomb has already been mentioned. In the passage between " Jerusalem " and " Jericho " appears the name S. Cypenham, etc.*

.   .   .   .   .

Woodwork.—Jordan the King's carpenter is named in 1229. Much is known of Simon the King's carpenter, who worked at Windsor (see Sir W. Hope's *Windsor Castle*) ; Alexander the King's carpenter is mentioned from 1239. Alexander was the carpenter engaged in the Westminster works (see *Craftsmen*). The original great roof of the church still remains. It is framed with stout rafters about nine inches square, every one of which has collars and raking braces. Tie-beams and additional timbering were introduced in Wren's time. A sketch of the roof by Carter, now in the Abbey collection, omits the added timbers.

* The inscriptions painted on the royal tombs and shrine in Abbot Feckenham's time were in well-formed Roman letters, but over each capital I was a dot.

WOODWORK

(For several minor roofs of the Abbey buildings see descriptions in the *Inventory*.)

The wooden partition in the Muniment-room is late fourteenth-century work. According to Carter, the oak screen of St. Edmund's Chapel was thrown down in his time and refixed without some of its details; this accounts for the bald modern cornice. An existing part of a door from the North Transept has been mentioned as having been re-used, and one or two smaller old doors exist.

Several early chests are preserved in the Muniment-room; one (illustrated in *Gleanings*) is so similar to another at Salisbury that they may have come from one shop. Another chest, with excellent late fourteenth-century ironwork, is in the Museum.

In the Muniment-room is a fine press, with somewhat similar ironwork, which is shown to have been part of the refitting of the room in the time of Richard II. by the painted pattern on it, which is similar to that on the partition. An old cope-chest of quadrant form, but plain, is in the north triforium. The renewed shrine of the Confessor (*c.* 1550), with its inlays of gilt glass, is a very pretty piece of work indeed. The pilasters had panels encrusted with small squares and lozenges of glass—mosaic, in fact; the larger plates of glass in the spandrels were spotted over at the back with paint imitating green porphyry. This was a very remarkable piece of furniture. Jacobean fittings in the Chapter Library are good, and there is some little-noticed Jacobean panelling in the space beneath the south-west tower.

We saw before that the stalls of the choir, of which fragments remain, were the work of Jacob the junctor, from 1253. William Joiner was an important citizen of London still earlier; in 1226 he bought vestments for the King. The house of Salamon le Joygnur in the parish of All Hallows at " la Heywarfe " is mentioned in 1283, and in 1291 John le Joynur had a house at " Douuegate " (Sharpe's *Calendar of Wills*). In 1327 a violent affray occurred between the trade of the saddlers of the city and the men of the trades of the joiners, painters, and lorimers, because of " a certain rancour."

In 1461 John Lynder " Joynour " willed that the Craft of Joynours should have the option of purchasing his tenaments in St. James, Garlickhythe, and St. Mary, Woolnith, if they wished. It is clear that the craft was separate from that of the Carpenters from the middle of the thirteenth century ; it was, I suppose, a shop occupation. An excellent illustration of a joiner's shop and tools is shown in a photograph from a MS., *c.* 1500, in the Woodwork gallery at S. Kensington Museum, but it is there called a carpenter's shop. The joiner is here using a plane. Now, the large painted panels of the sedilia (*c.* 1308) and that of the portrait of Richard II. (*c.* 1390) are so perfectly jointed and surfaced that planes must have been used in the work ; they are joiners' works. In 1307, Richard Godfrey and John Reed were junctors working at Westminster Palace, and it is probable that one or both of these made the sedilia. The coronation chair was undertaken by Master Walter the painter, but he must have employed a joiner.

Metalwork.—An excellent account of this is given in *Gleanings.* Several tall and heavy iron standards and rails preserved in the triforium, similar to those by Langham's tomb, probably came from the east side of Henry V.'s tomb. Some fine railings, removed a century ago from around the tomb of Mary, Queen of Scots, have recently been given back to the Abbey, and are now in the Museum. A small door to the stair turret of the North Transept in its N.E. corner still preserves its hinges, and some cupboards and chests in the Muniment-room and Museum have excellent ironwork.

A unique bronze dinner-bell, the shape of the cover of a pot, is in the Museum.

Bells.—The earliest account I have found of the bells

is in the manuscript (Sloane 904 at the British Museum) by W. Boghurst, written about 1685 :

" Of Belles in ye Abbey stepel, 6 belles, ye bigest is 5 yards in compas wanting 2 inches. St. Margaretes is 6 belles ye bigest 4 yards and a foot in compas."

The bells were repaired and some recast when Wren's renovations were done, and several entries regarding them appear in the books of accounts. At a meeting of the Society of Antiquaries in 1722 it was

Fig. 177.

reported that " the legend on the great bell was *Tertius aptavit me Rex Eduardus vocavit.*" (See also Malcolm, Westlake, and the *Inventory.*)

. . . . .

Tiles.—A further proof that the Chapter House tiles are of the same kind as the Chertsey tiles is afforded by the fact that Chertsey tiles have also been found at Hailes

Fig. 178.

Abbey, built by Richard of Cornwall, from 1246, in the style of Westminster Abbey. The fullest account of the tiles is that by Mr. Clayton in *The Archæological Journal,* 1912. Some specially interesting designs in the Pyx Chapel, including a knight on horseback and a dragon, have never been illustrated (Fig. 178).*

From time to time tiles are found in the Refectory, some of Henry III.'s date, and some of Abbot Litlyngton's ; one of the latter has his arms (Fig. 179).

. . . . .

* The dragon must represent the old Dragon Standard. A few of the tiles by variations show that separate pattern units were used (Fig. 177 is one of these, compare an illustration in Mr. Clayton's article).

u*

Heraldry.—An Armorial up to the year 1550 is included in the *Inventory*, but this is only a preliminary list. The recent cleaning of the tombs has brought out much that seemed to be lost, and a special study of the Heraldry would be valuable ; shields on the tombs of Crouchback and Aymer de Valence are in the very finest style of heraldic drawing.

The manuscript notes on Heraldry (Lansd., 874), which were mentioned before, are, I find, by William Camden, and date from the end of the sixteenth century. First come shields from the windows, then a late series from the screen of Abbot Kirton. Complete " tricks "

of the arms on the tombs of Edward Crouchback and Aymer de Valence follow. On the former, two varieties of the shield of Grandison appear on each side, one having three eagles on the bend and the other three scallop shells. It is still possible to trace the eagles of the former. On another shield the eagle of the Empire was single-headed. Then come the shields on the tomb of Edward III. (twelve smaller and four larger) and those

FIG. 179.

on Philippa's tomb (twenty-eight). There were twenty-four small enamelled shields around the effigy of William de Valence. The tomb of Bernard Brocas had eight shields, including his own, a ramping golden lion on a sable field.* The tomb of Sir Lewis Robsert had about fifty shields, all given. When the Keepe MS., which I have, was done, about 1680, only twelve of the little shields of William de Valence's tomb remained (this is an example of the losses in the Puritan period), but some of these are more clearly given.

. . . . .

---

* The shields, according to Keepe and Crull, were against the breasts of cherubs. These must have been painted on the panels.

SEALS

Seals.—The short account of Abbey seals, which I gave before, was drawn from the British Museum collection. It could be extended by a study of those at the Abbey. One of these, the seal of Abbot Gervase, is remarkable as a work of art for so early a time—*c.* 1140. It is a large oval, with the figure of the abbot before the Madonna and Child, and is, I should say, in the style of Touraine or Angers (Fig. 180).

A late-fourteenth-century seal of Abbot Colchester has an elaborate tabernacle con- taining chief figures of SS. Peter and Paul, side figures of the Confessor and Pilgrim, and a lower figure of a king carrying a church (Sebert ?). On either side of the last are two shields of arms, Colches- ter's own and that of the Abbey.

. . . . .

Regalia.—On the extensive lore of the coronations I can only set down a few chance observations while referring to special treatises. The most precious objects were the crown, sceptre, and tunic of

Fig. 180.

the Confessor (see Dr. Armitage Robinson's *Flete's History*).

The crown of St. Edward was surmounted by " arches " or bands crossing above it, rising to a central knop. Some- thing of the sort appears on his coins. In the thirteenth century paintings, once in the painted chamber of the Palace, arched crowns are indicated, and they are represented in the sculptures of the coronation of Henry V. at the Abbey (Fig. 181).* A recently uncovered painting of a large

* Crowns from a coin of the Confessor and from the Painted Chamber are also shown in Fig. 181.

figure of the Confessor, in Islip's Chapel, shows a similar arched crown.

In Lidgate's account of the reception of Henry VI. at the Abbey, it is said of the Abbot :

> "Among ye relics ye sceptre out he sought,
> Of Saint Edward and to the King he brought,
> Though it were long, large and of great weight,
> Yet on his shoulder the King bore it in on high
> In the mynster while all the bells rung,
> Till he came to the high altar."

In the Patent Rolls of King John, the sword of Tristram

F_{IG}. 181.

is mentioned as one of these in the Treasury (see also H. Hall's *Antiquities of the Exchequer*). Now, one of the state swords carried in coronation processions was called *Curtana* ; it was pointless, and it appears reasonable to identify this with the sword of Tristram, as has been done by Mr. Roger Loomis. On the other hand, *Curtana* seems also to have been known as the Sword of Mercy. Further, Matthew Paris, writing of the coronation of Eleanor of Provence, wife of Henry III., in 1236, says that the Earl of Chester bore the sword of St. Edward, *qui curtein dicitur*, in token of his being earl of the Palace. This is in the *Major Chronicle*, and there is a sketch of a sword and sceptre in the margin. I have not been able to see if the sword is here represented as pointless, but it seems that Curtana may not be accepted as Tristram's sword, although I cannot find any sword of the Confessor mentioned among the relics.

There were other legendary swords in the Treasury. "The sword with which King Athelstan cut through the rock at Dunbar ; the sword of Wayland Smith, by which Henry II. was knighted ; the sword of Tristram, presented to King John by the Emperor." * In a paper on Wayland Smith, Dr. Rendell Harris gives a reference for the Wayland Smith story as *Historia Gaufridi Comitis Andevagorum* in *Recueil des Historiens*, xii., p. 52. I have seen in some Patent or Close Roll that Richard I. made a present of the sword of King Arthur to a foreign king or the Emperor, but I cannot find my reference.

While the whole history of the Westminster buildings is a large matter to take up, the details such as those touched in this chapter would make subjects for particular research, which would be instructive and amusing to work at. I should like my last word to be a recommendation of these sectional studies.

.   .   .   .   .

" Again farewell, and may these essays have some influence over thy future welfare; Then shall I think my labours well bestowed; and my happy spirit when disrobed of mortal clay, will ever dwell a guardian genius to protect and guard thy architectural glories to time immemorial."

John Carter, on Westminster Abbey, 1799.

* Stanley's *Memorials.*

NOTES

1. *External Doorways.*—Details of the porch at Higham Ferrars, especially the sculptured medallions and square diapers, resemble the *North Portals* at the Abbey so closely that I could suppose that the porch was wrought by a Westminster mason. The probability that it was so indeed is increased by the fact that the lordship of Higham Ferrars was confiscated by Henry III after Simon de Montfort's rebellion, and given to the King's younger son Edmund Duke of Lancaster, who was afterwards buried in the Abbey. The porch must have been built about 1270–80, and it may have been a royal work. " It is practically certain that the work of Higham Ferrars Church was proceeding in the latter part of Henry's III reign."

The cleaning of the *Jesse-tree Doorway* to the Chapter House has in some degree brought out the details of the sculpture. The two upper figures of the Jesse-tree were not the Virgin and Christ, but ancestors ; the central statue on the tympanum must have been the completion of the tree. The fine statues of Angels on either hand of this central Virgin and Child are in blocks of Caen stone ; details of the wings and drapery show exquisitely sharp cutting. Most of the foliage carved on the tympanum can still be traced. Mr. Knight's measured drawings made in 1873 are not so accurate in regard to this foliage as they look, the scrolls and leaves were not so thin, and there are minor differences ; probably the carving was nearly as indistinct fifty years ago as at present.

Notice on the adjoining doorway to the Library stair the little corbels wrought on the lintel from which the tracery in the tympanum sprang ; the central one of these has been cut away. At the apex of this door is a deep hole, probably made for a lamp bracket.

If our present trivial fashion of " designing " sham " Gothic architecture " is to continue any longer, something a little more intelligent and worth while might be done by setting up copies of these precious Westminster doorways in new churches, so that accurate representations of them might be handed on. Such frank copies would have some value, sham Gothic has none.

2. *The Chapter House.*—The iron tie-bars of the Chapter House at Salisbury were $2\frac{1}{2}$ inches deep by $1\frac{1}{2}$ inches wide. The tension was so great that the central capital was shattered and a strong belt of iron had to be fitted round the group of hooks to relieve the strain from the stone. It may not be doubted that there was some similar failure at Westminster which caused the building of the flying buttresses.

3. *St. Erasmus' Panel.*—In the north ambulatory close to Islip's Chapel is an elaborate piece of tabernacle work which contained sculpture now lost; below were painted inscriptions, one in large letters being *Sanctus Erasmus.* A chapel of St. Erasmus was destroyed when Henry VII's Chapel was built, and in 1906 I accepted the view that the panel might have come from the old chapel; a recent examination of it, however, has convinced me that it is a work of Abbot Islip's time, and that his initials beside it were carved by the artist who made the panel.

4. *Cloister.*—Twenty years ago the cloister vaults were so badly decayed that at certain changes of weather there were large falls of scalings from the stone ribs, some of considerable size, and it was thought that the vaults would have to be rebuilt. About eighteen years ago we began to experiment with washes of lime carefully prepared and applied, and this has been so successful in arresting the rotting away that but few stones have had to be renewed. Moreover, the making it clean and fair has greatly increased its beauty. Many tablets have been removed from the wall-tracery and placed in the southern continuation of the east walk. When a large monument was taken from the panelled bay next to the Refectory door, we found that the tracery behind it had not been destroyed.

5. *Cleaning of Interior.*—About 1922 systematic cleaning of the interior, tombs, and paintings was undertaken, beginning with the tomb of Edmund Crouchback. By this means some unknown paintings, especially a large part of a noble Annunciation group on the sedilia, and figures of St. Peter and the Confessor in Islip's Chapel, have been recovered. The latter are in monochrome, as if representing sculpture and like the Eton paintings.

6. *Kings' Effigies.*—The tomb of King John at Worcester was examined in 1797. The body had been embalmed and "it was adjusted in the stone coffin precisely in the same form as the figure

NOTES

on the tomb. The dress appeared also to have been similar to that represented on the tomb. The left arm laid on the breast remained, and in that hand a sword had been placed as on the tomb." Compare the tomb of Edward I, p. 277.

7. *Elizabethan Sculpture.*—Cleaning has brought out the beauty of some of the Elizabethan and Jacobean tombs; the sculptors, of whom we know little, must have been artists of great ability. The effigy of the Duchess of Suffolk (1559) is a delightful and dignified work, and the recumbent statue of the Countess of Lennox is truly beautiful; the kneeling figures of the tomb of Sir R. Pecksall are charming. The effigy of Sir Thomas Heskett, 1605, is interesting, as having a moustache arranged in the fashion of the portrait of Shakespeare. These sculptures were still fully painted in the mediæval tradition.

8. *Stained Glass.*—In an account of the Abbey glass in the *Journal of the Society of Glass Painters*, April 1925, Mr. F. Sydney Eden says that the figure in the second light of the north-east apse window is partly ancient: "The upper half of a figure in a ruby tunic and green mantle (early fourteenth century); to this has been attached a late fifteenth-century head with a nimbus made up of pieces. The hands of the figure are also of fifteenth-century date, and it is set in fragments of patterned glass."

9. *Ironwork.*—The railing of the Daubigny tomb has been much restored; the initial letters on the angle standards appear among Powell's sketches in the British Museum.

10. *Tombs.*—Sandford and Dart illustrate the canopies once over the tombs of John of Eltham, Philippa Duchess of York, and Bishop Ruthall, and restored drawings of these might be made. Crull describes the painting of the Duchess of York's tomb. A painting of the Holy Trinity which probably came from the canopy of this tomb has been cleaned and hung in the Muniment Room.

11. *The Artists' Sketch Book*, mentioned on p. 256, has now been described in the last volume of the Walpole Society.

12. *Masons' Tombs.*—The most important of these now existing in England are incised slabs at Lincoln and Crowland. I have just been sent a rubbing of a small brass in Sudborough Church, Northamptonshire, to William West, marbler.

THE END

298